PRAISE FOR

THE TROUBLE WITH
BOYS

"Terrifically useful . . . A cogent, reasoned overview of the current national debate."
                                                    —PUBLISHERS WEEKLY

"A bible for those concerned about what is happening with boys."
                                                    —SANTA FE NEW MEXICAN

"Offers help . . . addresses the perils of growing up male."   —PEOPLE

"Keeping boys engaged is tough business. And many teachers are just missing the boat. . . . You'll want to get this book into some influential people's hands."
                                                    —BOOKREPORTER.COM

"Wise . . . Tyre calls for a realistic and nuanced definition of the problems boys face a   lating
equity   ccept
that b   less."
                                                    RNAL

"Peg   na-
tiona   h an
even

                                                    York

"Offe   ultimate   rls."

                                                    LIST

"A te   d to
under

                                                    hardt
                                                    nent,
                                                    form

THE
TROUBLE
WITH
BOYS

A Surprising Report Card on Our Sons, Their Problems
at School, and What Parents and Educators Must Do

PEG TYRE

THREE RIVERS PRESS • NEW YORK

Published in the United States by Three Rivers Press,
an imprint of the Crown Publishing Group,
a division of Random House, Inc., New York.
www.crownpublishing.com

Three Rivers Press and the Tugboat design are registered
trademarks of Random House, Inc.

Originally published in hardcover in the United States by
Crown Publishers, an imprint of the Crown Publishing Group,
a division of Random House, Inc., New York, in 2008.

Library of Congress Cataloging-in-Publication Data
Tyre, Peg.
    The trouble with boys: a surprising report card on our sons,
their problems at school, and what parents and educators must
do / Peg Tyre.
    Includes bibliographical references and index.
    1. Boys—Education—United States.   2. Motivation in
education—United States.   3. Sex differences in education—
United States.   4. Academic achievement—United States.
I. Title.
    LC1397.T97 2008
    371.8210973—dc22   2008002911

ISBN 978-0-307-38129-3

Printed in the United States of America

DESIGN BY BARBARA STURMAN

10 9 8 7 6 5 4 3 2 1

First Paperback Edition

CONTENTS

THE
TROUBLE
WITH
BOYS

INTRODUCTION

The Trouble with Boys

Trina Furgerson, who lives in Bucks County, Pennsylvania, was sitting on a small wooden chair listening to a first-grade teacher complain about her son Chance when it began to dawn on her that school has changed in a way that's bad for boys. The thought startled her. The Furgersons—she's a Pilates instructor and her husband is a software engineer—consider themselves strong supporters of education and big fans of their local school. Nonetheless, Chance's teacher had a laundry list of complaints: Chance never came to circle time when he was called; he needed to be asked at least twice. He frequently spoke without raising his hand. He didn't like to write for very long. He often asked when the class was going to get recess. Sometimes, he went to the bathroom without permission. During art, he used his plastic safety scissors to cut his own bangs. Worst of all, the teacher said, Chance didn't always pay attention. "He's never antisocial or aggressive and none of the things that are driving her crazy seemed that big of a deal," Trina thought to herself. But the teacher was finding so many things wrong with her son that Trina, the mother of two, felt cowed and stayed quiet.

The teacher had a suggestion about how to deal with Chance's "problems." When Chance did something wrong at school, she'd make

1

him put a sticker on a chart and recite his misdeed aloud. Then the teacher would write out a description of Chance's misdemeanor and give the note to him to take home for Trina to sign. Not knowing what else to do—and not wanting to seem uncooperative or resistant— Trina agreed to give it a try.

About three weeks later, when Trina met Chance's bus, she realized that she had made a terrible mistake. As soon as her six-year-old son felt her arms around him, he collapsed on the ground, convulsed in sobs. He showed her the list of misdeeds the teacher had written out. "Mommy," he cried, "I just can't be good!"

At that moment, Trina realized that it was her six-year-old son, Chance, not the school, who needed her support.

"I realized, deep inside of me, that something was very wrong—but not with Chance. The teacher didn't have bad intentions, but I had allowed her to make my son the problem when really the standards of the school were unrealistic." It was, she recalls, one of her very worst moments in parenting. As she dried her son's tears, she vowed to find a better way for him.

Maybe you have a son like Chance—a smart, capable boy—or maybe a teenager, who is starting to struggle in school. Possibly, you've had a wake-up call like Trina or are experiencing something that is less dramatic but equally troubling: a growing sense that your school-age son is falling out of love with learning. When he talks about his classroom experience, you've begun to notice that he seems fearful, bored, or frustrated. Or maybe you see ways in which he's disengaged from the classroom altogether. Perhaps you've begun to see small but persistent signs that it's gotten harder to be a schoolboy than you remember.

It turns out that more parents than you can possibly imagine are noticing the same things. For a variety of reasons, some obvious and some very subtle, a great many boys from all walks of life and every community are not thriving in school. Although your son's trouble may be setting off fireworks in your household, for the most part our schools, our communities, and our elected leaders are ignoring boys' widespread underachievement. Yet even as some folks turn a blind eye to the problem, the way boys struggle in school has begun to set off a cascade of effects large and small that are likely to change the fabric of our communities for generations.

Rethinking Ophelia

SURPRISED? I know I was. For the last seven years, I was a staff writer at *Newsweek* magazine covering social trends and education. In my job, I got to spend a lot of time in schools talking to teachers, principals, parents, and students of all ages. For several years, I didn't see what was in front of my face: the myriad ways in which boys are not thriving in the classroom. In my defense, it's not always easy to pick up on a national trend. Schools reflect the communities they serve, and no one kid, one class, one school, or even one district or state can reflect the colorful and chaotic mosaic that makes up the education system in the United States. Plus, I wasn't looking for it. As a grateful beneficiary of the feminist movement, I was steeped in literature about the lives and struggles of girls. I knew that poor African American boys had been lagging far behind most other demographic groups for decades. But books like Mary Bray Pipher's *Reviving Ophelia: Saving the Selves of Adolescent Girls* and Carol Gilligan's seminal work *In a Different Voice: Psychological Theory and Women's Development* were front and center in my consciousness. Those authors had alerted me to the perilous passage all girls traverse as they move toward womanhood. I'd read research promoted by the well-respected American Association of University Women that purported to show how boys dominate classrooms at the expense of girls. As a journalist, I try to stay aware of my own inevitable biases, but I was focused on the girls. And I wasn't the only one. I know many smart, sensitive teachers and wonderful principals who take special pains to ensure that their female students get a chance to shine. They are only too aware of the struggles women face in the work world. Those teachers are committed to creating a level playing field for girls in the 50 minutes or so of the world they control.

I'm also the mother of two school-age boys. I'm sure that most mothers of sons will understand me when I say that raising boys is an adventure. Even though I was raised with two brothers, having sons has given me a passport into a world that is sometimes dramatically different from my own. I've been amused and sometimes astonished at just how far Mars can be from Venus. My husband and I have been lucky. There have been a few bumps along the way, but for the most part, our sons are doing pretty well. But seeing their experiences, and the experiences of their friends, I began to realize that lots of intelligent boys from good, loving homes are poorly equipped to handle some of the things that schools are demanding of them. Behind their facades of indifference, they often feel a particularly acute form of pain—the kind that comes from knowing that you're not measuring up.

My aha moment, if you will, came when I was interviewing the headmaster at a prestigious New York private school—the kind that charges $26,000 a year. He was fretting about the lowest-performing students in his middle and high school. He had a real problem, he confided. All of the students in his school had the potential to be high achievers—the admissions office at this particular institution is notoriously selective. Still, students who fell into the lower quartile for grades tended to remain there until graduation. That wasn't a huge problem in itself. Even if you are educating the cream of the crop, every class is still going to have a bottom quartile. The trouble was that the lowest-performing kids were also unconnected from the rich extracurricular life of the school. Some were behavior problems. Others were simply checked out.

You don't get to be headmaster of a high-powered private school for nothing. This man was determined to pinpoint what was going wrong for those students. With the help of a researcher, he'd spent months trying to find out what these kids had in common. His results, which he shared with me, were intriguing. The low-performing kids didn't come from the same racial or ethnic background or even from the same neighborhood. They weren't scholarship kids from poor families or the Richie Riches who spent school vacations in Europe. They weren't the athletes, the Goths, or the arty kids either. The only thing those low-performing students had in common, the headmaster told me, was that all but one of them was male.

That triggered a series of questions in my mind. The key one was this: Is there something going on broadly across the population that is affecting the performance of young men in school? And if so, what is it? What I have learned from my many years as a journalist is that a handful of anecdotes and some personal observations don't make a trend. So I began to pour over data. Lots and lots of it. Here's what I found.

The New Gender Gap

How are boys doing? The answer, it turns out, is not very well. In Chapter 1, I detail how they are falling behind, and in the chapters that follow, I detail what that looks like close up and why it's happening. But for now, let me share with you in brief the statistics that caught my eye. Boys get expelled from preschool at nearly five times the rate of girls. In elementary school, they are diagnosed as having attention problems or learning disorders four times as much as girls and are twice as likely to get held back. Girls used to lag behind in science and math but lately have all but closed the gap. Boys, though, continue to lag badly behind girls in reading and writing, and this gap is growing and getting bigger, not smaller, as boys move from elementary school through high school. Boys' grades are worse than girls'. Boys are more likely to report being the victims of violent crime. They commit suicide in far greater numbers than girls.

By high school, girls rule. They take harder classes, do better in them, and dominate all extracurricular activities with the exception of sports. More boys than girls drop out. In college, the achievement gap is even more apparent. According to the U.S. Census in the fall of 2005, the most recent year they've looked at, 57.2 percent of all undergraduates in the United States were female. In the spring of that same year, 57.4 percent of all bachelor's degrees in the United States were awarded to women. I also uncovered an ugly and astonishing secret: There are so many highly qualified girls and so few boys at the same level that when selective and well-known colleges—such as Brown, Wesleyan, William and Mary, Tufts University's School of Arts and Sciences, Kenyon, and Providence College, to name just a few—put together their freshman classes, they favor boys over girls. Some colleges have even quietly begun to experiment with affirmative action–type programs to bring more boys to campus.

I began talking to educational researchers and school administrators to get some firsthand perspective on the "new gender gap." At one end of the spectrum, I met many competent principals who aren't aware of the problem. During a sit-down with a high school principal in his office in an affluent suburb of New York City, I heard about the pressures created by school reform, the changing curriculum, and measures this educator was taking to raise the achievement of all students. When I asked him about male underachievement, he contended the issue didn't exist among his students. At my urging, however, he opened his enrollment roster and counted the number of Advanced Placement classes taken by boys and girls, and he found that girls accounted for more than 70 percent of the enrollment. For a few moments, he appeared stunned. Male underachievement, he stammered, just might be a problem worth looking into.

At the other end of the spectrum, I met many principals—most notably from the lowest and highest socioeconomic sectors of our country—who were pulling out their hair about their underachieving males. "We know we have a boy problem," said Jeff Gray, the former principal at Foust Elementary School in Owensboro, Kentucky, who revamped the curriculum to address the gender-specific needs of his first- and second-graders. "We can't ignore it. We need to use every technique and tool at our disposal to address it." For others, the new gender gap is an issue just now coming into view.

For a lot of interesting reasons that I discuss in Chapter 1, there haven't been a lot of educators willing to openly discuss boys' underachievement. A few interesting thinkers—most notably Thomas Mortenson, a senior scholar at the Pell Institute for the Study of Opportunity in Higher Education—have been sounding the alarm about boys for some time. But for the most part, boy problems have not become part of the national discourse on education. I believe that is about to change. In elite institutions, high-powered, vocal parents of sons are starting to demand change, and principals and headmasters are scrambling to respond. The rest of us find that because of the No Child Left Behind legislation, our schools are engaged in some of the most dramatic efforts at widespread school reform that this country has ever seen. Principals in public schools are now responsible for showing the steady achievement of every pupil from every racial and ethnic subgroup. In an effort to move the needle on school performance, principals are starting to look at the underachievement of males. And they're finding that it's an issue well worth talking about.

On a national level, the response to the underachievement of boys has been to continue to focus on the achievement of girls, as if girls, not boys, were the ones having the biggest problems. Most of the elected leaders I've spoken to were familiar with the statistics on college matriculation, for instance, but they expressed profound skepticism about the public's capacity to perceive nuance. The politicians feared that if they raised concerns about boys they ran the risk of being misunderstood. In the 1990s, the struggles of girls were so vividly documented and widely reported that in the minds of most people, girls remain a vulnerable and disadvantaged group. Politicians also worried that any effort to improve the performance of boys might be interpreted as an attempt to interfere with the exhilarating achievements of smart, ambitious young females. From the statehouse to the White House, the elected officials I spoke to acknowledged the seriousness of the problem but believed that they lacked the political capital to take it on.

I also began talking to a lot of boys—probably 250 in all—in school and in their homes. I sat in so-called model classrooms where, for a full 50 minutes, the teacher led her girls in a lively discussion of Zora Neale Hurston's novel *Their Eyes Were Watching God* while the boys sat as still and silent as stones. I listened to the life story of a handsome young man, the son of Ivy League–educated parents, who described how he ended up at community college while his older sister went off to Duke. Some boys got tired of teachers telling them to sit down and stop fidgeting. Others believed their friends who told them that studying was "for girls." Others looked at school as a game they couldn't win, so they refused to play. Many boys told me their bleak tales of frustration, dejection, and—most of all—promise unfulfilled. Through these interviews, the data-driven portrait of male underachievement began to grow some sinew and bone. The new gender gap can take a big toll on a boy, of course, but it's hard on his parents, too. During many interviews, moms and dads of struggling sons teetered between frustration and fear. I listened to a mom weep as she recounted how her son's kindergarten teacher suggested her little boy might have "better days" if she gave him Ritalin. Some parents described the enduring pain of watching one disappointing school year bleeding into the next and seeing what their sons could not—that each D or F was an opportunity lost.

Most parents stood by as doors were slammed shut on their sons. Many blamed themselves. "I know it sounds crazy," said one mom who had a daughter attending an Ivy League school and a son who barely made it through high school, "but for the longest time, I felt like I just didn't do a good enough job with him." Most parents blamed their sons. "I thought it was just him" is something I heard over and over. Lately, however, I've been getting the sense that lots of parents aren't willing to stand by silently anymore.

In my research, I also uncovered a wide range of experts—psychologists, historians, demographers, school administrators, behavioral scientists, psychiatrists, sociologists, brain researchers, educational researchers, teachers, and therapists—who are analyzing the boy problem from every angle. I looked at newly founded organizations, innovative programs, consultants, psychologists, and academics, who were already thinking hard about how to attack the boy problem. Some, like psychologists Michael Thompson, coauthor of *Raising Cain: Protecting the Emotional Life of Boys,* and Michael Gurian, coauthor of *The Minds of Boys: Saving Our Sons from Falling Behind in School and Life* were already well known. Others, some of whom you will meet in these pages, were operating in relative obscurity. I began crisscrossing the country, conducting interviews with smart people who are looking for solutions to the boy problem.

In the winter of 2006, I wrote a cover story for *Newsweek* based on the research I had done so far. The cover featured a cluster of boys, struggling readers, from an elementary school in Colorado that is putting a big emphasis on boosting the achievement of low-performing boys. The cover bore the headline "The Boy Crisis." Inside, was a nine-page story titled "The Trouble with Boys." I worked hard to describe the issues as clearly as I could with as much nuance as possible. I tried to present a thorough picture of the disquieting trend emerging from Florida to California. My underlying idea was this: There are many ways in which boys are struggling at school. What is it about being male in today's schools that seems to confer such a pronounced disadvantage on so many? Have schools changed? Have boys changed? I described programs and approaches that were catching on with people concerned about the problem. I was unprepared for the response.

Within a day of my story appearing on the Web and on the newsstands, I was deluged with e-mails, calls, and letters. Most of the writers were moms. Many of these women were empowered, passionate, and articulate. All of them were mothers of sons. They wrote to thank me for writing an article that touched on the central drama of their family life—the subtle and sometimes profound ways in which their sons were mismatched with school. They asked me to write more on the subject and offered me lots of ideas about how the new gender gap took hold and why it is growing. They freely shared their families' experiences—some troubling, some painful, some inspiring, some deeply hilarious.

They asked me to look at specific questions: In what ways have our boys changed? Our schools are being transformed, but could these reforms actually be hurting young men? And what about society? Maybe today's parents, with their heightened expectations and close connections to their kids, were actually making life harder rather than easier for boys. Some put the blame squarely on the video game industry. Could these panoramas of hyperviolence actually dampen a boy's appetite for real learning? Why were boys lagging in reading and writing? What about single-sex school or single-sex classes in mixed-gender schools? Would they help? How could parents make their sons ambitious for a college education? Some suggested that I look at the changing gender roles. Perhaps one of the unforeseen by-products of the feminist movement was to leave boys rudderless in a changing world. I was amazed at the volume of mail and delighted at the richness and depth of the subject that lay before me. I was encouraged and energized.

A minority of readers didn't like the story. One woman wrote in complaining because *Newsweek* had dedicated so much space in the magazine to the topic. "Girls have been oppressed by men since the dawn of time," she commented wryly. "Now we're on top for a nanosecond and it's a crisis?" I sympathized. She's right, of course. But then I tried to imagine how difficult it would be to explain that position to the parents of a nine-year-old boy who is stuck in the slowest reading group. Yes, your son is not reading at grade level. But don't worry. After all, men have dominated women for centuries. That's a conversation I wouldn't want to be part of. It would be uncomfortable and offensive. One of the enduring effects of the civil rights and feminist movements has been to cement the idea in parents that all children, regardless of their race and gender, have the capacity to succeed in school.

I became aware that my story was being used as fodder in an ongoing debate. By writing about boys and school, I had inadvertently stepped into the protracted war between academic feminists and the people who despise them. Right-wing groups claimed my story was "proof" that feminists had somehow ruined public education. Feminist academics shouted "Backlash!" Talking about the underachievement of boys, they claimed, was simply a way of diverting attention from the needs of girls. Black and Hispanic boys are not faring well, they conceded, but women of all backgrounds still struggle for equity in the workplace. *Newsweek,* they charged, was mounting an effort to leach oxygen out of important workplace issues. One writer suggested that anyone who was concerned about the problems of boys was uncomfortable with the success of girls in school. I explore this criticism more closely in Chapter 3.

I began to wonder, Were the politicians I spoke to correct after all? Was the American public blind to nuance? I began to wonder if this kind of bare-knuckle gender politicking wasn't at least part of the reason why the new gender gap has grown unchecked. I began to wonder how we could look beyond ideology. Most of the parents I've met want the best for their daughters as well as for their sons. We're all proud of the gains girls have made and continue to make in education. Whether we make our homes in red America or blue America, most of us sympathize with the struggles women continue to face to get equal pay for equal work. Nevertheless, we need to have a rational conversation about what is ailing boys without being forced to take sides in a cultural debate left over from 1974.

In my research, I've found ample evidence that many boys at all levels of society are struggling. I've talked to principals from impoverished inner-city schools in Chicago and from affluent private schools outside Philadelphia, and I've found that they are asking variations of the same question: What is it about males that makes them achieve less in school than females achieve?

That's a vexing question, especially when we're talking about such different kids. The social capital of a black boy raised in poverty in Chicago, for instance, is very different from that of a fair-haired, football-playing boy attending a private school in one of the city's affluent suburbs. But when you compare those boys not to each other but to their female counterparts from similar backgrounds, it becomes obvious that something about being male is undermining their academic success.

What is it? Is it something in the way we're teaching them? And even if we can identify the problem, how can we help boys do better in school without hurting girls? As an education writer, I believe these are crucial questions—and their answers will shape our future. We won't find them, though, until we begin a thorough investigation of the problem.

What You Can Expect from Reading This Book

This is not the kind of book in which the author, having made up her mind, sets out in two hundred or so pages to prove to the reader that her initial ideas are correct. Since my cover story was published in *Newsweek,* I've had an opportunity to do more than a year's worth of detailed, thorough reporting and thoughtful analysis. I'm not trying to bolster or defend any particular ideology. I'll try to point out where my own biases shaped my thinking. I'll tell you what conclusions I've come to, but I'll also tell you when research about a particular topic is contradictory or simply not clear.

Before you begin, let me wave a flag: If you want to simply place blame or to read about someone grinding an ax, this book is probably not for you. To me, the problems with boys seem too broad and too serious to point an accusatory finger at teachers, schools, trends in parenting, feminism, or those old favorite whipping boys "the media" and "society." We raise our children in the way we do for some very good reasons. There's a fascinating story behind the reasons why schools do what they do. To understand the problem, it was helpful, maybe even necessary, for me to take a step back, to see how we got here in order to see where we might go. My goal is to look at the boy problem fairly, clearly, and compassionately—and to take you along for the ride.

I've come to believe that the biggest roadblocks to change are three myths that our culture is perpetuating about boys. The first myth is that for males, school achievement doesn't matter. That is an outdated notion and demonstrably false. The second myth revolves around the idea that boys who struggle early on eventually will catch up. At this juncture, that is probably true for boys from the richest families—those who enmesh their sons in support services like tutors, psychopharmacological aids, SAT coaches, and academic camps, to ensure they get into some kind of college. But the majority of middle-class and poor boys who struggle never catch up, and the consequences for them are devastating. The third and possibly most powerful myth is that schools "have always done it this way." To the contrary, schools are social institutions, and they constantly change to reflect the prevailing wisdom of the day. Today's tradition was yesterday's fad. And believe it or not, that's good news. If schools are failing boys, they can—in fact, they must—evolve to better serve all children.

What should we do? I've come to distrust the easy and obvious solutions, and I urge you to do the same. Some terrific innovative thinkers are looking at the boy problem, but a great many ideas are floating around about boys and school that ultimately may do more harm than good. I'm going to show you why you should think deeply about this problem, and I'm going to help you separate useful programs—ones that actually help our boys—from ones that merely make parents or teachers feel better. Remember: In many cases, there's a big gap between what we think will help boys and what has proven to be effective. This book will sensitize you to the ways in which boys run into trouble, provide you with information on how some schools have adapted, and give you some ideas about when and how to press for change.

If you're anything like me, your time is at a premium. If you are an educator, I know your days are jam-packed. If you're a parent, I realize that reading a book can take a backseat to working, getting a hot meal on the table, or holding up your end of the carpool. With an eye on the busy reader, I've worked hard to boil down a great deal of information into an accessible form. In Chapter 1, I hit you with a lot of facts and figures, but I think it's important for you to understand the scope of the problem. From time to time, I offer a little history about gender and education, too. Women's Studies 101 might not seem too important if you and your son are locked in a battle royale over math homework, but bear with me. There are good reasons why some smart people get twitchy when they hear talk about programs to help boys. You're going to run into those folks, so you might as well know where they're coming from. I believe the more we understand about this problem and where it comes from, the better and more efficient our response can be.

I thought a lot about how to lay out the information in this book so it will be most useful to you. With a couple of exceptions, I structured the book so that you come across issues and debates in the order in which they are likely to touch a boy—and his family—as he grows and moves through school. After I lay out the problem, in Chapters 7 to 11 I address specific issues that bedevil young boys—too much fidgeting, scattered attention, problems in reading, the lack of male teachers— and I consider what we can do about them. Chapter 12 on the "boy brain" comes at the end of that series because late in childhood is the time when many parents seem to realize that there's something going on with gender that is larger than simple environment and condition- ing. Chapters 13 to 15 are aimed at parents and teachers of adolescent boys and focus on video games and some broader psychosocial con- cerns. If your son is struggling in his middle school years and you are considering an alternative such as a single-sex school you may find Chapter 14, about boys' schools, helpful. Chapters 16 to 19 are about high schools and college and the problems that sometimes affect young adult males in those settings. Interspersed throughout the chapters are short vignettes dubbed "Notes from the Front." They will give you ideas about what is being done to help boys around the country. At the end of some chapters, I pass along specific suggestions that teachers, school administrators, and parents of boys have made to me in the course of my research. I'm aware that your son's issues are unique to your particular family, school, and community, but the suggestions seemed to be useful and sensible ideas that are well worth a try.

What almost everyone quoted in this book can agree on is that we need to change things—some big and some small—in order to help young men who are struggling succeed. We need to figure out what those changes must be. Then we need to take action. I hope this book gives you not only information but some inspiration, too.

CHAPTER 1

NOTES FROM THE FRONT

The Edina Experiment

Throughout his thirty-nine-year career in education, Superintendent Kenneth Dragseth was guided by a single rule: Do what's right for the kids. So a couple of years ago, when he began to see signs of the underachievement of boys in his schools, he knew he had to do something about it. It first came to his attention in 1999 during the end-of-the-year awards ceremonies for high school juniors and seniors. "I couldn't help but notice that nearly every honor and every award was going to a young woman." The habits of old math teachers die hard, and Dragseth, who spent eight years in front of a blackboard before heading up the schools in the well-to-do community of Edina, Minnesota, began to keep a tally of how boys and girls in his schools were faring. Impressions, he knew, are fleeting and don't always tell the whole story. "So I began to save every bit of documentation I got which compared the achievement rates between genders. Within a year or so, I looked at what I had collected and I thought, 'Wow, we really have a gender problem. This school might really be skewed toward girls.'"

Dragseth is a plainspoken man with an even smile, which can disguise the fact, at least at first, that he's something of a visionary. He prides himself on looking at the whole kid. In 1996, he noticed something that parents have remarked on for centuries: Adolescents simply aren't at their best in the morning. "You could tell just by looking at them," he says, that they weren't engaged in optimum learning before nine o'clock or so. Dragseth consulted the experts—in this case, scientists who study sleep cycles, hormones, and diurnal clocks—and he found out that there were good biological reasons why his sophomores came to school looking bleary-eyed and his juniors were swilling coffee in first-period calculus. So he did something that tends to be pretty unusual in the world of public education: He took it upon himself to change the way things were being done. Armed with the latest scientific information about teenagers and sleep, he persuaded his school board to allow him to move the opening bell of high school from 7:20 to a more humane 8:30. In doing so, he made national headlines.

"It was just common sense," Dragseth says. "We're trying to get the best out of our students."

On the subject of gender differences, though, Dragseth's notions about what was best for kids flew smack in the face of conventional wisdom. Across the nation, most educators acknowledge that impoverished black and Latino boys are lagging badly behind white boys and all girls in school. But Dragseth's students hardly fit that demographic. There aren't many minority kids in Edina, and there aren't many poor kids, either. In fact, the average family income hovers around $93,000 a year. The school system is one of the top-performing districts in the country—a full 96 percent of graduates attend college. The parents tend to be highly educated, and scholastic achievement seems to be a dominant gene. A study conducted on Edina high school students ten years after graduation found that about 45 percent of them were pursuing advanced degrees. "These aren't poor kids from urban Minneapolis," says Dragseth. "These are rich, suburban kids."

Dragseth is a worldly man. He knew all too well that gender can be a political hot potato, especially in a field where concerned women have pushed hard to widen the academic and professional horizons for young girls. But he was convinced that his schools had a serious problem. He decided to dig deeper. In 2001, with the blessing of his school board, Dragseth launched a task force aimed at putting the boys and girls of Edina under a microscope. The study group, made up of teachers and administrators, took its job seriously. They were nothing if not thorough. They looked at four years' worth of records and summarized the grades, class rank, standardized test scores, and behavioral issues for boy and girl students from second to twelfth grade. They figured out how much homework girls were doing compared to boys. They conducted careful polls to elicit feedback on how much students actually liked school, whether they felt encouraged, and how frequently they engaged with teachers. They asked students about their lives beyond school as well—how much they read for pleasure, for instance—and they tried to gauge students' civic involvement by asking if they attended a church group or volunteered in the community. They probed the kids on aspects of life they tended to keep hidden from the high-achieving adults of the town, asking whether they engaged in violent or risky behaviors and whether they drank alcohol or smoked pot.

The final report was troubling. It showed that boys and girls performed about the same on aptitude and IQ tests. By every other measure, however, boys' experience of school was startlingly different from and far more difficult than the experience of their female classmates. The report laid out the difference in black and white. Boys and girls started off about the same. Around fourth grade, though, girls pulled ahead. By sixth grade, many boys had fallen behind in reading, writing, and sometimes math, but rather than overcoming the challenge, those boys seemed to tune out. By middle school, girls spent more time doing homework, and many more females than males were in the top 10 percent of the class. Although there were almost equal numbers of boys and girls in gifted programs, many more boys received remedial help, and there were many more boys than girls in special education classes.

In high school, the split between boys and girls grew even more dramatic. On standardized tests at all levels, boys were equally or slightly more proficient in math than girls. Girls were equal to or slightly better than boys in reading. In the classroom, though, girls dominated every subject. Many more girls took Advanced Placement courses. Girls made up the majority of names on the honor roll. They participated in more after-school activities and received far more school or districtwide recognition and awards. Boys engaged in risky behaviors at far greater levels. They drank, smoked pot, and used other people's prescription drugs more. They reported being physically injured at greater rates. They were suspended more frequently and spent less time reading for pleasure. Given all that data, you won't be surprised to learn that the task force found that boys in Edina reported liking school less than girls do.

The report confirmed Superintendent Dragseth's fears. He'd been operating a school system that gave every appearance of doing very well—a cohesive community that cultivated rigorous academic standards. But in reality, his schools were offering the children of Edina a two-tiered experience. Many more girls than boys were engaged, active, and happy learners.

Dragseth wasted no time. He made a full presentation to the school board. "Some members were concerned about girls, and we were, too," recalls Dragseth. "But this wasn't about bringing them down or keeping them from succeeding." The evidence was incontrovertible. Boys needed help. The board agreed that something must be done.

In the fall of 2002, Dragseth set out to change the culture of his schools in a way that would ensure that both boys and girls would thrive. He started by meeting with his kindergarten through twelfth-grade teachers. At that meeting, he witnessed a world-class game of pass-the-buck among his otherwise enthusiastic and dedicated early education staff. Because the data showed that boys began faltering in fourth grade, the early education teachers figured they didn't need to change.

"But I knew that wasn't right. From walking in and out of first-grade classrooms, I could see the problems boys were facing," says Dragseth. He asked the teachers to reflect on their own classroom experiences: "What do you see in a reading circle? A teacher reading and the girls sitting and the teacher stopping to say, 'Stop moving around, Matt. Pay attention, Jules.' Boys who need to move around attract lots of negative attention. They get beat down early. They lose their spark."

Dragseth asked all his staff members to come up with ideas to weave boys of every grade more tightly into the academic and social fabric of the school community—especially when it came to reading and writing. "We wanted to look at how we were turning boys off." They launched a boy-friendly book club, they revised their reading lists in high school, and they decided to experiment with single-gender classes in some subjects. Then Dragseth brought the gender study data to the parents. "We realized if we wanted to change things we needed parents on board." Specifically, he asked parents to encourage their sons as well as their daughters to get involved in the arts. Then he made his appeal to the wider Edina community. When Kiwanis and other groups were recognizing academic achievement, Dragseth asked them to expand their criteria so more boys could be recognized for achieving in school. Was this strategy fair to the girls? "The girls still got awards," says Dragseth. "But we felt it was important to reinforce certain positive behaviors [among males]."

Did it help? The results are mixed. These days in Edina, many fewer boys are being identified as needing special education. Boys who previously ran about a half a year behind girls in reading and math achievement have closed the gap. Other measures indicate only partial success.

On average, the male GPA still lags behind the female GPA, though less than in the past. Boys still pose the majority of behavioral problems, and the male writing deficit remains unchanged. Dragseth, who retired in 2006, says the most profound and longest-lasting changes may be the most difficult to measure. "We're changing attitude and awareness," he points out, "and that's going to continue paying dividends down the line." He knows he succeeded on the most important level: doing what's right for the kids.

CHAPTER 2

THE SCOPE OF THE PROBLEM

It's Not Just Your Son

Let's take a closer look at how boys are doing. What we find is that, on the whole, in crumbling public schools in poor neighborhoods, in elite schools that serve the very rich, and in many middle-class suburban schools around the country, boys are doing less well than girls. Not every boy is struggling. Everywhere you look, some high-performing boys are doing as well as, in many ways even better than, the smartest and most accomplished girls. But generally, boys, for a number of reasons—some new and some that would be familiar to our parents and to their parents—are not keeping pace with girls when it comes to learning.

How are they failing? In Edina, many more boys than girls were identified as having learning disabilities and were relegated to special education classes. That disparity is nationwide. Across the United States and in every socioeconomic grouping, boys make up the overwhelming majority of kids who get that special ed label. Why? Part of the reason has to do with simple biology. Pediatricians find that more boy babies than girl babies are likely to be born with vision problems, hearing impairment, and gross motor disabilities, which can interfere with learning. But there also are good indicators that boys, for reasons we'll discuss later, simply aren't fitting into the flow of the school day in the same way as girls. Boys represent the overwhelming number of behavioral problems. They are prescribed medicine for attention-related disorders at twice the rate of girls, and far from leveling out, the number of boys taking attention-related drugs continues to climb—growing 48 percent between 2000 and 2005. Boys themselves report that they are more likely to be the target of bullying and even violent crime like assault.

Think boys can handle it? The pressure is on boys to appear stoic, but there are worrisome signs that at some deeper level, boys are not OK. There has been much in the popular press about high rates of depression among adolescent girls, and indeed girls are more likely to report feeling blue. But boys are much more likely than girls to kill themselves. According to epidemiologists and the Center for Disease Control, suicide rates among adolescent boys skyrocketed from the 1950s to the 1980s and remained high. Currently, between the ages of 5 and 14, boys are three times more likely to die by their own hand than girls. Between the ages of 15 and 19, boys kill themselves at four times the rate of their female classmates.

Boys learn less than girls in school. How do we know this? The educational system in the United States is highly fragmented. Public schools get some money from the federal government—about 10 percent of their operating budgets or about $71.5 billion a year—but for the most part public schools are administered and funded by state and local governments. Still, the federal government wants taxpayers to know what they're getting for their money. The feds also need to keep a sharp eye on how well schools around the country are preparing the workforce of the future. So, fortunately for us, the U.S. Department of Education churns out data on the nation's students by testing and questioning a representative sample of school-goers and then breaking the results down by ethnicity and gender. Periodically, the National Center for Education Statistics (NCES) issues a report—*The Nation's Report Card*—to let us

know how the kids are doing. According to the U.S. Department of Education, the academic underachievement of boys that Kenneth Dragseth uncovered in affluent Edina reflects an entrenched national problem.

To understand this crucial point, let's examine the data more closely. Since the early 1970s, the data-collecting wing of the Department of Education has been keeping a close watch on how children perform on standardized tests for all major subjects at ages 9, 13, and 17—ages that roughly correspond to fourth grade, eighth grade, and the senior year in high school. All of this information is available online at http://nces. ed.gov/nationsreportcard/ltt/results2004.

As you can see from looking at Figure 1, a great deal about student achievement changed in the last thirty years. In 1973, girls lagged badly behind boys in high school math. Back then, their underperformance meshed smoothly with societal expectations, and many smart thinkers had plausible-sounding theories about why girls should not be expected to achieve in math at the same rate as boys. Their minds didn't work that way, some educational policy makers argued. Reputable scientists

Figure 1. Trends in Average Math Scale Scores by Gender, Age 17

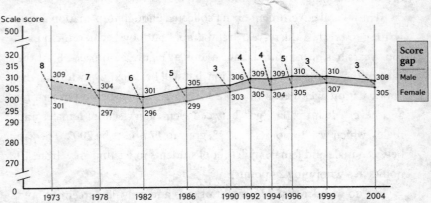

SOURCE: U.S. Department of Education.

suggested that girls didn't have the "math gene." Maybe not. But if they didn't have it, it turns out they didn't need it. Once a critical mass of teachers put raising girls' achievement in math in their sight lines, girls learned math and learned it well. By the early 1990s, girls had all but closed that gap. In 2004, high school girls scored within 3 points of the boys.

In the same time period, the NCES data on reading, the linchpin skill for academic success, shows boys lagging far behind. Let's look at the data in Figure 2 carefully. The longer boys stay in school, the farther they fall behind the girls. What's frustrating is that these numbers are not immutable. Since the 1990s, when schools began to focus on improving early literacy, both male and female fourth-graders have improved in reading competency, and boys have narrowed the gap. In 2004, fourth-grade boys scored better but remained 5 points below fourth-grade girls. Now look at the gender gap between boys and girls in the years that follow. In middle school, the gap widens to 10 points. By high school, the gap has widened to 14 points—and in high school, boys are actually doing worse in reading than they were thirty years ago. We know that schools can improve reading levels, as they did for kids in fourth grade, and can effectively shrink the gender gap. The question then arises, Why on earth don't they do it for middle and high school boys?

The federal government hasn't collected enough information about writing to create a thirty-year trend graph, but boys' achievement over four years has been plotted. Take a look at Figure 3 on page 28. At the start of the twenty-first century, in what will be called by historians the "information age," here's what we see. Boys start far behind in writing and never catch up. The gap between elementary school females and males, which was 16 points in 1998, grew to 17 points by 2002. The gap between male and female high school students in writing grew from 19 points to a whopping 24 points.

It's no wonder that 72 percent of girls and only 65 percent of boys graduate from high school.

Figure 2. Trends in Average Reading Scale Scores by Gender, Ages 9, 13, and 17

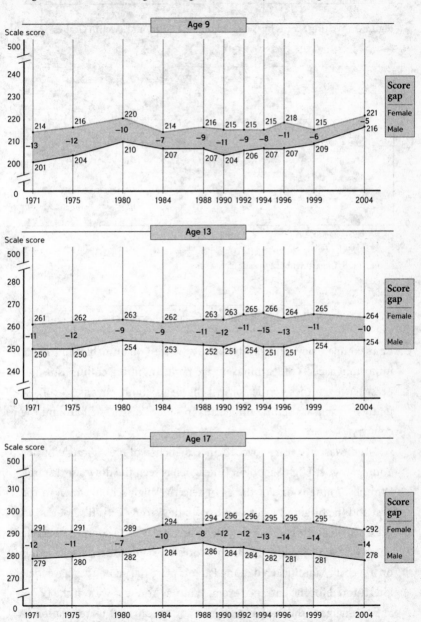

SOURCE: U.S. Department of Education.

Figure 3. Writing Scores by Gender: Fourth, Eighth, and Twelfth Grades

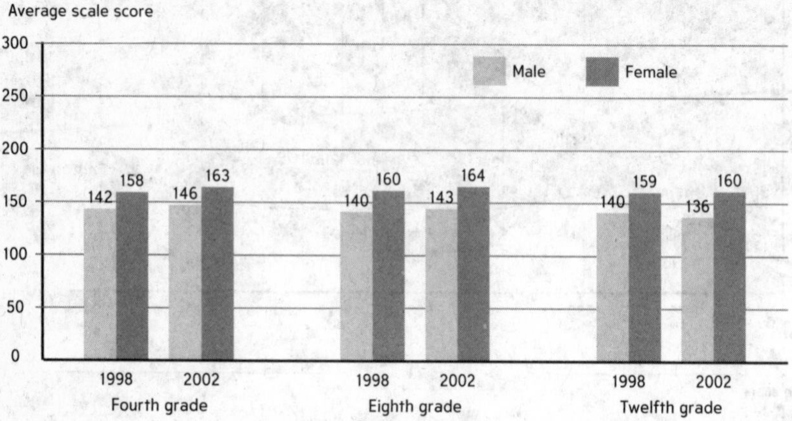

Average scale score

	Male	Female
Fourth grade 1998	142	158
Fourth grade 2002	146	163
Eighth grade 1998	140	160
Eighth grade 2002	143	164
Twelfth grade 1998	140	159
Twelfth grade 2002	136	160

SOURCE: U.S. Department of Education.

The Feminization of College Campuses

LET's compare boys and girls by some other, less quantifiable but equally important aspects of learning: engagement, ambition, enthusiasm, and persistence. In these critical areas, the news about boys is so consistently bad that it's setting off alarms in school districts all around the country.

In the last five years, Joyce Kenner, principal of prestigious Whitney Young Magnet High School in Chicago, has seen the downward spiral. Whitney Young is one of the eight selective high schools open to the best and the brightest eighth-graders in the Windy City. It's not easy to get in. Rising eighth-grade candidates are ranked by a complex formula based on GPAs, reading and math scores on statewide tests, and scores on a specially administered exam. Parents pay $100 an hour to have their kids tutored for the entrance exam. Whitney Young is west of the Loop, and the neighborhood is a little gritty, but because of its reputation—famous graduates include Michelle Obama, wife of Senator Barack

Obama, and *The Matrix* directors Andy and Larry Wachowski—it tends to attract more white and more middle-class families than most institutions within the Chicago public schools.

In the spring of 2003, slightly more males than females were accepted to the incoming freshman class. In the spring of 2006, though, the balance tilted solidly in favor of girls: 38 percent of the coveted seats went to boys, 62 percent to girls. Principal Kenner is proud of her smart females, but worries about what the gender imbalance is doing to her school. "It's becoming a little uncomfortably girls over boys," she says.

Whitney Young isn't the only selective high school in Chicago with a gender imbalance. At Gwendolyn Brooks College Preparatory school, the percentage of boys accepted in 2006 dipped to 30.6 percent. For social reasons, school administrators want to maintain something of a gender balance in their school community. In a pattern that mirrors the college application process, they've begun discriminating against girls. If you're female, it's harder to get into a selective school in Chicago. Rejected girls averaged a 2.82 GPA; rejected boys averaged 2.45. "One is closer to a B and the other is a C," John Easton, director of the University of Chicago's Consortium on Chicago School Research told the *Chicago Sun-Times.* "It seems like a meaningful difference."

The CEO of Chicago public schools, Arne Duncan, has been monitoring the plummeting achievement of boys with growing concern. "It seems to be getting worse," he says. Duncan asked his staff to figure out the legalities of establishing a formal affirmative action program for boys.

Researchers who study the education pipeline—the progression of students into secondary school and on to higher education—say that a significant cross section of boys fall down early and never catch up. "We call them the missing boys," says Thomas Mortenson from the Pell Institute, who's been studying the underachieving males in school for years. Boys, it seems, stumble badly in school in the earliest grades.

They read less well than girls, and they read less. As they get older, they study less, too. They hand in less homework than their female counterparts. In high school, their grade-point averages are lower—a gap that has widened since 2000. Eighteen years ago, the kids at the bottom of the class consisted of nearly equal numbers of boys and girls. In 2005, more boys than girls were at the bottom. By high school, families and communities reap what they have sown. In order to get to college, students are expected to take rigorous courses in high school to prepare them for challenging college work. In the last thirty years, that message seems to have been increasingly lost on young males. In 1980, girls took slightly fewer science courses and many fewer math courses than boys. Since 1992, girls have been taking more science and math courses and doing better in them than boys. Girls now take more geometry, algebra II, precalculus, biology, AP honors biology, and chemistry. (Slightly more boys than girls take calculus and boys still dominate in physics.)

Admission to highly selective colleges has grown more competitive. High schools, eager to show that they have a rigorous curriculum, have expanded their Advanced Placement programs, enabling juniors and seniors to take at least one or two college-level courses. A high-schooler who does well in an AP class and scores high enough on the AP exam can receive college credit before even graduating from high school. These days, in most schools, classrooms where AP courses are taught look like a branch of a local sorority. Girls often outnumber the boys, sometimes by two to one in AP English and AP foreign language classes. In 1985, about the same number of girls and boys took the final AP exam. By 2002, 56 percent of the exam takers were female.

Gradually, young males have withdrawn from extracurricular activities, with the exception of competitive sports. This is not a small thing. Students who participate in activities at school but outside the classroom develop confidence, exercise leadership skills, and tend to engage more in their studies. Females are now much more likely to run the school paper, piece together the yearbook, participate in music and the performing arts, and get themselves elected to the student council. Carlos Laird, associate admissions director for Texas State University-San Marcos, spends a chunk of each year visiting high schools in all kinds of communities. He says the stereotypical Big Man on Campus is gone. Instead, he sees the disengagement of boys writ large. "It's almost like boys have conceded the playing field. High school is something girls do well and boys are going to just step aside and let them do it," Laird says.

UCLA freshman Karen Teng saw firsthand the defensive and ultimately self-defeating attitudes boys develop toward school. She attended high school in economically and racially mixed Charlotte-Mecklenburg County, North Carolina. Parts of Mecklenburg County are very wealthy. Colleges around Charlotte and big employers like Wachovia and Bank of America have brought large numbers of affluent families to the area. Yet the county also suffers from a boy problem. In 2006, an astonishing 26 of the 31 valedictorians from the twenty-one public and the ten largest private high schools in the county were young women. Karen Teng was one of them: She led her class at South Mecklenburg High school with an impressive 3.9 grade point average while taking the most rigorous courses, including twelve APs.

"I worked for it," she says matter-of-factly. She is unquestionably ambitious for herself. She's motivated, in part, by a kind of reverse peer pressure. Instead of influencing her to skip school or stay out late, Teng says, her closest girl pals made her success possible by supporting each other and by competing against each other, too. Being smart was part of their self-image. "You want to look good, you want to dress well, and you want to have good grades," she says. Her brother, now a sophomore at the same high school, is having a different experience. He's as smart as she is, "but he acts more like a typical guy," she says. Instead of studying hard, he prefers to play tennis and acts like he's satisfied with his B's. "He acts more laid back," Teng says, "like school doesn't matter."

Mac Cramer, 17, who attends high school in the same county, is a self-described "slacker" when it comes to getting his schoolwork done. His parents—his father works in advertising and his mother works for the chamber of commerce—want him to do better, but *Halo 3*, not books, is his thing. "Some of my friends work hard," he says. "But most of us, well, put it this way: We're not fans of homework." Cramer says that for him, and many guys like him, the purely social aspect of school is what keeps him showing up each day.

School matters, though, if you want to go to college. Not surprisingly, many more girls than boys are getting there. It wasn't always this way. In the 1950s and 1960s, only a small percentage of people attended college at all—and most of them were wealthy, white, and male. In the 1970s, the number of men and women attending college began to rise dramatically. By the 1980s, bachelor's degrees were awarded to males and females at about the same rates. Since then, more young adults— male and female—have been enrolling in college, but women have been enrolling faster. In 2005, the most recent data the government has published, 57.2 percent of the undergraduates enrolled in American colleges and universities were women. In pure numbers that translated to about 2.5 million more girls than boys enrolled in college, and that gap has been growing at a rate of about 100,000 students a year. Once women get to college, they are more likely to graduate, too. Most people can tick off a list of differences between men and women, but here's a new one: For the first time in history, women are better educated. At present, 33 percent of women between twenty-five and twenty-nine years of age hold a four-year degree compared to 26 percent of men.

We'll drill farther down into these numbers later. For now, suffice it to say that unless there is some large-scale change in the way we educate our children, that gap will continue to widen. Figure 4 shows projections by the U.S. Department of Education.

The gender imbalance in education is not only an American prob-

Figure 4. Undergraduate Enrollment in Degree-Granting Institutions with Projections

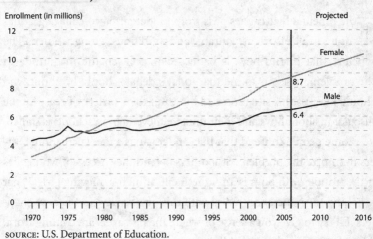

SOURCE: U.S. Department of Education.

lem. Almost everywhere in the industrialized world, in places where boys and girls have equal access to education, the underperformance of boys is not just an uncomfortable fact but a real and pressing problem. In 1998, the British government made the problem of boys in schools a top priority. "We . . . should not simply accept with a shrug of our shoulders that boys will be boys," said Stephen Byers, the school standards minister, when he announced a new national boys' initiative. "Failure to raise the educational achievement of boys will mean that thousands of young men will face a bleak future in which a lack of qualifications and basic skills will mean unemployment and little hope of finding work." Other governments also have recognized the massive economic, social, and cultural fallout that will result from letting the new gender gap grow. Government officials in New Zealand, Australia, Canada, and Jamaica came to the same conclusion: Helping boys in school is a matter of grave importance to the future of their respective countries.

———

The pipeline that carries girls from kindergarten to college graduation is full of bright, vibrant, and ambitious young women. The pipeline that carries boys is badly leaking. Given the magnitude of the problem, it seems to me that today's debate should be about who should address this situation and how. But for a variety of reasons, the discussion about boys and their underachievement in schools is stalled.

Some people contend that the gender gap is a media creation. Others minimize the problem. Still others defend the success of women, as if the trouble with boys is an indictment of high-achieving girls. What is behind the reluctance to deal with this new reality? In the next chapters, I'll try to give you a sense of where the naysayers are coming from, what they're afraid of, and I'll try to explain why some otherwise smart people react the way they do when the conversation shifts to boys.

CHAPTER 3

THE DOUBTERS

Why Some People (Mistakenly) Say Boys Are
Doing Just Fine

In this chapter, I provide a thumbnail sketch of the history of gender and education. If you just got finished looking at your son's dismal report card and then reached for this book, you might feel that you don't have time for this digression. You might find it more useful to skip ahead to Chapter 4 to find out more about what I learned goes on inside the classroom. But if you can, stay with me. The reason I want to give you a little history here is that the problem is bigger than your son alone. To understand how schools got this way and why the problem has gone unaddressed for so long, it is going to help you a lot to understand the harrowing struggles women went through to get access to education. You'll learn how the challenges women faced and to a great extent overcame in order to become educated continue to shape many aspects of our schools. After you read this chapter, you'll be able to more accurately assess how we might change things about schooling for the benefit of our sons without hurting our intelligent and ambitious young girls.

Until recently, any discussion about formal education was really a discussion about wealthy men—poor boys and girls were pretty much shut out. Boys from rich families went to school or had tutors. Slightly less affluent men were educated in guilds, at royal courts, and in monasteries—usually in a particular profession or trade. The odd noblewoman might have learned reading, writing, languages, and maybe a smattering of math, but only in the last three hundred years or so did anyone consider poor males and any females worth educating at all.

About 250 years ago, it became more common to educate upper- and middle-class women, but they were taught different things than boys. Males were educated in order to improve their minds and support their families. Women were educated to be good wives, run efficient households, and be good mothers. Academic rigor for girls was considered not only unnecessary but unnatural. In the early twentieth century in the United States, the suffrage movement called attention to the rights of women and gradually they gained more access to schooling.

Still, women remained second-class citizens and their education—which emphasized courses in home economics, typing, and cooking—reflected that status. Until the 1950s, more men than women graduated from high school, and many more men than women went on to college. Except during a brief period after World War II, when the GI Bill gave working-class young men access to higher education, college was reserved for wealthy males, and those guys never had to compete head-to-head with females. Rich white guys ruled, and no one complained.

In the early 1970s, the women's rights movement returned with great ferocity. Taking a cue from the successful civil rights movement, women began organizing, petitioning, and campaigning for equal rights in education and on the job. At the time, discrimination against women in all walks of life was overt and pervasive. The June Cleaver–style stay-at-home mom was the societal ideal, but many women worked outside the home for money—they just didn't get paid very much for their labor. Inequity was written into the law. Working-class women were subjected to so-called protective laws, which in theory were supposed to prevent employers from abusing women by forcing them into harsh physical labor or long hours. In practice, the protective laws kept women out of supervisory positions and limited their income without affording much protection at all. Ambitious young women were steered into clerical classes, nursing school, or education. Forty years ago, 8 percent of scientists, 7 percent of physicians, 3 percent of lawyers, and 1 percent of engineers and architects were women. Colleges and universities practiced systematic discrimination against women, using quotas to limit enrollment. Even when women managed to get into higher-paying careers, from scientist to salesperson, women usually earned substantially less than men.

Feminists in the 1970s realized that to level the playing field, women needed to get more education. These visionaries used the courts to force colleges and universities to provide it. The first court case to suggest what was then the novel theory of gender discrimination was brought in 1969 against the University of Maryland by part-time psychology professor Bernice Sandler, who was sick of applying for full-time faculty jobs and getting passed over in favor of men. She brought her complaint to the Women's Equity Action League, a group of well-connected lawyers and politicians. Together, they began filing a series of complaints with the U.S. Department of Labor for gender discrimination. Sandler's cause struck a chord with women around the country. By 1970, about one hundred other groups and individual women had filed their own gender discrimination charges against colleges, universities, and the federal government. That summer, the House Committee on Education and Labor held hearings aimed at prohibiting discrimination against women in federal-assistance programs and women employed in education—testimony that laid the groundwork for legislation that would help outlaw discriminatory practices against women in education: Title IX of the Education Amendments of 1972.

TITLE IX

> *No person in the United States shall, on the basis of sex, be*
> *excluded from participation in, be denied the benefits of, or*
> *be subjected to discrimination under any education program*
> *or activity receiving Federal financial assistance.*
>
> *—From Title IX*

IN THE spring of 1972 the country was still up in arms about the desegregation of formerly all-white public schools. The nightly news was packed with images of hard-faced white women who on another day might have baked cookies for the PTA bake sale but instead were turning out to "defend" their schools by throwing rocks at busloads of frightened black children. In April, when Congress convened to reauthorize the Higher Education Act, all eyes were on a doomed amendment to stop busing. What little debate there was focused on a provision aimed at providing funds for needy students—what would become Pell Grants. When Republican president Richard Nixon signed the Education Amendments of 1972, reauthorizing the Higher Education Act, there wasn't any discussion about an innocuous little provision concerning equal rights for women.

"Most people didn't realize the wide implications of a sex amendment," says Representative Edith Green (D-Oregon), who slipped Title IX in among other amendments, "and it was better that way."

Lawmakers figured Title IX would transform the world of education, though they weren't exactly sure how. The concept of gender discrimination was still relatively new. Feminists were in a battle to persuade at least the female citizenry, if not the general public, to support the cause of women's rights. American women, they calculated, would be able to recognize some of our country's fundamental and most deeply held principles—fairness and equality—inherent in the newly enacted law.

As it turned out, Title IX had about the same effect on antifemale discrimination in higher education as David's rock had on Goliath. It was a long shot. It was a lucky shot. But it changed the balance of power between men and women more abruptly than anyone thought possible. Although colleges and universities were given six years to change their discriminatory enrollment practices, most threw open their doors to all qualified applicants almost immediately. Women began applying to the most prestigious universities, were accepted, and began to thrive. Title IX also opened the floodgates to new federal laws and provisions—including the 1974 Women's Educational Equity Act and amendments to the Vocational Education Act in 1976. Throughout the 1970s and 1980s, those laws provided a massive funding stream for projects aimed at fighting the bias against girls in education. State legislators got in on the action, too. In 1993, one-third of the states had legislation that equaled or exceeded the provisions of Title IX, and thirty-one states had legislation that supported gender equity in education.

Today it's hard to comprehend how fast the educational prospects for girls changed. Education is a field in which money is perennially tight and old ideas, even bad ones, die hard. Suddenly, there was willingness to engage girls more thoroughly in school, and there were well-funded, well-organized programs and materials with which to do it.

Teachers ensured that the new societal order, one that viewed girls as worthy equals of boys, was reinforced at every opportunity. In elementary schools, they discarded reading primers that pictured girls as stewardesses and boys as pilots and replaced them with books that encouraged both John and Jane to be pilots. Before Title IX, it was common practice for high school guidance counselors to hand out vocational worksheets color-coded by gender. On the pink version, the choices for girls included model and actress but not veterinarian and psychiatrist. After Title IX, teachers raised a fuss, and soon, girls and boys were getting the same sheet.

And it worked. In 1975, for the first time, the number of high school seniors who took the SATs was almost equally divided between men and women. In the more than thirty years since then, more girls have taken the SATs than boys, and that gap continues to widen. By 1978, six years after Title IX was enacted, girls were enrolling in colleges in numbers almost equal to boys.

Shortchanging Girls

IN THE mid-1980s, as young women continued to make extraordinary gains in schools, Republican president Ronald Reagan began whittling away at Title IX funding. In response, some feminists renewed their call for more programs to fight off what they saw as an especially pervasive and previously unknown kind of anti-girl bias. Feminist psychologist Carol Gilligan, then a professor at Harvard University, conducted a study of a group of wealthy girls at a boarding school outside Albany, New York, and discovered that adolescent girls were not empowered by their success but were suffering from a crisis of self-esteem. In 1990, when Harvard University Press published *Making Connections: The Relational Worlds of Adolescent Girls at Emma Willard School*, coedited by Gilligan, educational policy makers, by now finely attuned to the feminist agenda that had so successfully buoyed females, were all ears. That same year, the American Association of University Women commissioned a study and in 1991 concurred with Gilligan's findings: "Most [girls] emerge from adolescence with poor self-image."

The AAUW commissioned a second study, which was released in 1992 as the book *How Schools Shortchange Girls*. The 223-page book cataloged shocking, systemic discrimination against girls, ranging from the ways in which teachers interacted with students (when boys called out, teachers listened, but when girls called out, they were told to "raise your hand if you want to speak") to the curricula that teachers chose. The study found that educators chose classroom activities that appealed to boys' interests and selected presentation formats at which boys excelled. As a result, girls, according to the study, experienced a "debilitating loss of self-confidence." The AAUW report cited studies that "proved" that "boys are more likely to feel mastery and control over academic challenges, while girls are more likely to feel powerless in academic situations." What resulted, the report said, was a kind of "learned helplessness" that explained why "boys [and not girls] persistently pursued academic challenges for which both groups were equally qualified." As young girls moved from childhood to womanhood, they were gradually being drained of their confidence and their ambition. *Reviving Ophelia* and other pop psychology books picked up where Gilligan and the AAUW left off, describing a silent crisis among white middle-class suburban girls. The idea that girls were in trouble became imprinted on the national consciousness. If we wanted to help our daughters to be educated, successful, and happy, we needed to make sure our schools and our communities paid special attention to meeting their unique and individual needs.

Serious social scientists questioned the validity of Gilligan's work and the AAUW studies. Girls, they pointed out quietly, had never done better. Indeed, around that time, high school girls, who were besting the boys in literacy and writing, had narrowed the gap in math to 3 points. Still, the AAUW report kicked off a second wave of feminist activism in schools. At the AAUW's urging, the U.S. Congress passed the Gender Equity in Education Act in 1994, which provided schools with new funds to train teachers to help girls succeed.

In order to create a level playing field, schools promoted the interests of girls by embedding pro-girl strategies in the English, science, and social studies curricula. Communities helped, too. When the Ms. Foundation launched "Take Our Daughters to Work Day" in 1993 to combat the crisis of self-esteem among young girls, corporate America embraced it. The tenets of feminism had moved into the mainstream:

If girls were getting shortchanged, schools, parents, and corporate America wanted to do something about it.

Ironically, according to most available statistics—academic, psychological, and social—girls were doing fine. Yes, they needed, and continue to need, encouragement to explore computer science, physics, and higher-level math. But they were achieving better in school than ever before. In 1994, girls were almost matching boys in math, and boys' downward slide in literacy had begun. Among schoolgirls, the confidence gap, which feminists, the media, and then teachers and school administrators had seized on, didn't seem to exist. The situation was ripe for a correction and in 2000 conservative writer Christina Hoff Sommers delivered it in *The War Against Boys: How Misguided Feminism Is Harming Our Young Men*. It was hardly a sneak attack. Six years before, she'd published *Who Stole Feminism: How Women Have Betrayed Women*, a lacerating portrait of the extreme fringe of the women's movement in which she targeted and relentlessly mocked prominent feminists.

In *The War Against Boys*, Hoff Sommers launched another full-frontal attack, this time targeting the notion that schools were shortchanging girls. Her book was meticulously researched, venomous, and unyielding. A heated debate followed, and battle lines were forged: Hoff Sommers and other conservatives charged that feminists promoted the achievement of girls at the expense of boys. Feminists accused conservatives of having a secret agenda—of trying to silence the feminist movement and shift attention away from girls out of concern that men were losing their economic advantage over women.

Shortchanging Boys

SINCE then, boys' struggles in schools have come more sharply into view. Women's rights organizations began to realize what was at stake for both boys and girls when boys fail. They continued to press for programs to help girls, but many widened their scope and began asking, "What is ailing our boys?" In 2003, the Ms. Foundation expanded Take Our Daughters to Work Day to include sons. In 2004, the Ms. Foundation launched a symposium titled "Supporting Boys' Resilience." At Harvard, Carol Gilligan, whose research had set off alarms about the girls' crisis, began steering her graduate students to researching the struggle of boys as well as girls.

It is the extremists, those who interpret real concern about boys as an anti-girl jihad, who still get the ink. Not long ago, in response to an editorial in *USA Today* about the underachievement of boys in school, Kim Gandy, president of the National Organization for Women, wrote, "Part of the boys-crisis alarm is about competition and about women's changing roles in our society. Too many men have a problem seeing women as equals, and would just as soon not have to compete." Fiery words. But she continues, "we see this in employment discrimination, sexual harassment, rape and all forms of violence against women." How can concern about boys in the classroom be linked, even tangentially, with rape?

In 2006, the well-regarded bipartisan Washington think tank Education Sector issued a position paper titled "The Evidence Suggests Otherwise: Truth About Boys and Girls" that purported to debunk the "myth" of boys' underachievement. The report was picked up widely and uncritically by the press, garnering a front-page story in most major newspapers, including the *Washington Post,* and was at the center of a clash between op-ed writers at the *New York Times.* The report, written by policy analyst Sara Mead, suggested that the crisis with boys is merely hype spread by antifeminist factions. "The hysteria about boys is partly a matter of perspective. While most of society has finally embraced the idea of equality for women, the idea that women might actually surpass men in some areas . . . seems to be hard for many people to swallow," Mead wrote. Then she cited the NCES data (see pages 25–28), giving it her own girl-centric interpretation: "The real story is not bad news about boys doing worse. It's good news about girls doing better . . . Girls have narrowed or even closed some academics gaps that previously favored boys while other long-standing gaps that favored girls have widened, leading to the belief that boys are falling behind."

Please flip back to pages 27 and 28 to take a look at those graphs of reading and writing scores; then reread Mead's sentence. The "good news" that she mentions is that on average, a sizable portion of our 45 million American schoolchildren lags behind a sizable portion of others in key subjects, learns less, gets worse grades, and attends college in smaller numbers. Increasingly, the portion at the bottom is failing to keep pace with the demands for an increasingly educated workforce. It's exasperating.

In an op-ed piece written for the *Washington Post* in the spring of 2006, Caryl Rivers, a journalism professor at Boston University, and Rosalind Chait Barnett, a senior scientist at the Women's Studies Research Center at Brandeis University, showed the same lack of nuanced thinking: "The alarming statistics on which the notion of a crisis is based are rarely broken out by race or class. When they are, the whole picture changes . . . White suburban boys aren't significantly touched by it."

Rivers and Barnett do raise a point worth looking at. Almost every ill that befalls schoolchildren in America—from learning disabilities, to dropout rates, to rickets—disproportionately affects poor black and Hispanic children. And the boy problem is no exception. We should not downplay the heavy burden that poverty and racism place on poor kids and kids of color. That said, it's useful to hold this bit of data in your mind: Please take a look at the graph reflecting college enrollment prepared by the U.S. Department of Education on page 46. As you can see, boys in every racial subgroup do worse than girls in school *even though they come from identical environments.*

Now let's break it out by class. To suggest that middle-class boys are not "significantly touched" by the crisis is simply false and shows just how ill equipped some once-progressive thinkers are to participate in a discussion of gender equity that considers the needs of both girls and boys. According to the American Council on Education, the percentage of white male undergraduates from middle-class families with incomes ranging from $32,500 to $97,500 has dropped to 47 percent, and the percentage of black undergraduates from middle-class families is 44 percent. If Rivers and Barnett aren't sure what the impact of those numbers might be, they need only stroll around their own campuses. What they must know but fail to acknowledge is that the proportion of (the mostly white middle- and upper-class) men at Boston University and Brandeis is dipping—their freshman classes in 2007 were 42 percent and 40.8 percent male. Because boys—middle-class and upper-middle-class white boys—do so poorly in school and girls do so well, many private colleges now handicap the applications of girls in favor of boys in order to maintain a gender balance on campus.

Why do so many fewer boys apply? To answer that question, I traveled to schools in Boulder, Colorado; Greenwich, Connecticut; and Wilmette, Illinois. I checked in at elite private schools such as Haverford, outside Philadelphia, and Episcopal High School in Alexandria, Virginia. Not every boy is struggling. But administrators at those schools have identified a serious and growing gender gap and are making a prodigious effort to redress the imbalance. Despite what the doubters say, these school administrators are not operating out of any secret conservative agenda. What motivates them motivates most educators: They want to make sure all kids succeed.

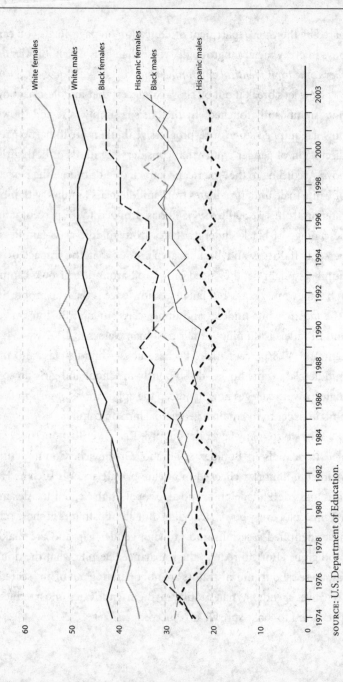

Figure 5. Participation Rate Trends for Adults Ages 18–24 by Combinations of Sex and Race/Ethnicity, 1974–2003

SOURCE: U.S. Department of Education.

A Changing World

ANYONE who dismisses or downplays the trouble with boys is ignoring a changing world. While girls are stampeding into college and boys are lagging behind, the job market is becoming decidedly less hospitable to people who lack a college degree. During most of the twentieth century, the economy relied on a solid agricultural and manufacturing base, which depended on large numbers of unskilled or semiskilled workers. But in the last thirty years, the manufacturing sector has been shrinking, replaced by service-based industries that favor workers with more than a high school diploma. As globalization has driven many low-skilled jobs in textiles, manufacturing, and auto parts overseas, the proportion of reliable, well-paying manufacturing jobs, which once provided a middle-class lifestyle for high school–educated workers, has declined—from 32 percent of all jobs in 1959 to 17 percent in 2003. According to U.S. Bureau of Labor Statistics projections, by 2014 that rate will drop to 5.4 percent. Getting a college diploma has become prerequisite for a middle-class lifestyle. Boys who don't thrive in school, who disengage, and who fail to reach their potential not only are suffering an assault to their self-esteem and confidence, but are setting themselves up for a life of economic insecurity.

Perhaps the old feminist slogan holds true: The personal really is political. Perhaps the trouble with boys begins to resemble a crisis only when it affects someone you know: a brother, a son, a grandson. Penny Rusk, 42, an office manager at a car dealership outside Chicago, a self-described "staunch feminist," and the mother of three boys, says she understands boy trouble now. She was raised in a female-centered environment by what she calls "a super-feminist mom." Her teachers, she remembers, were determined to show her that girls could achieve in high school, in college, and in the world beyond. She grew up understanding that achievement in school equaled economic independence.

Girls, she says, were groomed to succeed. But watching the education of her son Matthew, now nineteen, has given her a different perspective.

In elementary school, Matthew was slow to read. Penny was dismayed to see him falling behind, but the school seemed to have different standards of achievement for girls and boys. "I got the classic 'Oh, he's just a boy.' And I said, 'He might just be a boy, but he's my son and he's not learning to read and we need to help him.'" But no one did. "He was one of those kids who just floats along under the radar. They don't get great grades, and they don't get horrible grades." After fourth grade, Rusk says, "Nobody really noticed him."

Gradually, Matthew disengaged from school. In high school, he worked hard but was met with mixed success. He got mostly C's but a few B's in courses that had hands-on components (like science labs) or real-world applications (like an economics course in his senior year in which there was a lot of discussion of current events). At sixteen, Matthew started working after school at Taco Bell. A year after high school, he is working at the drive-through and the register full-time. He's proud that he's earning money and relieved that the constant struggle of middle and high school is behind him. His mother hopes college is in his future. Someday, she predicts, he'll want a family, and if he doesn't have a degree, he'll have a hard time supporting them.

Penny Rusk sounds wistful when she compares the mentoring and encouragement that she and other girls routinely received at school to her son's experience. Matthew seemed to get lost in the post–Title IX world. "People just take it for granted that boys have opportunities," she says. "But sometimes that's not clear to the boys themselves."

During my school visits, while I was talking to experts and interviewing boys and their parents, a few questions kept cropping up: What happens in school that makes boys learn less? Are girls simply smarter or more neurologically adept at formal learning, or does something in the way boys are taught put them at a disadvantage? What psychological and social factors may be at work? Why is this problem arising? And why is it arising now?

There are no pat answers, but there are many tantalizing clues. Let's start by taking a close look at boys' very first experience with formal education: preschool.

CHAPTER 4

PRESCHOOL BLUES

The First Signs of Trouble

It was hard to tell who was more excited about the first day of preschool—thirty-something parents Reed and Kyle Karen or their chubby-faced three-year-old son, Ray. The Karen family had recently moved from a city townhouse to a leafy suburb outside New York City, and Kyle, an art director, and Reed, a cabinetmaker, were looking forward to the leisurely pace of life in their new community. Ray was eager to make new friends, and the preschool the Karens had selected seemed like a great place to do so. It was bright, cheery, and conveniently located in the basement of a local church. The program would give Ray a chance to experience a little independence before he started "real school," reasoned Reed and Kyle. It also offered a natural way for them to meet other families with young children.

At first, Ray seemed to love preschool. But soon Kyle began to get an uneasy feeling when she picked him up at the end of the day. Ray's teachers began handing him off to her with cryptic remarks such as he'd "had a hard time" or "it was rough on the playground today." Kyle was puzzled. She knew that Ray could get a little wound up at times. Maybe he was reacting to the move. Perhaps, she reasoned, he needed time to get used to the new program. But troublingly, she was also detecting subtle changes in Ray's behavior at home. Before the start of preschool, Ray was what his mother describes as "a typical boy." He liked motion—the more the better. He liked noise, too. As a toddler he would let out joyous laughing whoops that could be heard above the roar of New York City traffic. He wasn't particularly mannerly or compliant. He was a curious kid, and responding to his temperament, his parents gave him plenty of leeway to explore the world. He was always active, but lately Ray at times seemed almost frenetic. Kyle could tell something was troubling him. But her sunny, big-hearted son was finding it hard to meet her eye, much less tell her what was going on. He'd even started to act aggressively toward his little sister, squeezing her a little too hard or patting her with too much vehemence.

A soft-spoken, levelheaded woman, Kyle decided to check out what was happening to Ray during his school day. As the teachers' comments morphed into complaints—Ray had thrown a toy at another child—Kyle arranged to "help" in the classroom, and on other days she hung around after morning drop-off, trying to get a sense of what might be bothering her son.

What she saw made her worry both less and more. Ray wasn't doing anything antisocial, but almost everything that came naturally to Ray seemed to be an affront to his teachers. They didn't seem to understand what he needed. He was bursting with energy, and sitting still at circle time was an ordeal for him. One of the regular activities—crafts—was torture for the little boy. He struggled to manipulate the scissors and glue.

"It seems like the school was trying to follow a particular model of what a preschool should be," said Kyle. "But they were fitting a round peg in a square hole." What troubled Reed and Kyle most of all was this: It was clear that their bright, perceptive, curious, energetic boy was being bombarded with negative attention from teachers who regarded his natural behavior with thinly veiled impatience. In the Karens' new community, Ray was getting branded as a troublemaker.

Shortly after the Christmas holidays, the preschool expelled Ray. His crime? He had resolved a dispute over a swing by biting a classmate. Unfortunate, but hardly a felony for a three-year-old. The school wanted him out anyway. Kyle told herself and her friends that Ray and the program were simply a bad fit. Privately, though, she fretted. Was there something wrong with her son? Every time she picked up a parenting magazine, she read articles about ADHD. Could he have an attention disorder? Kyle arranged for Ray to have a neuropsychological workup to see if he had a diagnosable problem. The doctor's verdict? Ray was a little anxious but otherwise was a perfectly normal boy. Kyle was relieved, but as she watched other moms cheerfully walking their kids to preschool in the morning, she reviewed her son's difficult experience. When did the range of acceptable behaviors for little boys get so narrow? Kids in her new neighborhood had full schedules. If Ray didn't meet kids at school, it would be hard for him to find a peer group. How would Ray learn to make new friends? More important, how would he ever learn to love the classroom?

Ray is a normal little boy, Kyle reminded herself over and over. But she felt she'd been handed a verdict. "He was barely out of diapers," she says, "and he'd already had a negative experience with learning."

After a few months, Kyle and Reed found a different kind of preschool. Although it was farther from their house, "they seem to have more understanding and tolerance for boys," says Kyle. She suggested that Ray give school another try, and he gamely agreed. A few months after the first go-round, the sun rose on Ray's first day of School 2.0. To the great pleasure of Reed and Kyle, Ray seemed to fit in immediately. The program featured plenty of movement—outdoor play, yoga, dance—and lots of music. The staff wasn't fazed by Ray's behavior. Gone was endless circle time. Crafts were more free-form. When Ray failed to follow directions, the teachers provided him with subtle prompts. If he couldn't figure out how to manage a social interaction, the staff found a gentle way to redirect him.

"We were lucky that we had options," recalls Kyle.

Slowly, the Karens have begun to exhale. But Kyle still has strong feelings about what her family went through. She is grateful to have had the means to find both good doctors to reassure her and a more appropriate program for her son. But she wonders what happens to boys whose families don't have those resources.

"In too many preschools these days," she says, "being a perfectly normal, loud, active boy just isn't acceptable."

Changing Childhood

YOUR son's face is freshly scrubbed. His sneakers are brand-new. You pull the tag off his backpack and, tremulous with pride and anticipation, send him from a cloistered home where he's adored and accepted into a new and unfamiliar environment: preschool. The experience was once relatively rare. In the 1960s, only 500,000 kids attended preschool. Now, it's a milestone of a normal childhood. These days, more than 5 million youngsters attend preschool, and that number continues to grow. States like Georgia, Oklahoma, and Florida are passing legislation to make preschool available to all. Today, the benefits of preschool are considered so obvious that they go unquestioned. Preschool can help children make an important transition—moving from family life to a world where they are one among many. A thoughtful program provides opportunities for children to develop independence—finding their own cubbies, tying their own shoes, and buttoning their own raincoats. It also provides a kind of intellectual fertilizer for young minds, making sure children spend their fourth and fifth years of life in the language-rich environment that turns out to be crucial to their becoming proficient readers and writers. Preschool can stoke a child's natural curiosity, generate openness toward formal education, and lay the cognitive building blocks to help the child become a lifelong learner.

Except when it doesn't. A typical four-year-old boy heading to preschool may find himself caught in a cultural riptide that may affect him deeply—and not in ways his parents would endorse. In the last thirty years, we've experienced a rash of changes in the structure of our families, in our communities, and in our schools. As a result, our very youngest children now face challenges and expectations very different from those faced by their parents or grandparents.

What has shifted? The changing workforce and fear of rising crime have substantially changed the way kids play, making play itself more structured, more adult-driven, less imaginative, and less active. In the 1980s, scientists figured out that children begin responding to, even learning from, experiences shortly after birth. Eager to exploit this "breakthrough," policy makers advised parents to ensure that all children experienced plenty of stimulation in order to enhance their cognitive development. Preschools, working without much oversight and without clear direction, have tried to embrace these changes. Some offer play-based, child-centered curricula. Others adopt academic-focused programs. Many preschools, particularly the academically focused ones, are proving intolerable for some kids—and many of those kids are boys.

That means that when you send your son off to preschool, he may repeatedly experience things that he finds frustrating, uncomfortable, or alienating. He may encounter expectations that are so at odds with his natural development that they leave him bewildered and angry. His preschool experience may plant in him the seed of a bitter weed, which may grow into the conviction that formal education is simply not for him. Instead of fostering a love of learning, his days in preschool may shake his confidence to the core.

Let's take a look at how things have changed.

The End of Free Play

Unstructured play activities were at least as common as the formal games. We observed children playing stickball, "line soccer," "duck, duck, goose," hopscotch, jump rope, "red devil," "box," "freeze tag," "cooties," and "hide and seek tag." We also watched them pretend the concrete overhang above the basement door was a shower, that the set of steps in the backyard was a bus, that the stonewall was a fortress from which to fight an imaginary battle. —Amanda Dargan and Steven Zeitlin, from *City Play*

UNTIL the middle of the twentieth century, adults didn't pay too much attention to kids' play. Parents—usually mothers—were responsible for feeding children, clothing them, giving them a bath, taking them to church, and providing them with a basic education. No one spent a lot of time fretting about a child's cognitive development. No one had to. Children were assumed to be intellectually dormant. The work of childhood, experts believed, was physical maturation and social development, and that would be accomplished without much effort. Communities were set up in a way that encouraged casual interaction among children. In cities, children were at liberty to move around the neighborhood alone or supervised by a slightly older sibling or friend. In the post–World War II era, a generation of young couples was bootstrapping themselves out of cities, and the suburbs, with their kickball-friendly culs-de-sac, were considered the ideal place for the new middle-class families to raise kids. Family structure allowed kids to play freely, too. Poor moms toiled for money, but the thrifty wife of a working-class man could feed a family with three or four kids from her husband's salary and was able to divide her time between housework and a sort of laissez-faire oversight of the children.

Before the early 1970s, 60 percent of all mothers with school-age children stayed at home. Despite the physical presence of a parent back then, children and adults inhabited separate spheres. The first five years of a child's life were devoted to free play—pretend games, toys, and board games on rainy days, and endless ball games, building tree forts, bike riding, and maybe swimming on sunny ones. Siblings, cousins, and neighborhood kids formed a de facto peer group. Kindergarten was a child's inauguration into formal learning, and plenty of kids had their very first classroom experiences in first grade.

In the late 1970s, families began to change. Birth control became widely available and commonly used. Women began postponing marriage and childbearing. The average age of a first-time mom rose from 21.4 years in 1970 to 25 years in 2000. When women had children, they had fewer. In 1967, the average household consisted of 3.3 people. By 2006, that number had shrunk to 2.6. Women began entering the workforce in greater numbers. By the mid-1990s about 70 percent of women with school-age children were earning wages. Who was minding the children? Parents in two-income households—most often the moms—were under tremendous pressure to cobble together safe, adequate child care. Playgroups, day care, and preschool—their cost, quality, and convenience—became a preoccupation for most American families.

By the mid-1980s, another set of issues assumed center stage in the family drama: fear of crime and concern about the safety of the children. An epidemic of crack cocaine addiction seized the nation's inner cities. The rate of violent crime in urban America—bloody homicides and brutal assaults—began to spiral out of control. Tabloids and newly established twenty-four-hour cable news television were full of tales of drug-fueled gang wars and of innocent children caught in the crossfire. Americans grew wary and then fearful. For two centuries, crime had been mostly a homegrown affair leaving behind a few unfortunate victims and a traumatized community. Suddenly, crime and especially crimes against children were not tragic anomalies but national news.

Pedophiles and child killers, it seemed, lurked everywhere. The peaceful suburbs, once a haven from urban ills, began to seem dangerous—especially for kids.

Of course, not much crime was actually happening in middle-class America. Aside from an occasional DUI or a break-in at the local Radio Shack, the crime rate in suburban communities remained about the same. But people's perception of safety was altered. People not only locked their doors but began paying for private security systems and local guards. Brand-new cars came equipped with antitheft devices, and the whoop of the automatic safety alarm became as common in the suburbs as birdsong.

Those fears changed the way adults allowed kids to play. Kicking a ball around the front yard suddenly seemed dangerous. The backyard was preferable, but the living room was safer than either. In fifteen short years, the touchstone leisure-time experiences of childhood—pickup ball games, games of competition, fantasy battles, bike races—the kinds of activities that boys have long enjoyed, were transformed into something frightening. In the 1970s, if you noticed a nine-year-old boy riding his bike on the street, walking to the corner store alone, or scooping frog eggs out of the mud slick in an uncultivated patch between two housing developments, you might have marveled at his energy, his independent spirit, or his curious mind. If you saw a nine-year-old boy doing the same thing in the 1990s, you'd most likely wonder where his parents were—and why they were letting him out alone.

The Myth of Zero to Three

As opportunities for free play in children's lives began to recede, parents were handed another set of child-rearing nostrums—this time by cutting-edge scientists. For decades, psychologists who specialized in human development had been showing, using behavioral-type experiments, that the early experiences in a child's life matter. Test after test indicated that babies and toddlers who were cuddled, given consistent and responsive care, kindly and frequently spoken to, and who had plenty of exposure to singing and books, did better in school and later in life than babies and toddlers who didn't have that kind of care.

In the late 1980s and early 1990s, the nascent field of neuroscience began to provide a hard scientific gloss to all that soft and squishy behavioral science. At that time, state-of-the-art brain scan technology required physicians to inject radioactive substances into their subjects. Not surprisingly, few parents would subject their kids to those kinds of tests. In 1987, though, brain scientists started to get glimpses of what was happening inside a child's head. Dr. Harry Chugani, a researcher at Wayne State University, injected radioactive glucose into twenty-nine epileptic children ranging in age from a few days to fifteen years old in order to measure brain function through positron-emission tomography (PET) scans. The area of the brain that takes up the most glucose, he reasonably assumed, was most active and therefore requires more energy.

What Chugani "saw" with his PET scans astonished the scientific community and set off a cascade of actions and reactions that impact our view of childhood to this day. Far from being dormant, the brain of a two-year-old consumes glucose at approximately the same metabolic rate as the brain of an adult. That rate continues to increase, reaching rates twice the adult level by age three or four, and continues to blaze away until a child is about nine. After that, the rate of brain glucose metabolism starts to decline, and it stabilizes at the end of the teen years. The "high plateau" period of metabolic activity extends roughly from age three to age nine.

There were questions the PET scans couldn't answer. The patterns created by radioactive glucose didn't tell us much about ease and depth of learning. Could a five-year-old learn more easily or more quickly than a fifteen-year-old? Most people assumed the answer was yes. It made sense. Everyone could think of violin protégés or pint-size polyglots who were introduced to their subjects early and grew up to play concert-worthy Mozart or speak the Romance languages perfectly.

Chugani's work, and the work of other neuroscientists, captured the attention of the Carnegie Corporation and then–first lady Hillary Clinton. Shortly after graduating from Yale Law School, Clinton had worked at the Yale Child Study Center, which had pioneered some of the behavioral science connecting early experience and optimum learning. The PET scans seemed to prove in black and white what behavioral scientists had been saying all along. The research galvanized Hollywood powerhouse Rob Reiner, too. He created a public awareness campaign and a foundation called I Am Your Child. In April 1997, Bill Clinton was president, and the Clintons hosted Chugani and other doctors at the White House Conference on Early Development and Learning to discuss the latest neuroscience findings. Somewhere in the excitement, though, the message began to morph.

From birth until age three, children experienced windows of opportunity during which they were particularly sensitive to learning. So far, so good. But here's where it went wrong: Some scientists and science writers began to suggest that the windows remained open for only a finite period of time, during which a child could learn things that would set his or her course for life. After age three, they warned, the windows shut. By the time Reiner began successfully lobbying for Proposition 10, which imposed a tax on cigarettes to fund child development programs in the state of California, the idea of finite windows of opportunity for optimal learning had become conventional wisdom. Proposition 10, which read, "It has been determined that a child's first three years are the most critical in brain development," codified this notion into law.

The press spread the word. Major newspapers covered this breakthrough. The newsweeklies published special issues. *Time* ran a cover story titled "How a Child's Brain Develops and What It Means for Welfare Reform." *Newsweek*'s special issue was titled "Your Child: From Birth to Three." One of the television networks aired a prime-time special. Colorful graphics explained the research findings to American parents: The brain undergoes a period of extraordinary growth. Thickets of new neural pathways are laid down while others are pruned back in a process called "synaptogenesis." Every time a synapse fires, that neural pathway is fortified and becomes sturdier. Synapses that aren't used die away. To achieve maximum brainpower, a child needs enough stimulation to keep his or her neural pathways plush and efficient. A child who doesn't receive the right stimulation in those early years, parents were told implicitly (and sometimes explicitly), might never reach his or her full intellectual potential.

The "Birth to Three" message was aimed squarely at policy makers controlling the federal and state dollars that supported the 25 percent or so of Americans with children living in or near poverty. Children who grew up in homes without books or much conversation seemed to lose out on some critical learning opportunities, and many never fully recovered. Middle-class parents, though, were the ones who heard the message loud and clear, although for the most part they already were giving their children exactly what they needed to grow and thrive: a consistent, warm connection to a caregiver, a language-rich environment, and everyday experiences such as trips to the corner store or the zoo. Highly educated and ambitious, middle-class parents interpreted the "Birth to Three" message through the scrim of their own shifting values and generational anxieties.

And there was plenty of anxiety to go around. The economy was changing, and middle-class Americans were getting squeezed. At the bottom end, the manufacturing sector began to erode. At the top end, the era of the free-spending corporation was coming to a close. The word *downsizing* entered the national lexicon. A college degree from a prestigious four-year university, which had long been reserved for white males from elite families, was now a desirable credential for all kinds of children. Colleges became more selective as distinguished, brand-name institutions were inundated with applications. In 1945, Harvard University had received 1,467 applications and admitted 1,043 students. In 1985, Harvard received 13,614 applications and admitted 2,175.

Parenting was becoming a competitive sport. Middle-class parents began grooming their kids to play the game. Summer camps featuring canoeing and crafts began to close and were replaced by camp programs promising academic enrichment, "gifted and talented" programs, and computer technology. SAT tutoring became commonplace. Parents began thinking about the Ivy League—not when their kids headed into high school but when their kids were still in Pampers. Generation Xers who followed—the Latch-Key Kids grown up—seemed especially hell-bent on providing their children with every advantage. As teenagers, they had watched their own parents get laid off, then rebound as lesser-paid consultants before getting bounced again as corporations lightened and finally slashed their payrolls. They had seen the early and unsettling effects of an increasingly global marketplace. They had grown up to be adults who craved above all things a warm, consistent family life. These young parents—goaded by skillful marketers—accepted as gospel the idea that early enrichment would make or break a child's future achievement. Their anxieties were inflamed.

Jump-Starting Childhood

IT TURNS out, though, that many of the conclusions about early childhood development that scientists, science writers, policy makers, and parents drew from the "new" neuroscience were wrong. During childhood, the brain *is* actively growing neural pathways and pruning others, but neuroscientists now know that the process continues throughout life. Learning, it turns out, is continuous. It extends from the first few days of life into late middle age and beyond. PET scans, the "proof," measured the rate at which the brain uses glucose. But today most neuroscientists believe that a brain that uses a lot of glucose is not super-primed for learning but rather is operating with less efficiency. When people perform tasks fluidly, their brains are almost on idle. (Curiously, there does seem to be a "window" in childhood when it is easier to acquire, say, a second language, but adults learn new languages, too.)

Unfortunately, most middle-class parents missed all that scientific backpedaling, and they did what middle-class parents do: They bought stuff. The stuff they bought was intended to get Junior to read and count early. The "Birth to Three" message moved markets. Overall, retail toy sales had been dropping for several years, but between 2003 and 2004, so-called learning and exploration toys (not even a category in 1980) rose an astonishing 19 percent to $510 million a year. Many of those products were aimed at the youngest children. Baby Einstein videotapes and CDs and *JumpStart Preschool,* which promised to "boost a child's brain," became as common as Cheerios in the households of many toddlers. In 2005, sales of Hooked on Phonics early reading CDs doubled. Christopher Paucek, a division chief at Education Inc., which markets Hooked on Phonics products, is frank about what is driving the trend. Twenty years ago, he says, "your kid started to read in first, second, even third grade. Now everyone feels like they have to get their kids started early." Parental anxiety, he says, is "driving a lot of sales." And Education Inc. is ready to meet the ever-increasing demand by expanding its line to include more CDs and reading and math workbooks for preschoolers. Parents' appetite for early academic learning "is limitless," says Paucek. "Really, when I think about it, I get giddy!"

In middle-class communities, early academic learning has become an obsession. If you take a look at the bulletin board at Starbucks in any affluent neighborhood, you'll find it's covered with notices for toddler chess instruction, Komputer4Kids, Mommy & Me Spanish classes, Mandarin playgroup, and Suzuki violin lessons.

The same parental anxieties that are making Paucek rich and are creating a crush on Mommy & Me Orientation Day have also restructured preschool. All over the country, traditional play-based learning activities such as rhyming, sorting, and block building—which have important skills embedded in them—have been replaced by formal, elementary school–type lessons scaled down for three- and four-year-olds. These days, many parents believe that learning to read and to compute early—usually before the age of five—gives a child a lifelong academic advantage. Parents believe that by age three or four a kid is either on the bus or off the bus to educational success.

Day care centers and preschools have become battlegrounds between early childhood educators, who know that children learn best through play, and vigilant parents who want to see worksheets and spelling tests. The day care behemoth KinderCare, which enrolls about 100,000 preschoolers across the country, recently introduced an academic program called "Kelsey's Learning Adventures." For twenty-five more dollars on top of the $250 weekly fee, children as young as three get thrice-weekly lessons in phonics, reading, mathematics (including, the website says, algebra and data analysis), and Spanish.

"Our parents were expressing to us that they didn't think it was right that their children were just playing all day," says Sharon Berger, who developed the program for Knowledge Learning Corporation, KinderCare's corporate parent. "They felt they should be getting instruction." How useful is it to teach a three-year-old algebra and data analysis? "All our programs are developmentally appropriate," insists Berger.

But developmentally appropriate isn't really the point. "Our parents were demanding it."

Little Boy Blue

WHILE expectations for early academics have been ratcheting up, little boys' abilities have remained about the same. In these anxiety-ridden times, the natural development of young males turns out to be wildly at odds with what some parents and teachers want them to do.

Although boy and girl babies hit most of their developmental milestones at about the same time, girls tend to be more verbal. As toddlers, females learn to speak earlier and learn words faster than their male counterparts. There is great variability between boys and girls, of course, but in general, once girls gain the advantage, they keep it for a critical period before things even out at around age eleven. At eighteen months, boys' vocabularies ranged from zero to 220 words, girls' from 2 to 318 words. At twenty-four months, a girl's average vocabulary is 40 percent greater than a boy's.

Why do little boys speak less than little girls? The evidence points in two directions. In a study conducted in 1991 at the University of Chicago, the influential developmental psychologist Janellen Huttenlocher and her team tried to figure out exactly how gender impacts language acquisition. After running an ad in a local paper, she found 22 educated, middle-class mothers of toddlers—12 boys and 10 girls between the ages of fourteen months and sixteen months—who (perhaps out of sheer boredom) agreed to allow a researcher to follow them and their kids around for a few hours every couple of months, diligently audiotaping every word the mom or child spoke. The results, published in the peer-reviewed *Developmental Psychology,* were as follows: Mothers spoke about the same amount to boys and to girls, but boys spoke less than girls and used fewer words. This finding suggested that something intrinsic to males makes them less verbal than females. Subsequent studies, though, including groundbreaking work by human development expert Betty Hart and psychologist Todd R. Risley, make a persuasive case that verbal fluency is a product of a child's environment.

Hart and Risley spent two and a half years recording the number of words spoken between parents and children between the ages of one and three in forty-two diverse families. They found that across racial and socioeconomic lines, the number of words that parents speak to a child is directly related to the size of the child's vocabulary, regardless of the child's gender.

Why is this finding important? Learning, retaining, and using language, it turns out, create the cognitive foundation for reading. And on that score, preschool boys are at a disadvantage. Researchers at the U.S. Department of Education found that parents offered their sons less exposure to books, storytelling, and reading than they offered their daughters. But the Education Department survey sheds no light on an important issue: Did the participating parents practice a subtle form of gender stereotyping by taking their daughters to story hour at the public library while their sons tossed a ball around in the yard with Dad? Or did they provide a sensitive response to what they perceived as their sons' preferences, interests, or capacities?

Ants in the Pants

Boys talk less than girls. Their fine motor skills tend to be less well developed, which can make it hard for them to hold a pencil or a paintbrush. But perhaps the greatest natural deficit that little boys exhibit in preschool is their seeming inability to sit still.

Most parents who have both boys and girls acknowledge this as a fact of life. Some little boys seem to be born with a severe case of the "wiggles." They are always on the move. They're the ones who climb out of their cribs, who dash headlong across the playground, who throw and catch balls as reflexively as most people breathe.

Sharon O'Donnell, a writer and mother of three boys in Raleigh, North Carolina, has one of those.

"All my three sons were very active preschoolers but my youngest, Jason, now six, is the most active of all," she recalls. "When he was three, he got a hand-me-down play tool bench with a roof, and instead of using the bench, he climbed on the roof. He learned to walk downstairs, then started sliding down the banister, and then he started jumping down a flight. Even when he lands hard or hits his knee, he just says, 'Cool!' "

Kinetic. Spirited. Irrepressible. Maddening. Many teachers don't seem able to tolerate that kind of boy. It's imperative, of course, for classrooms to be run in a way that ensures safety. Too much movement and activity can overwhelm the children in the class who are naturally more reticent. But too many teachers expect all boys to sit still like the girls—and to like it. And they become exasperated and even angry if a couple of high-energy boys "refuse" to do so.

What they don't know is that some boys simply can't sit still. Canadian developmental psychologist Warren O. Eaton, a professor at the University of Manitoba, has done some of the best research on gender and "the wiggles." In the late 1980s, he set out to answer a question that has been bandied about the teachers' lounge for decades: Are boys actually more active than girls? Eaton is a good scientist. He knows how complicated that question can be. He asked himself the right questions. Are boys conditioned that way? Or is that simply a myth based on cultural stereotypes of passive women and active men?

"My hypothesis was that boys were more active—that is certainly what I saw when I observed a playground," Eaton says. He consulted the literature and found it less than comprehensive. Much of it connected boys to higher levels of activity, but the studies were inconclusive. So he put his hypothesis to the test. He located an engineer from Timex, the old watch-making company, who had adapted wristwatches in order to measure movement. Then, in a series of well-designed experiments, he strapped the primitive motion sensors to the wrists and ankles of pre-school and school-age children and then recorded how much they moved around. His findings? The typical boy moves around a little more than the typical girl. Then Eaton plotted a graph of the most-active and the least-active kids. The most-active ones, he found, are almost always boys, and the least are much more likely to be girls.

Intrigued, Eaton dug deeper. Abandoning his modified Timex watches, he began using electronic motion detectors and did some fas-cinating follow-up studies on gender, motion, and normal human de-velopment. Male and female fetuses move around at about the same rate in utero. But after birth, Eaton was able to record slight differences in motor activity between boys and girls—even among very young in-fants. The difference between the normal activity levels of boys and girls, he found, grows pronounced at age two and peaks when boys are about seven or eight years old. That is why, says Eaton, preschool and early elementary school are "often a poor fit for some young boys." Little boys are more active than girls, but the children who are bounc-ing off the walls are almost invariably male.

Free to Be . . . Just like Me

THE demands of an academic preschool classroom can rapidly outpace a boy's natural development. Slower than girls to develop verbal skills and possessing a smaller vocabulary, boys are told to "use your words" to express affection, anger, or frustration. When they are "tested" on phonemes—when teachers ask them if they know, for instance, that "C" makes the first sound in *cat*—boys often draw a blank. Holding a pencil for any length of time can be tricky, but filling out a worksheet can be torture for a boy. Boys respond in ways that seem oppositional: They move around during story hour, they slump off their chairs instead of sitting at the desk, and they space out during calendar study.

But another factor is often at work when boys fail at preschool—and at elementary school, too. Most early education teachers are female. Although many are gifted and empathetic, some others don't appreciate—or are profoundly uncomfortable with—the ways in which boys naturally express themselves. I imagine right now that many of you are about to throw down this book in disgust. Bear with me. I know all too well that women are the ones who have children and by and large raise children and educate children, and that it hardly seems fair to criticize women when they are selflessly taking on the lion's share of the responsibilities connected to bringing forth the next generation. But well-respected experts from across the political spectrum worry about early education teachers who have a zero-tolerance attitude toward boisterous behavior. That unexamined prejudice, they say, is hurting our sons.

Early education expert Kathy Hirsh-Pasek, a developmental psychologist at Temple University in Philadelphia, says it's about time for an open discussion about the problem. As she sees it, well-intentioned teachers simply do not know enough about boys to devise a classroom environment that engages them. Not long ago, Hirsh-Pasek was asked to visit a friend's son's preschool. The school administrator, the worried friend confided, had stiffly informed the family that she suspected their impish and beloved four-year-old was "violent." After sitting in the classroom for less than an hour, Hirsh-Pasek figured out what had gone wrong.

"What I saw was a female-driven classroom," says Pasek, "that focused on female-centered activities and allowed no expression for normal males. Boys didn't fit the routine. When the boys tried to be normal males, the activities felt out of place to the teacher."

Girls were praised for sitting compliantly at desks, and boys were constantly shushed for being noisy and chided for moving around too much. The art activities were prefabricated—pasting already cut-out leaves on already cut-out tree trunks. The gym class consisted of a teacher shouting out commands: "Run to the right! Run to the left!" The day Hirsh-Pasek visited was "Sit Where You Like Friday." The rest of the week, Hirsh-Pasek noted dryly, "was sit where you were miserable." Hirsh-Pasek's advice to her friend was emphatic: Get your son out of that preschool!

In the field of child development, Hirsh-Pasek is a progressive, compassionate voice for children. No one who knows her work, including her terrific book *Einstein Never Used Flash Cards: How Our Children Really Learn—and Why They Need to Play More and Memorize Less* could remotely construe her as being antifeminist. But when it comes to the bias against boys and preschool, she's unequivocal: "The stakes are too high to worry about political correctness. Many early education teachers need help seeing boys for their strengths and abilities."

Famed boys' psychologist Michael Thompson, coauthor of *Raising Cain*, agrees: "Too often, the behavior of girls is the gold standard. Boys are simply treated as defective girls."

Playing Soldier

NOT long ago, George Washington University law professor Jonathan Turley, father of two, saw firsthand how threatened some adults feel by the fantasy life of little boys. Aidan, his four-year-old son, brought his orange Buzz Lightyear plastic ray gun to the neighborhood playground. As Aidan began pursuing Jack, his six-year-old brother, Turley says, a mother froze with an expression of utter revulsion. Glaring at him and then at Aidan, she grabbed her son and proclaimed loudly that he couldn't play "if that boy was going to be allowed to play with guns."

Turley was puzzled, then annoyed. Then he began to get sensitized to the negative attention that rains down on little boys in their most playful, affectionate, and unguarded moments. "I've seen it in mothering magazines as well. I was flipping through one of those magazines and I read an article that advised women to encourage their sons to pretend their guns are magic wands," says Turley.

These days, there is a palpable sense—in school and on the playground—that the ways in which boys play need to be suppressed or rigidly controlled.

Why do we want to keep such a tight lid on our little boys? It's almost as if some adults these days interpret a boy's pretend play as an expression of a nascent propensity for real violence. Condemning it, then, seems like part of an effort to help boys become more civilized. But there are smart people who believe that when teachers and parents put the kibosh on a rousing game of Capture the Bad Guy and Send Him to Jail they are badly misunderstanding little boys and depriving them of an important psychological tool. Rather than outlawing violent play, psychologist Michael Thompson suggests, we should pay close attention to what the violent play is really about. Usually, it reenacts the age-old struggle between good and evil, "but," says Thompson, "it's really about something more. It's about courage, loyalty, risking all to save friends in the face of powerful foes." Little boys are playing at being the best, most compassionate, most heroic kind of men imaginable. Thompson and others believe that at least some of that fantasy-type play has a place in schools.

Jane Katch, a veteran kindergarten teacher and educational consultant from Grafton, Massachusetts, knows such play can be challenging for the teacher. Still, she preaches a gospel of tolerance to the young, mostly female teachers who populate the ranks of early education. She asks them to be a little less rigid, and, instead of being critical, she suggests that those teachers get curious. Boys, she suggests, always are preoccupied with fantasy action, aggression, and violence.

"Most of their games are about imaginary aggression but they aren't aggressive, and they can play together cooperatively. They understand the games are fantasy," she says. "Thinking about violence, playing about violence, is not the same as being violent. When we tell them not to pretend to shoot things, we don't teach them not to do it, we teach them to lie—to pretend the pointed finger is a fire hose."

Katch is mindful that teachers are responsible for maintaining a safe environment for all children—boys and girls, active and not so active. But she asks teachers to strike a better balance: "It's not reasonable to allow boys to tackle each other when they're walking to the gym. But on the playground, as long as everyone is laughing, pretending to shoot other kids with your outstretched finger is OK. Let's not make little boys feel like they're bad for imagining violent things. When we tell boys not to play about their violent fantasies, this is what they understand us to say: that it is not acceptable for them to be who they are."

Storm Clouds at Preschool

WHAT will happen if we don't create a better alignment between early education and little boys? Walter Gilliam, Yale University professor of child psychiatry and psychology, says that little boys will continue to get expelled at the same shocking rates at which they're getting expelled now. A former public school teacher himself, bespectacled and bearded Gilliam is one of the country's foremost experts in early education. In the last ten years, he has observed the changing preschool agenda.

"It used to be the place where kids were socialized to be with other kids and learned to love school," he says. "Now, in many programs, preschools are teacher-led environments given over to lessons in early literacy skills and math fundamentals." Some three- and four-year-olds blossom in this kind of academic environment. But a few years ago, Gilliam noticed a disquieting trend. Many preschoolers were not blossoming. They were hitting other kids, acting aggressive or oppositional. Because no formal judiciary process was in place, preschool troublemakers, he noticed, were often summarily expelled.

Gilliam collects national data from 3,898 state-supported preschools through a regular survey. In an effort to get a handle on what he sensed might be an emerging trend, he added a few key questions about expulsion rates to the survey to figure out which kids were cutting it and which were not. The data he collected was astonishing: Among public school students in grades K through 12, the expulsion rate is 2.09 per 1,000. For preschoolers, the expulsion rate is more than three times higher. Who is having the most trouble in preschool? Boys are 4.5 times more likely to be expelled than preschool girls.

When Gilliam published his findings in the spring of 2005, they were widely reported in the national print media and on TV. The reporters and producers who did the stories, though, must have just disembarked from coast-to-coast flights with toddlers kicking the backs of their seats the whole way. "Preschools Troubled by Unruly Tots, Study Reports" was the headline in *USA Today*. The *New York Times* report quoted California child-development expert Karen Hill Scott: "What the data tells us, as does the show *Supernanny*, is that there are a lot of out-of-control kids out there." CNN's Jack Cafferty kicked off his interview with Gilliam by asking, "What do we got here? A generation of unruly three-year-olds?" No one seemed to question exactly what was happening in preschool that was causing so many boys—boys barely out of diapers—to act in such a disruptive way.

Gilliam did not have enough data to make the connection between academic-focused preschools, teacher-led classrooms, and the high failure rate of boys, but other researchers have been able to do so. Still, preschools continue to push early academics. School administrators, especially in economically disadvantaged areas, say they have no choice. By early elementary school, most poor kids trail middle-class kids in reading and writing in large part because they have had so little exposure to early literacy skills at home. In these neighborhoods, early reading and math instruction becomes a kind of instructional triage: Educators are willing to accept some casualties to help some kids get ahead. Yes, they admit, you might lose a few high-energy boys who simply can't bear circle time and get crazy when it comes to worksheets. But some kids—mostly girls—may benefit from the reading and math skills they learn in preschool and get a leg up in kindergarten and beyond.

In middle-class neighborhoods, where parents pushing Bugaboo strollers are already projecting their offspring's SAT scores, preschool administrators use a different calculus. They know that many boys—and some girls—are not ready for the kinds of early academic programs they now embed in their curricula. Anxious, competitive parents, however, make it clear that they want those programs. School administrators know their enrollment rates and financial futures are contingent on keeping those parents happy.

The strategy may backfire for rich and poor kids alike. Researchers have found that children who attend preschools that emphasize direct instruction experience more stress at school. At ages five and six, children from academic-type preschools knew more letters and numbers than their peers who attended nonacademic preschools, but by first grade those advantages had disappeared. Researchers have also found that children from academically oriented preschools are less creative and less enthusiastic about learning than their peers who attended nonacademic preschools. And here's the clincher: Kids who attend academic preschools may also, in the long run, do more poorly in school, and those kinds of schools may be handicapping boys in a way we could not have anticipated.

Dr. Rebecca Marcon, a developmental psychologist and psychology professor at the University of North Florida, followed 183 poor African American children for six years as they made their way from three different types of preschool—one that was academically focused, one that favored child-initiated activities, and one that combined both approaches—through to fourth grade. Her study, published in 2002 in *Early Childhood Research and Practices*, is enough to give even the most enthusiastic proponent of early academics pause.

By third grade, Marcon found no significant differences in performance among the three groups, although kids who attended academic preschools were held back less frequently. By fourth grade, though, children who attended academic preschools earned significantly lower grades—and behaved worse—than children who attended play-based or mixed-approach ones. And boys? Marcon expected boys to do worse than girls in all groups, in keeping with national averages. But when she broke her data down by gender, she saw that something more interesting might be going on. The boys who were best able to keep pace with the girls had attended the child-initiated schools. The boys who fell farthest behind girls were the ones who had attended the academic preschools.

Despite the research, schools that allow boys to function in accordance with their own natural development are a vanishing breed. Maria Amorosino is old enough to remember a time when kids were allowed to play in the front yard. She believes that all kids—including her three sons—should have a childhood shaped around movement, play, and love of learning. As director of the Churchery School, a preschool for 92 two-, three-, and four-year-olds at the United Methodist church in Avon, Connecticut, a bedroom community ten miles outside Hartford, she is constantly made aware of parents' accelerated expectations for their children. Although Amorosino is careful to make sure her teachers integrate literacy and numeracy into every class, she knows that real learning occurs when kids can touch, smell, move, and taste the lesson. She's confident that she can supply an environment in which all kids can thrive—even active, impulsive, aggressive boys—and learn, too.

One of the favorite activities of the youngest kids at the Churchery School is the water table—a large red trough of water. The kids roll up their sleeves and take turns pouring water from brightly colored tumblers, measuring with various sizes of measuring cups, and making waves. They're learning about volume, but they're also preparing for math. Each of the four positions around the water table is marked with a number written on a piece of cardboard. Each day, the children attempt to decipher the number before participating in the activity. Initially, there is always some confusion. The children form little committees to discuss how many should stand at the table and what the number of their spot might be. Some struggle for weeks to figure out which squiggly line on the paper denotes 2 and which is 3. Sometimes, they hang back and wait until other kids take their spots before jumping in. They forget to roll up their sleeves properly once in a while, and despite their smocks their clothes get damp. Without the use of flash cards, chalkboards, number 2 pencils, or computer software—and with much giggling and splashing—children as young as three learn to recognize the numbers 1, 2, 3, and 4 and figure out, without much stress, the sum of 3 plus 1.

For the last few years, though, more and more parents of Churchery School kids have been demanding to see worksheets. Perplexed, Amorosino began kicking off each school year with a parents-only meeting to explain what a developmentally appropriate preschool day should look like. "We talk about the importance of hands-on learning and our commitment to keep kids active and moving," she says. During the meeting, the parents nod appreciatively. But by the third week in September, the same parents begin to complain that their three- and four-year-olds "are just playing all day." Anxiety about their children's future has become an epidemic. Amorosino says she and her staff have become "like part-time therapists. We're trying to get parents to calm down." The sad part is that parents are so worried about the future that they are often blind to the amazing development of their kids.

Lately, she's spent hours counseling a parent of one of the most active boys in the school. "He needed a lot of movement," Amorosino said. "There wasn't anything wrong. It wasn't something he was doing. That's just the way that he is." His mother, though, wanted the teachers at the Churchery preschool to train him to sit in a chair and to write more legibly. "It's hard for parents to hear," says Amorosino. "But he just isn't ready for it."

So if you're thinking about preschool for your son, choose wisely. His earliest classroom experiences may shape the kind of learner he becomes. To get him ready for school, talk to him, rhyme with him, and sing with him. After kicking the soccer ball, take him to the library for story hour. Before you enroll him, visit the school. Put your anxieties about college acceptance aside, and make sure the curriculum is play based and not too academic. Take a tour and make sure you see some kids engaged in noisy, boisterous play. Make sure the school has some tolerance for "play violence" as long as classroom order is maintained. Make sure his daily schedule will include plenty of time and space for movement.

CHAPTER 5

NOTES FROM THE FRONT

Fixing the School, Not the Boy

Not long ago, Susan Horn, a longtime early education expert, got a call from a preschool teacher in downtown St. Louis. One of the children, a little boy, was acting aggressively—hitting and kicking teachers, even throwing chairs—and the teacher was at her wits' end about how to contain the child. Horn, who wears her sandy brown hair tucked behind her ears, has plenty of experience with little kids and school. She spent fifteen years in the classroom, ran a Head Start program, and supervised an early education program for an entire district. The job she has now—preschool troubleshooter and inclusion consultant for the city of St. Louis—requires every bit of the wisdom and tact she's accumulated in her thirty-five years as an educator.

Horn is supposed to help preschools and day care centers identify kids who might have serious developmental or neurological problems, help the administrators and teachers adapt classrooms to meet the needs of those kids, and help schools connect families with early intervention services. In the eight months that the program has been running, she has been called to observe fifty problem students—every one of them a boy. All fifty times, she found no diagnosable problems. She made no referrals. To her eyes, none of the "problem boys" had anything remotely wrong with them. Instead, she's begun working with teachers and administrators to try to persuade them to become more boy-friendly. "What I'm finding," she says, "is that many early teachers I talked to, especially ones that don't have brothers and don't have sons, simply don't understand what little boys are like."

After securing permission from the school and the child's parents, Horn went to the preschool in St. Louis to see the troubled boy in action. At first, the teacher and the twenty-four or so children—including the offender, a thin, sweet-faced four-year-old with big eyes and brown curly hair—were well behaved. Horn took advantage of the relative calm to look closely at the layout of the room and at the toys and activities available to the children. Soon, the teacher announced it was time for recess. Six or seven kids who were very eager to get outside moved rapidly to the door. They waited, impatiently shifting their weight from foot to foot, as their slower-moving classmates finished their activities and pulled on their coats. By this time, the kids at the door had begun to sway, then bump against each other. Very quickly, bumping became shoving and pushing. In the confusion, the four-year-old boy whom Horn had been called to observe hauled off and struck a friend.

The teacher, who had been watching the boy out of the corner of her eye, was on him in a second. She pulled him out of line, but instead of containing his behavior, her actions seemed to set him off. He began howling and kicking at her. The teacher brought the curtain down on the scene by hauling the boy down to the principal's office while the other kids went out to play. The principal's assessment of the little boy? Incorrigible. Horn, however, sees things differently.

It simply wasn't developmentally appropriate for the teacher to ask a group of four-year-olds—especially four-year-old boys—to wait by the door for so long, she points out. But the problem didn't begin there, From the moment she walked in the room, Horn thought the environment was set up for little boys to fail. The classroom looked big enough, but after closer examination, she saw that half the room was sectioned off for an after-school program and that the preschool kids, mostly boys, didn't have enough room to move around. The block area was too small. There were no hoops and balls or opportunities to build things. The daily schedule wasn't very boy-friendly, either. There wasn't enough free play. Instead of being allowed to blow off steam on the playground in the morning and settle down for quiet activities when they came inside, the kids were supposed to sit still and listen for long stretches of time.

Horn felt some sympathy for the teacher. "I'm sure she was doing her best; it's hard work and it can be very frustrating," she says. But she reserves special sympathy for the "troubled" boys. "Most educators don't consider that they need to fix the environment that these boys are learning in," says Horn. "They'd rather try to fix the boy."

The sister of four brothers, the mother of a son, and the grandmother of five grandsons, Horn has a pretty good idea about what boys need to thrive. From her years on the front line in the classroom, she knows the difficulties teachers face, too. Lately, Horn has been speaking out more and more to parents and teachers in the St. Louis area about making early education more boy-friendly. In a presentation she calls "Let Boys Be Boys," she lays out guidelines for keeping boys happy and engaged in the classroom—guidelines that many teachers have forgotten or never learned.

First and foremost, the day has to include plenty of active play. She begs teachers to allow a little more leeway for physical contact, rough-and-tumble activities. She even cites examples where teachers have let boys use swimming noodles to sword-fight. Each classroom, she insists, should have ample room for building—with blocks, with Styrofoam, with Duplos—and room enough so kids can knock over their towers with abandon. They also need a place to play with cars. She suggests that teachers set up an "aggressive play" area—a large box and some action figures—and let boys use it as a play-boxing ring. Teachers should allow boys plenty of opportunity for sensory development—incorporating mud, Silly Putty, and other messy concoctions into the day's activities. Because boys tend to get confused when confronted by several tasks, Horn suggests developing rituals to mark the beginning and end of school as well as transitions from one activity to another. If the teacher is going to plan the day around "themes" such as learning about food groups or kinds of trees, she or he should be sure to include themes that boys relate to such as kickball or camping. Teachers also need to help boys develop an emotional vocabulary—to use and talk to them about words such as *excited, overwhelmed,* and *sad*—so that little boys become less of a mystery to themselves.

Recently, Horn's talks have been drawing enthusiastic crowds. Members of the African American community, she says, know they have a problem with their young boys in school and are happy to hear her message. Middle-class parents are starting to wake up to the problem, too. "I think the pendulum is starting to swing again," says Horn. Parents and teachers are starting to realize that, when it comes to preschool, sometimes little boys and little girls need different things.

CHAPTER 6

KINDERGARTEN

The New First Grade

When Natalie Leitch enrolled Harry, her kindergarten-age son, in an after-school tutoring program, she felt she had no choice. Harry is a bright boy with burning curiosity about the world. He loved the Montessori preschool he attended—the program put a premium on social and emotional development. But kindergarten in Leitch's suburban Seattle neighborhood was a pressure cooker. The push to ensure that all children became readers was intense.

That wasn't the way Natalie remembered school. "I remember kindergarten fondly—sitting in circles, singing songs," says Natalie. Harry's experience was much more academic and more rigid. The classroom layout signaled that the teacher meant business: The desks were lined up in rows facing a white board. The school day was given over to academics—reading, writing, math, and science. Recess? Forget it. During the school day, five-year-old Harry Leitch got 15 minutes of free time.

A few weeks into the school year, Harry's teacher approached Natalie about her son's "reading problem." He recognized all the letters, the teacher reported, but he wasn't clicking with the school's reading program.

Natalie was puzzled. Harry loved stories. Their house contained books—lots of them—and she read to Harry almost every day. He wasn't ready to read independently. "To him, reading was a very abstract concept," Natalie recalls. "He just wasn't there yet."

Getting homework done was nearly impossible. Every evening, Harry had ten problems in math and a daily writing assignment—for instance, writing capital Y's, then lowercase Y's twenty times each. On top of that, there was reading and a weekly math game. Instead of recognizing that children in her class were at different levels, the teacher seemed to assume that if she assigned homework they'd get it done. To Harry, says Natalie, "homework began to seem almost like a punishment. He'd put his head down and get quiet."

His troubles at school were eating away at Harry's self-confidence. By Halloween, the teacher reported, he was starting to play the clown. "I could tell what was happening," says his mother. "He was frustrated and acting out."

With great misgivings, she enrolled Harry in a twice-weekly tutoring program that focuses on reading. Harry's doing better, but Natalie wonders if some damage has been done. "The whole thing was too much. I felt like a lot of his youth had been zapped out of him."

The Hurried Child

ELEMENTARY school is a conveyor belt. It moves kids from the magical world of childhood toward a more complex universe where reading and writing, concrete reasoning, abstract thought, and time-management skills are the currency of the land. In the last ten years, that conveyor belt has been speeded up. Our children are being pushed to reach the milestones of literacy and arithmetic earlier and earlier.

If you doubt this is true, talk to any veteran kindergarten, first-grade, second-grade, or third-grade teacher. Fifteen years ago, kindergarten was a place for social and emotional development. Reading was reserved for first grade. First-graders were expected to learn their letters and slowly, over the year, master letter sounds, begin to recognize some words on sight, and read short sentences. Second grade was given over to developing math concepts and reading fluency. These days, in many schools, principals urge parents to be sure that their incoming kindergartners already know the letters—uppercase and lowercase—and to make sure they have the corresponding letter sounds solidly under their Hello Kitty or Power Ranger belts. Many parents are warned that in order to stay at grade level, kindergartners should be able to read on their own by the end of the year. Today, first-graders are routinely pushed through a curriculum that fifteen years ago was considered standard for second or sometimes third grade.

Some kids can handle it, but many can't. The fortunate ones have experienced, sensible teachers who can protect them. Good teachers know that within certain parameters, different kids learn at different rates. But many kids are not so lucky. Inexperienced teachers or teachers in overcrowded or failing schools are required to teach from rigid lesson plans targeted at the middle range of abilities.

How does the acceleration of the curriculum affect little boys? Many teachers believe it has been nothing short of a disaster. Ro Costello, a robust-looking woman with Mediterranean features, chin-length brown hair, and large, cappuccino-colored eyes, has seen the effects firsthand. These days, she teaches special education and fifth grade in public schools in suburban Oakland, New Jersey, but she was a kindergarten teacher for almost twenty-five years. You can still hear it in her calming, comforting tone of voice. What she has to say, though, is not reassuring at all. Much of the work that teachers routinely assign children in early elementary school, she believes, borders on developmentally inappropriate for many kids but is especially bad for young males.

"Perfectly smart boys tend to come to reading and writing a few weeks or months later than girls," Costello says, but fewer and fewer allowances are made for differences in their learning timetable.

The ever-narrowing range of expectations makes boys unhappy. How? She's happy to provide an example. Not long ago, she was observing a classroom full of second-graders at an elementary school in her district. Their assignment? Write a one-page essay in their writing journals. Most of the children sat hunched over their black-and-white marble composition notebooks. Some kids, though, simply stared into space. Then she noticed a small, fearful-looking boy who'd crawled under his desk and was curled up, unnoticed and silent, with his pencil tip in his ear. She bent down and looked him in the eye.

"What are you doing?" she asked quietly.

He stared at her for a moment, then whispered, "Scratching my ear."

Costello tried again. "Why are you under the desk?" she said, keeping her voice low.

The boy tried to explain. "The teachers said we should write about anything," he said, then fell silent.

"And?" prompted Costello.

"I don't know what to write."

Costello recounts the conversation with a sigh. Writing a full page can be a formidable task for a second-grader. "It's good to set a high bar," she says. "All good teachers want to take kids as far as they can go. But you also have to remember that not every child is the same."

What happens to a second-grade boy who spends writing period hiding under his desk? Costello has seen the heartbreaking pattern repeated with boys year after year. By third grade, a second-grade boy's fear has turned to frustration. By fifth grade, he's the class clown. In middle school, he's aggressive and begins to get labeled a behavior problem. By high school, he's in special education if he's still in high school at all.

"It starts with a little boy under a desk," Costello says.

The effect of the accelerated curriculum on boys has been immediate and dramatic. In the early years of elementary school, boys are twice as likely as girls to be diagnosed with learning disabilities. They make up two-thirds of the children relegated to special education, often an instructional ghetto of the worst kind. In a national sampling taken in 2003, the most recent data available, boys were 60 percent more likely than girls to get held back in kindergarten. Since then, schools have gotten even more demanding, and the number of boys who are retained around the country has risen even higher. In Texas, which has the largest number of elementary-school children after the state of California, twice as many kindergarten boys as girls were held back in 2005. That's an astonishing rise and a sickening one if you know the research. It turns out that a student who gets retained is much more likely to be identified as learning disabled or as having a behavioral problem and is more likely to eventually drop out. "That the system is saying that boys are failing kindergarten at twice the rate of girls is problematic," Paul Kelleher, who chairs the Education Department at Trinity University, told the *San Antonio Express-News*. Failure breeds failure, he warned: "It can influence parent expectations, teacher expectations and student self-esteem."

What has changed about the kindergartens in Texas since those astonishing failure rates for boys were made public? Absolutely nothing.

A Nation at Risk

WHY are we rushing our children? To understand where schools are coming from and why we're in such a big hurry, it helps to know a little bit about how our nation's view of learning—especially early learning—has evolved. I realize that if you wanted a full-blown History of Education course you'd enroll in a local community college. So in the interest of brevity, I'll give you the Sparks Notes version of how our thinking about what we teach, how we teach, and when we teach it has changed. The payoff will be this: The next time you sit down with your son's teacher, you'll have greater appreciation for why she does what she does.

In a nutshell, what's happening in classrooms today is a response to revolutionary ideas about education that swept through American schools forty years ago. The 1960s were a bad time for barbers and Army recruiters, but they were even worse for tradition-loving academics. Skirts got short. Trouser legs got wide. The sexual revolution caught fire. Rock music ruled. For many young people, recreational drugs became a way of life. The tune in, drop out message was an affront to many traditions, institutions, and social convention. Rates of marriage dropped, women's roles changed, and church attendance plummeted. There was a direct assault on what educational historian Diane Ravitch, in her book *Left Back: A Century of Failed School Reforms,* calls "the very foundation of a solid education—a thoughtful, challenging curriculum delivered in a well-calibrated fashion by well-trained teachers to students who would endeavor to master the material with ingenuity, discipline and perseverance." Hierarchy was out, and the walls seemed to be tumbling down.

"To bore a child," wrote George Leonard, a senior editor at *Look* magazine and author of a best-selling book called *Education and Ecstasy,* "is as cruel as beating him." In place of the dusty Western canon, Leonard advocated for a new kind of educational model based on freedom, self-expression, and "the ecstatic moment" like the kind that hippies were experiencing in the hot tubs of Esalen. Responding to the times, educational theorists called for a reversal of lines of authority within schools and for "open" classrooms. Learning, they insisted, should be collaborative. So walls were knocked down, and movable furniture replaced rows of desks bolted to the floor. The vocational track and the college track of high school lost their luster. Increasing numbers of students began pursing what was called "general education"—a path of study replete with electives and for-credit courses in such subjects as "bachelor living," cooking, health, driving, and banking.

To the consternation of college presidents, as well as state and federal policy makers, national standardized test scores began declining precipitously. Although more people were interested in pursuing a college education, high schools weren't preparing college-goers for high-level academic work. Fewer students were taking college-prep courses in English, science, history, and mathematics. Thirty percent of the most selective colleges reported that they were lowering their standards for admissions. SAT scores swooned. The situation was a source of national embarrassment as well as a national defense concern. The head of recruitment for the U.S. Department of the Navy reported to Congress that one quarter of the Navy's prospective recruits could not read at the ninth-grade level, the minimum needed to understand written safety instructions.

Media coverage of this education slump was intense. By the 1980s, the federal government realized something must be done. In 1983, President Reagan's secretary of education, Terrel H. Bell, formed a National Commission on Excellence in Education made up of college presidents, academics, and educational policy researchers. In short order, the committee held hearings in Washington, D.C., then issued a report called *A Nation at Risk*. It asserted that all young people, regardless of race or economic background, deserved a decent education, then, in language calculated to inflame the passions of the American public, warned that "a rising tide of mediocrity" in public education was eroding our economy, our society, and our very democracy.

If an unfriendly foreign power had attempted to impose on America the mediocre educational performance that exists

today, we might well have viewed it as an act of war. As it
stands, we have allowed this to happen ourselves. We have
even squandered the gains in students' achievement made in
the wake of the Sputnik challenge. Moreover, we have dis-
mantled essential support systems that helped make those
gains possible. We have, in effect, been committing an act of
unthinking, unilateral educational disarmament.

The commission suggested that schools reduce general education courses, realign their priorities with the needs of the nation, and return to the basics—English, math, science, and social studies.

Around the same time that *A Nation at Risk* was rattling Americans, momentum began building to address the achievement gap between poor black children and middle-class whites. In 1972, social scientists at the University of North Carolina launched the Abecedarian Project, perhaps the most intensive intervention ever attempted in the United States. They identified 109 very high-risk infants and put 57 of them in a five-year program where highly trained teachers provided them with social, emotional, cognitive, and language enrichment. Later, at key intervals, the two groups of children were assessed. Social scientists found that the children who had received the services did much better in math and English, attended college at more than twice the rate of the control group, and were more likely to delay the birth of their first children until they had finished high school. In the mid- to late 1980s, social scientists involved with that study began to lecture on and publish their results. The findings of the Abecedarian Project gave new hope to people who fervently believed that all children, regardless of their economic circumstances or racial background, could do better. It was up to schools to provide the right kind of instruction.

In 1989, President George H. W. Bush held an education summit for governors in Charlottesville, Virginia. There, Arkansas's Governor Bill Clinton took the lead in drafting national goals—many of them already successfully implemented in states around the country. The goals included promoting school readiness for young children, raising the standards for academic achievement for all students, and lowering high school dropout rates. After Clinton was elected president, Goals 2000, his first major educational legislation, enacted in 1994, provided funds to encourage all states to develop their own standards and assessments that would make schools responsible for educating all kids, including poor and minority ones.

The governors and the federal government were demanding that curricula in schools become standardized. But was there a single best way to teach, say, reading? For decades, some reading teachers had championed phonics—decoding each word by sounding out letters—while others hotly insisted that the whole-language approach, in which students used context clues to figure out meaning, was a better way to go. To end the "Reading Wars," the U.S. Department of Education asked a panel of experts to comb through twenty-five years of scientific research and provide the nation with a list of best practices for teaching early reading. In 2000, the National Reading Panel issued its report, which said, in essence, that the fundamental components of good instruction are phonics, plenty of out-loud reading in small groups, and explicit vocabulary instruction.

In 2001, President George W. Bush signed into law the groundbreaking No Child Left Behind legislation. If Goals 2000 was the carrot, No Child Left Behind was the stick. By the school year 2013–2014, the law declared, every school would be required to show that every child—regardless of race, economic background, or disability—was reaching state standards on important academic content. Schools that failed would face reorganization, and teachers would lose their jobs.

No Child Left Behind

So EVERY state developed a set of rigid academic standards and began to administer a battery of standardized tests to ensure students were meeting those standards. In Texas, for example, in order to move up to first grade, kindergarten students must now demonstrate that they are able to do the following: make predictions about stories and events; distinguish between different kinds of texts such as lists, newsletters, and signs and explain the function of each; distinguish between stories, poems, and nonfiction books; begin to read words and simple stories and to write phrases and sentences; and in math, make and use graphs, identify the symbols for greater than, less than, and equal to, and add and subtract.

Standards and assessments are why at the Lafayette Elementary School in a middle-class section of Boulder Valley, Colorado, soon-to-be kindergartners and rising first-graders come to school on the last day of summer vacation to take a reading test. First, parents fill out a form that asks whether they've been reading to their children and how much. From that information, the teachers decide the level of test that each child should take. According to Principal Holly Hultgren, the early testing is aimed at establishing a baseline portrait of ability for each child. That information will indicate how much ground a teacher can cover and how fast, in order to meet the state requirement when the race officially begins on the first day of school.

In a classroom down the hall from Hultgren's office, a boy wearing a striped jersey is sitting with his soon-to-be kindergarten teacher and trying to identify letters and words. The teacher points to an F. The boy squints thoughtfully. "Sometimes I forget that one," he offers. "That's why you come to school," the teacher says encouragingly. He's relieved to recognize the letter M. "That one's on the M&M's," he reports. He finishes the exercise by writing his name although he clutches the pencil awkwardly.

The standards have been set, and Principal Hultgren knows it's her job to make sure kids reach them. She was assigned to Lafayette from a better-performing elementary school, at least in part to raise test scores. A lively woman with an easy smile, she exudes an air of certainty as she walks through the hallways of her school. Privately, though, she feels deep ambivalence. As in most public elementary schools around the country, at Lafayette tests have become a way of life. The end-of-summer reading assessments are only the start. Districtwide reading tests are administered three times a year. By third grade, students will be measured against regional and statewide norms, and standardized tests—multiple-choice questions and a number 2 pencil—will be regular features of the school experience.

If you think this system seems too test-driven, remember that it has the blessing of the community. In wealthy areas like the Boulder Valley school district, parents can enroll their kids in any one of thirty-four public and charter elementary schools. Schools with good test scores attract young families moving into the area, and real estate prices go up and stay up. Parents seem to like the tests, too. The scores help them see how their children are progressing. Sometimes, though, Hultgren worries that the constant testing makes it hard for teachers to stay sensitive to the important qualities in children that tests can't measure—diligence, creativity, and potential—or to nurture kids who develop more slowly. "I worry," she says, "that we're creating school environments that are less friendly to kids who aren't ready."

And as the national numbers show, the kids who aren't ready tend to be boys.

Redshirting

SOME parents have found a way to, if not stop the madness, then at least postpone it a year. They opt to delay their sons' and daughters' entrance into what has become the early educational rat race. That is why, not long ago, Ron Montaquila, the principal at Clemmons Elementary School in an affluent suburb just outside Winston-Salem, North Carolina, surveyed the roster of his incoming students and was astonished to see that the average age of kindergartners had risen from five to six and some kids were almost seven. Twenty years ago, most kids started at age five, the minimum age at which you can enroll a child in school in North Carolina. Today, between 46 and 50 percent of Montaquila's incoming kindergartners are at least six. They were held out of school a year by their parents.

This practice is called redshirting in the world of college sports—athletes enroll in college later in order to get an extra year of conditioning. And it isn't new to elementary schools. Teachers, who see the ways in which boys trail girls developmentally, have redshirted their own kids for years. But lately, Montaquila notes, the trend is out of control. In response, private schools around Winston-Salem began catering to redshirters, offering junior kindergarten as a kind of bridge year between preschool and the rigors of kindergarten. "Those programs," says Montaquila, "are practically a boys' club."

The problem with redshirting is that it accelerates the academic conveyor belt even more. The weakest student in Montaquila's school would be considered a high-achieving kid. The high-achieving parents in the community, most of whom have college degrees, would expect nothing less. And it's easy to lose perspective. With academics being introduced to kids as early as age three, in the last few years, new kindergartners come to Clemmons Elementary School having already had plenty of instruction in reading. "Most kids come to us with a four-year degree from preschool," Montaquila jokes. Then he adds, torn between admiration and disbelief, "We had nine kids reading chapter books in kindergarten last year." That is a good thing except that it helps people forget that perfectly smart kids develop at different times. And slow-to-mature kids, who tend to be boys, find that they can't keep up.

Redshirting takes money. Families need to be able to afford an additional year of tuition, day care, or a caregiving parent staying out of the workforce. But most who can afford it figure that redshirting is a worthwhile investment to help their sons avoid trouble. Families who can't make that financial sacrifice try another strategy to protect their boys. As the drumbeat for early reading grows stronger, an entire industry of private tutoring companies—Score, Sylvan Learning Center, Kumon—have sprung up to support kids who are struggling in school. In the last five years, those companies have begun offering programs to help kindergartners and first-graders grasp the reading basics. The majority of their pupils are young males.

Most boys, however—the ones from families who don't have the resources or the sophistication to game the system—begin school at the earliest age, full of excitement and enthusiasm. Then their teachers ask, then insist, often again and again, that they behave in ways that are beyond their natural developmental abilities. In short order, they become confused, upset, and sometimes dejected. They may be slow to read, but they are not stupid. The experience of kindergarten and first grade delivers to them an implicit message that careful curriculum planners probably never considered. The message they get is this: School is not geared for boys.

No Time for Blocks

LIKE them or hate them, educational reform laws, including the sweeping No Child Left Behind legislation, have accelerated the early elementary school curriculum. They also have made it more narrow and test-driven. Not long ago, researchers at the Center on Education Policy, a privately funded nonpartisan Washington think tank that advocates for more effective public education, evaluated changes in school programs since No Child Left Behind was enacted. They described elementary schools that were replacing breadth with intensity. They found that nearly two-thirds of elementary schools were spending more time on reading and math—the subjects that will be measured by state tests. Forty-four percent had reduced the time kids spent on social studies, science, art, music, lunch, and gym.

In many schools, especially in historically low-performing districts, the school day resembles a basic skills boot camp. In Coronita Elementary, in a working-class section of Corona, California, sixty miles outside Los Angeles, kids focus on reading, writing, and math. The principal, Alma Backer, says there's no choice: The challenge laid down by No Child Left Behind—getting all children to read at grade level— is a massive one. Seventy percent of children who attend Coronita Elementary live below the poverty line. Thirty percent don't speak English at home. The school offers parents of kindergartners a "readiness program," and each year about fifty families attend. Even so, most kindergartners don't know their letters, can't name colors, and don't recognize their own names when they are written in big letters on their cubbies. So from day one, says Backer, "our kids are playing catch-up." The school day starts at 7:45 and ends at 2:05, and teachers spend most of their time teaching kindergartners and first graders to read. Music, dance, art, social studies, and science—even gym and recess—get shoved aside for reading and writing. At the end of the day, about one-fifth of students go to an after-school program, where until 5:30 they get even more instruction: tutoring, reading group, and homework help.

Woe to the little boy at Coronita who doesn't have the muscle tone to sit at a desk or the impulse control to look at a book about Dot and

Spot. In the past, kids who struggled to make sense of a narrative on the printed page might learn how to organize a story by learning to sing a simple ballad in music class. A boy might improve his fine motor skills by holding a paintbrush. Another boy might grit his teeth through reading so he could get to the science lab and play with frogs. Some boys might have blown off steam during recess. The single-minded focus on the basics—reading, writing, and math—is harmful for many kids. For boys, it further erodes the common ground between what interests them and what is happening at school.

It's a perplexing problem. As a nation, we are committed to making sure kids whom we once ignored—poor kids and black and Hispanic kids—reach proficiency in reading and math. This is a noble goal, and it's long overdue. For the most part, parents and teachers connected to traditionally low-performing schools welcome the change. But parents of boys may find that, at least in some cases, the cure for ignorance may prove lethal to the patient. What we have to remember is that No Child Left Behind doesn't explicitly require that teachers throw out a well-balanced curriculum in favor of a single-minded focus on standardized tests. At badly managed schools in underserved neighborhoods, though, that kind of narrow focus goes unquestioned. Poor schools attract the least-experienced teachers, who almost by default end up teaching rigid "standards-based" lessons—and almost nothing else.

It takes an experienced teacher like Kay Kobbe to teach state standards in an age-appropriate way. For the last thirty-five years, she's been a second- and third-grade teacher at Mamaroneck Public Schools, in an affluent suburb of New York City. She has long been a champion of women's rights, but she is, she says, "at a place in my career where I can stand up for boys." Four decades of teaching have provided her with ample evidence that when it comes to learning styles, there truly are differences between boys and girls. And in many ways, those differences receive less attention these days than they did in the past. "Is this a particularly difficult time to be an elementary school boy?" she asks in her rich contralto. "Yes, it is."

On the whole, Kobbe supports school reform. She wants all her kids to learn as much about reading, writing, and math as they can. But she's also determined to prevent filling out worksheets and quiet desk work from taking time away from active play and hands-on learning—things, she points out, that are important to all kids but especially to young boys. So nearly every year, she puts aside test prep and spends four months studying Africa. The children report on animals, they become pen pals with Namibian schoolchildren, they study migratory patterns of animals, and they look at African art. The culmination of the unit is a pretend trip to Africa: Some kids run a virtual airline; others are baggage handlers, pilots, food servers, and tour guides. The principal, who has actually visited Africa, is an honored guest in the classroom, and the highlight of the celebration comes when she shows students slides from her trip.

"Real learning takes engagement, and engagement—and activity—is key for boys," Kobbe says.

Kobbe is the last third-grade teacher in the school to have chunky, wooden blocks and a block construction area. Younger teachers, she says, don't understand her approach. They haven't been given the liberty, she says, or the support to explore this kind of learning with their classes. Most third-grade teachers are locked into the drill-it-till-you-kill-it mode, preparing kids for regional and state tests. They were taught that a teacher-led—and sometimes even scripted—curriculum is a more powerful one. Not Kobbe.

"I believe in blocks," she says simply. And she believes in the third-grade students—mostly boys—who build with them. She considers block building a sophisticated activity—teaching the rudiments of fractions, geometry, and even physics and art. Nine-year-old block builders, she says, aren't just stacking, they're "managing dimension." Wasted time?

"My block builders are engaged in important cognitive development," she says.

Kobbe is trying to protect all her students and especially her boys. "They shouldn't be made to feel like there is something wrong with who they are just because at this particular time in history, our system doesn't provide for them."

What can parents do? Be aware: The goal of early elementary school has changed. That's a good thing, but make sure your son is ready. Don't be afraid to hold him out a year if you can. Remember that some kids need more time to develop reading and writing skills. On the whole, it's a good thing that states are developing standards. Schools need to be held accountable for making sure all kids are proficient in basic skills, but the way in which those standards are administered is important. If your son is attending a cram-school (one that solely focuses on the rote teaching of state math and English test standards), take heed: It may be time to organize fellow parents to pressure the school to add teacher development and to widen the curriculum—and bring back art, music, science, and social studies. Or it may be time to look for another school.

CHAPTER 7

REQUIEM FOR RECESS

Yes, They Need It—More Than You Think

In 2006, PBS ran an hour-long documentary about boys and school called *Raising Cain*. The producers asked boys what part of school they liked best and spliced their answers into a rapid and hilarious montage. A chorus of boys of different ages, different ethnicities, different heights, and different hairstyles gleefully uttered the same word: "Recess!" "Recess!" "Recess!" Yet, students in many elementary schools are in danger of losing what boys say they like most about school. As a result of school reforms in the last decade, many elementary schools are reducing or dropping recess.

Twenty years ago, in most public elementary schools, recess offered a daily or even twice daily respite. These days, according to the U.S. Department of Education, 39 percent of all first-graders in the country get 20 minutes a day or less of recess. Seven percent get none at all. By fourth grade, nearly half of students get less than 20 minutes a day, and 9 percent get none at all. Physical education class, which is usually required by the state, is provided one or two days a week, for less than 30 minutes.

What remains uncounted, though, is how the rapid erosion of recess hurts kids and especially active boys. Paula Bulwidas, of Middlebury,

Connecticut, knows. As the mother of twins, a boy and girl, she has seen the ways in which both her kids benefit from physical activity. Her daughter, Daria, enjoys boisterous outdoor activities but is content to spend the day in quiet play. Her son, Joseph, needs almost constant motion and continuous speed. Both kids are intelligent and able learners, but in first grade, Joseph began to struggle. "I need to move around more," Joseph complained to his mother.

Paula paid a visit to the teacher. Could Joseph get up from his desk more, Paula wondered, or record his answers on a chalkboard once in a while instead of sitting at a desk and writing on a piece of paper?

The teacher's response was chilly. "Moving around," the teacher told Paula, "is for recess."

How much recess did the children get? Exactly 20 minutes out of Joseph's six-hour school day.

Daria tolerated the school day as best she could, but Joseph, bright-eyed, big-hearted, and full of ideas, began boarding the bus each morning as if he was facing a firing squad. Looking back on the year, Paula thinks that her son was being asked to work in a way that was at odds with who he is. "The school," she says, "needs to understand boys a little better."

Principals are torn. They know that kids need activity, but physical movement—jumping, screaming, whooping, skipping rope, throwing a ball, roughhousing with friends, or simply taking a quiet walk around the perimeter of the playground—is no longer considered a productive use of the school day. In some schools, principals allow a kind of conditional recess—physical movement in the service of larger, No Child Left Behind–worthy goals. Grade-schoolers at Kensington Avenue Elementary in Springfield, Massachusetts, don't have art or music anymore. Instead, first-graders get three hours of reading and an hour of math. Recess is a miserly 15 minutes, but it is not an opportunity for the active games or frenzied running and shouting that allow kids to tone muscles, increase blood flow, or improve social skills. At Kensington, recess is as highly instructional and teacher directed as reading. One day not long ago, teachers spent the 15 minutes of recess leading first-graders through a game of Fishy, Fishy. The game, says principal Mary Thompson, helps kids practice following the teacher's directions.

Thompson says that she's glad she didn't grow up that way. "When I went to kindergarten, recess meant you'd sit on the playground and talk to your friends," she recalls nostalgically. Thompson knows the school schedule is at odds with child development, but she's caught between state and national mandates: "This is what our government tells us that it wants us to do."

In Atlanta, Georgia, and elsewhere, recess has become such a marginal part of the school day that elementary school buildings are being erected without playgrounds. Taking test scores seriously means giving up recess. Benjamin O. Canada, superintendent of schools in Atlanta, told the *New York Times*, "We are intent on improving academic performance. You don't do that by having kids hanging on monkey bars."

Most parents of boys recognize that it's a bad idea to try to keep children—especially boys—cooped up in a classroom doing desk work. But most don't see the long-term effects. From her lofty perch at the University of Pennsylvania, President Amy Gutman is keeping a sharp eye on the shortage of males in higher education. A pioneer and an innovator at one of the most prestigious universities in the country, she draws a straight line from physically restrictive environments in early education to the postsecondary school male shortage, which, though not acute at Penn, is increasingly evident in colleges around the country. Says Gutman: "The tallest hurdle facing early childhood education is the creation of . . . learning environments that are responsive to a broad spectrum of personalities, behavior and learning styles." Whittling away recess and doing away with playgrounds "penalizes all children who have difficulty sitting still in the classroom for hours on end, and disproportionately puts little boys at a disadvantage. That simply is not good schooling."

Even when schoolchildren are allowed recess, the rough-and-tumble interaction that boys seem to love is often frowned on—and sometimes banned outright. Contact sports such as soccer and touch football were forbidden at Freedom Elementary School in Cheyenne, Wyoming, because, principal Cindy Farwell told *USA Today,* "it progresses easily into slapping and hitting and pushing instead of just touching." In Broward County, Florida, running has been banned on all playgrounds at all 137 elementary schools. At Barnes Elementary School in Beaverton, Oregon, tag was deemed too dangerous for children. In downtown Los Angeles, Local District 4, which serves 100,000 children, didn't ban tag, but school administrators discourage it. Why? According to District Superintendent Richard Alonzo, "The game can bring out aggression in kids."

Why are we so paranoid about boys and aggression? There was a time when boys' noisy, boisterous expressions were seen as natural parts of their psychological makeup. Even a little scuffling, as long as it didn't lead to a bloody nose, was considered to be a sign of a boy's vitality. But then came a series of tragic school shootings, starting at Columbine High School in 1999 and continuing straight up to Virginia Tech in 2007. Instead of beefing up community mental health resources to get help for kids who need it, schools began to adopt zero-tolerance policies toward any behavior that they could construe as aggressive or potentially aggressive.

Have we taken this approach too far? Consider this: In New Jersey, an eight-year-old boy used an L-shaped piece of paper in a game of Cops and Robbers during recess. School officials called the police, saying the child had threatened to "kill other students." He was held for five hours and forced to make two court appearances before the charges were dropped. In Arkansas, an eight-year-old was punished for pointing a cooked chicken strip at another student and saying "Pow! Pow!"

Teachers who are grappling with overcrowded classrooms filled with excitable young kids know that management is key. But when a boy is arrested for pointing a chicken strip, what are we really afraid of? Do we believe that a nine-year-old boy who raises his thumb and extends his pointer finger is training to be a serial killer? If that were so, then why aren't murder rates higher? After all, the overwhelming majority of men in this country probably played that way as boys.

Some teachers may believe that roughhousing boys create an unwelcoming environment for quiet boys and girls. That concern seems legitimate. We want to find a way to make all kinds of kids feel comfortable. But should we do so by making boys play more like girls? After seeing my nieces mix it up on the soccer field, I have to wonder: Are our daughters really so fragile and sensitive that they cannot tolerate the kinetic, goofy way that some boys play?

Let's be clear about what we are losing when we reduce recess and ban tag. We rob children of free play that is really free. There's a cost— and it's a steep one for many boys.

Anthony Pellegrini, an educational psychology professor at the University of Minnesota, has made a career studying the effects of recess on elementary school children. In a series of well-controlled experiments over the last two decades, he discovered that what looks like carefree time may be a critical component of the educational experience for many children. One big benefit is academic. In one study, Pellegrini followed kindergartners and first-graders in the classroom and on the playground. He found that even after controlling for kindergarten test scores, successful peer interaction at recess was an excellent predictor of success on standardized tests. Another benefit is that recess helps children experience mastery, which boosts their performance across the board. When children, but especially boys, establish competence in the schoolyard, Pellegrini found, they do better in school.

Who pays when recess is cut short? Boys do. Pellegrini and his researchers manipulated the length of sessions of "seatwork" and recess. What they found was that recess helped kids pay attention. All children were less attentive before recess than after, but recess was especially crucial for boys.

Dr. Kenneth Ginsburg, an associate professor of pediatrics at the University of Pennsylvania School of Medicine, says play—especially for young males—is a public health issue. Ginsburg, a former nursery school teacher, is a sought-after speaker on the subject of building resiliency in children. Not long ago, he authored an American Academy of Pediatrics position paper urging schools and families to weave more free play into a child's day. In his high-energy way, he's happy to talk about the academy's recommendations. But his personal story is even more compelling.

Movement, he says, provides a way to help him focus. He has grappled with attention issues his entire life. Listening to patients is easy. Sitting in a chair listening to teachers lecture? "Forget it!" he says. What he tells the boys who he sees in his practice is that movement is important for the healthy development of all kids, but for them it's crucial. "On the average," he says, "girls can handle a sedentary school day"— although he's quick to point out that it's not good for them, either. He then reiterates what so many people who study boys eventually conclude: Boys need movement to survive.

At your son's school, recess should not be optional. Nor should it be given as a reward or taken away as a punishment. Protect recess. There is a strong connection between recess and the well-being and academic achievement of all children but especially of young boys.

CHAPTER 8

PAY ATTENTION

Your Son, His Teacher, and ADHD

As six-year-old Kai Farquhar tells it, he ran into a bit of trouble in first grade. Mostly, he wants you to know, he likes school, "especially P.E., library, music, and art." He likes to read, too—and his parents will proudly tell you that he devours books at a fourth-grade level. So what's the trouble?

"I can't complete a journal entry," Kai confesses, his blue eyes and thick eyelashes growing moist. Why not? He thinks for a minute, then looks down at his hand, which often starts to ache when he writes for a long time. "Oh, man!" he says, flexing his fingers. "I just get sick of doing it!" What happened when he didn't finish his journal? The teacher, he says tremulously, "would give me a look." A look? "She'd be doing her papers and I'd be not doing my work and she'd give me a look." He shakes his mop of brown hair as if he's still amazed that he survived it.

Kai's parents are a little frightened of the teacher, too, but for other reasons. For the last eight months, they've been caught in a vise: They believe their son is a bright normal boy, but the teacher and the school think Kai has an attention deficit and should be on Ritalin.

Kai's problems, such as they are, are a relatively recent development.

Kindergarten and the first half of first grade were a breeze. Back then, Kai's teacher had nothing but wonderful things to say about him. Shortly after Christmas break, though, Kelley and Tim Farquhar, who live in a suburb outside Kansas City, noticed that Kai was struggling to get his math and writing homework done. "Writing has always been a problem since he can't really control his pencil yet," says Kelley, who works in a bank. She gives a little laugh. "He's got the handwriting of a serial killer." He's also bored to death with the drill-it-till-you-kill-it approach to math homework. "The same problems, with the same numbers over and over again," says Kelley. "We've had lots of tears—both his and mine."

When Tim, a stay-at-home dad, picked Kai up from school, the teacher began signaling that there was trouble. "He's not getting his work done," Tim kept hearing. "The teacher said, 'He's daydreaming. He's out in left field,' and 'even when I stand on top of him, he's not paying attention.'" Tim started to worry.

Soon, the teacher started sending Kelley and Tim notices that Kai had a "red day," meaning he hadn't finished his work in the allotted time, he was talking to other kids, or he was acting silly. "None of those infractions seemed all that serious to me," says Kelley. Tim, though, decided to sit in on class one afternoon and try to get a sense of the problem. "I couldn't help but notice that all of the kids who were having 'red days' were boys," he says. Around that time, the teacher and the school nurse began a steady patter of "suggestions" urging Kelley and Tim to "get Kai tested." Kai is Kelley's only child, but she knew what that meant. She had heard plenty of other parents talk about taking their children for an evaluation, getting a diagnosis of ADHD, and then trying various medications.

"I wondered if it was really necessary," says Kelley. She stalled, but the "suggestions" grew more pointed. It's against the law for school personnel to pressure parents into giving a child attention-enhancing drugs, but Kai's school got the message across.

"The teacher would say, 'Kai had a bad day today. Have you taken him to the doctor? You know, [Kai's classmate] is on Ritalin and he's been having mostly good days,'" says Tim, his voice filled with anguish and self-doubt. "Growing up, you're taught that a teacher is an authority figure. And you figure she probably sees lots of kids. They act like you just don't know what they know because you're an inexperienced parent. They act like they know what's good for your kid more than you do."

Kelley and Tim resisted.

Finally, in the spring, they broke down. They asked the teacher for a note detailing Kai's problems. She listed Kai's frequent daydreaming and failing to complete his journal. Then Kelley, Tim, and Kai went to their local pediatrician. The doctor spent 10 minutes examining Kai, read the teacher's note, and handed Kelley and Tim pamphlets for different ADHD medications. "Sounds like ADHD to me," she told Kelley and Tim. "Take a look at these and see which one you want to put him on."

The couple looked around the examining room. Logos for popular attention deficit drugs were emblazoned on the notepads, the pens, the posters, the pencil holder jars, the Kleenex box, the doctor's own stethoscope, and the little hammer she used to test Kai's reflexes. They grabbed up their son and backed out of the office.

That afternoon, Kelley called a renowned hospital in Kansas City and put Kai on the waiting list to get a second opinion. He'll be evaluated—in eight months. Tim is dreading it already: "I feel like we're all getting sucked into something we don't think is right for Kai." It seems to him that the school doesn't have enough tolerance for typical boy behavior. "But at the same time you worry because maybe there is really something wrong with my kid."

The "Epidemic" of ADHD

FEW discussion topics around the sandbox can spark a controversy more quickly than the diagnosis and treatment of attention-deficit/ hyperactivity disorder. The National Institutes of Health describe ADHD as a lifelong mental disorder that affects approximately 3 to 5 percent of the population. Although the disorder was largely unheard of before the 1950s, attention deficit medication in the United States is now a $2.7 billion industry. Plenty of people, including some well-known research scientists, think that the widespread acceptance of ADHD marks a step forward in our understanding of human behavior. Plenty of other people, including some well-known research scientists, believe that the diagnosis and treatment of ADHD in this country is an example of junk science run amok. But there is one point about which both sides agree: There's no medical test for ADHD. The identification of the disorder results from a series of highly subjective judgments.

Drug companies and Big Pharma–sponsored ADHD support groups insist the squishy diagnostic process means that ADHD is underdiagnosed—that many people have the disorder but never get sensitive medical care and the proper treatment. But when you look at the national data, one subgroup of the American public is getting identified and treated for ADHD at a truly astonishing rate: school-age boys.

Before you sit down to write me a nasty letter describing how ADHD is real and how ADHD meds helped your son, let me say this: I'm not pulling a Tom Cruise here. I've met very few responsible thinkers on this topic who believe that ADHD doesn't exist at all. For some people— including some school-age boys—the arsenal of ADHD medications is nothing short of a godsend. That said, let's take a harder look at who is being medicated for this disorder, who is doing the diagnosing, and why.

According to the Centers for Disease Control, in 2003, 14 percent of boys across the nation were identified as having ADHD by they time they reached their sixteenth birthday. And the percentage is continuing to grow. Between 2000 and 2005, the number of boys from birth to age nineteen who were being prescribed ADHD medication grew 48 percent. That such large numbers of boys are being diagnosed with a central nervous system disorder suggests two things: Either we are witnessing the largest pandemic in our country since influenza struck in the United States in 1918, or school-age boys are being overidentified and overdiagnosed.

Why are boys in the crosshairs? Maybe it's all about biology. We know that for complex biological reasons, boys are more vulnerable to genetic anomalies than girls. It's possible, then, that they also might be more susceptible to as-yet-unknown environmental or chemical causes of the disorder. But other factors—including the higher academic expectations, zero-tolerance policies, and shrinking of recess that we've been talking about—may be making boys' behavior seem less normal and more pathological.

According to researchers who study dosage patterns, affluent white boys (who attend the schools where expectations for academic achievement are most intense) and poor black boys (who attend underfunded, overcrowded schools with a high proportion of inexperienced teachers) are most likely to be identified as having attention problems and given medication. In two southeastern Virginia school districts—one poor and one affluent—a researcher at Eastern Virginia Medical School in Norfolk found that 20 percent of white elementary school boys, one in five, line up at nurses' offices at lunchtime to take stimulants in order to get through the day. In a follow-up and as-yet-unpublished study, the researchers culled information from nurses and parents at three middle schools in the same area and found that an astonishing 38 percent of white boys were diagnosed with ADHD and 100 percent of them were taking medication for it. For boys, getting a neuropsychological workup or "getting tested" and trying out attention-enhancing medication is becoming a perverse right of passage.

From Daydreaming to Ritalin

WHO does the diagnosing? What training do they have to determine which attention spans need enhancing and which do not? Let's take a step back and see how it works.

In order for a child to be identified as having ADHD, the child has to have six of the following nine symptoms:

> Fails to give close attention to details or makes careless mistakes.
> Has difficulty sustaining attention.
> Does not appear to listen.
> Struggles to follow through on instructions.
> Has difficulty with organization.
> Avoids or dislikes tasks requiring sustained mental effort.
> Loses things.
> Is easily distracted.
> Is often forgetful in daily activities.

The child has to exhibit these symptoms in at least two out of three areas of life: home, social settings, or school. For school-age boys, that usually means home and school. In order to elicit feedback from schools, doctors provide teachers with a checklist of behaviors: often fidgets with hands or feet, often runs about or climbs excessively, often has difficulty playing quietly, often fails to give close attention to details or makes mistakes in schoolwork. In a quiet moment between classes, a teacher reviews the behavior of one of her or his one hundred or so students and checks off "Never," "Rarely," "Sometimes," "Often," or "Always." After talking to the parent and to the child and reviewing the checklist, psychologists and physicians interpret the checklist to determine if a boy is "normal" or not.

How important is the teacher's input? Bryan Goodman, a spokesman for Children and Adults with Attention Deficit/Hyperactivity Disorder (CHADD), a support group funded in part by drug companies that make popular attention-enhancing drugs, says, "Our position is that only medical professionals should make a diagnosis for ADHD. But teachers do provide crucial information that parents can then take to medical professionals."

But not too much information. For a time, teachers, backed by eager drug company marketers, were playing too big a role in getting kids identified, diagnosed, and put on medication. In 2003, when Jonah Hoover attended first grade in Memphis, his teacher called in his parents, Brian and Kate, to discuss Jonah's pattern of behavioral infractions: horsing around in the hallways, talking out of turn, and poking other kids. Recently, he'd gotten two half-day suspensions: one for squirting a ketchup packet at another kid, another for jumping in a puddle. "Exactly the same kind of stuff I did when I was a boy," says Brian, who works in retail. The assistant principal was there, too. He lectured the Hoovers on the school's code of behavior, then concluded their brief meeting by handing Kate and Brian a promotional pamphlet and DVD about Ritalin. "I had a pretty emotional reaction," says Brian. "My son was six. I think long and hard before I give him an aspirin."

This scenario was repeated so many times in so many schools that in 2003 a federal law was enacted to prevent schools from discussing ADHD medication with families—or risk having their federal funding yanked.

Bryan Goodman, the spokesman for CHADD, says, "We hear rumors about [schools pressuring parents to drug their children] all of the time, but we rarely find cases of it. What we do find are parents who spend years trying to figure out what the teachers are trying to communicate because of the rules of what teachers can and cannot say." To that end, many teachers and school administrators point out that they have been carefully trained NOT to suggest to a parent that a child might have an attention problem or require medication. But the Farquhars and Hoovers and scores of parents like them from all over the country are not hard to find. They tell harrowing stories about teachers who repeatedly hint, suggest, insist, and even demand that parents give their kids—usually their sons—drugs.

What gives? I'm not sure. Some principals, school nurses, and teachers may be going out on an ethical limb, violating federal law and school policy because they have very real concerns that a child has a serious lifelong mental condition and they feel compelled to help. But what teachers and principals see as a gentle suggestion might be being interpreted by parents as a requirement.

"Parents really see teachers as having a medial authority," says Dr. Ilina Singh, a lecturer at the London School of Economics, who studies ADHD. "Parents find it hard to resist a statement from a teacher concerning the normality of their child. In my experience, parents take it very seriously."

What parents, psychologists, and physicians forget is that when a teacher checks off "Often" next to "Climbs excessively" she is saying something about your son but she is saying more about her expectations for your son's behavior in her class. As schools ratchet up their expectations, says Lawrence Diller, a psychiatrist in the Bay Area who has been an outspoken critic of the ADHD industry, "more kids—and particularly more boys—look as if they might have a problem. Teachers now demand a standardized level of performance from all students. Many can't tolerate too much motion, too much noise, too many questions—even within the range of normal—if it interferes with the pace of their class. They forget what's normal."

Then there are kids who won't pay attention. Diller says, "For most kids, there is a natural downturn in motivation as they approach middle school. Kids who have been trained in good habits weather the change with no problems in school. For others, who by nature or nurture have not developed good habits"—Diller estimates their numbers to be about one in five—"school performance plummets." And that puts them under stress. "When girls are under increased stress, they fold their hands and get quieter. When boys are under stress, they become a behavior problem." If their parents are wealthy enough, the boys end up in Diller's Walnut Creek office, where Diller says he produces medically enhanced compliance in those boys by providing them with attention-enhancing drugs.

"Do I like it?" he asks. "No. But I do it. And as a consequence, I feel compelled to speak about it publicly."

A teacher's opinion of your son's behavior is a subjective one. When it comes to identifying boys with ADHD, it turns out the teacher is often wrong. In 2005, psychologist J. Michael Havey and his team from Eastern Illinois University surveyed 52 regular K–6 classroom teachers from eight different rural midwestern elementary and middle schools. Most of the teachers were experienced; 35 percent of them had been on the job over twenty years. Havey asked them to fill out a questionnaire on ADHD in the classroom and then complete a rating scale on 121 randomly selected boys and girls to identify the ones who they thought were suffering from the disorder. In the opinion of these experienced, well-meaning teachers, 24 of the 66 males they evaluated had ADHD. Other studies have found that teachers from private schools, and teachers with large classes where maintaining order in the classroom is key, also report implausibly high rates of ADHD. Guess who gets identified (wrongly) most often? Boys.

Small Changes, Big Results

SOME experts say that instead of medicating boys, it may be time to change some of the routines of schooling. Lisen Stromberg, a former ad agency executive from Northern California, says she's trying. A few years ago, she founded an advocacy group called Supporting Our Sons in Northern California in an effort to encourage schools to be more tolerant of typical boy behavior. "All my friends who had active boys were being told, 'This boy is out of control. This boy needs to go on Ritalin right away,'" recalls Stromberg. So she began to raise money—almost $600,000 in all—and launched a series of training sessions for teachers hoping to get the best out of their young male students. One hundred forty-six teachers from public and private schools in Northern California attended. "We started with the idea of helping teachers understand the gestalt of a boy—what makes up the boy dynamic, the bandwidth of boy behaviors, how boys interact, and about boys' cognitive and physical needs," says Stromberg.

The training continues to have a big impact on teachers at the Ohlone Elementary School, a public school in Palo Alto, California. As is so often the case in any discussion of schoolboys, the link between well-being and movement was front and center. "The way schools are run we have kids sitting at desks for a very long time," says principal Susan Charles. So Charles and her teachers began changing how things were done. If a kid wanted to stand instead of sit while he wrote, no problem. If he was wiggly during circle time, he got something to lean against. Poor fine motor skills? He got a fat pencil to hold instead of a thin one. The changes cost nothing, says Charles. "Sending a child out for a run break costs nothing. Allowing them to work outside instead of at a hard table costs nothing. You have to change the mind-set of the school and what it should look like." Does ADHD exist there? Sure. But the principal and teachers at Ohlone want to make sure the school environment isn't part of the problem.

Of course, you want to give your son the tools he needs to do well in school—and that's especially true if your child is struggling. Your son may be suffering from ADHD, but remember that teachers aren't always the best people to make that diagnosis. Sometimes, the school, not the boy, needs the overhaul.

CHAPTER 9

NOTES FROM THE FRONT

The Wilmette Solution

A few social ills must be lurking in the hallways of the public schools in Wilmette, Illinois, a pristine suburb outside Chicago. But they certainly aren't obvious. The classrooms are brightly lit, and the teaching seems remarkably intelligent, thoughtful, and engaging. The children, who range in age from seven to thirteen, look well rested and well groomed—a high bar for any group of youngsters. To a child, they seem cheerful, and while they are filing from one class to another class, they speak to a visitor in a confident tone that is at once direct, open, and respectful.

The public schools of Wilmette reflect the values of the community. The parents of Wilmette are fiercely child centered and unequivocal in their desire to get the best education possible for their kids. Local officials support them all the way and for good reason. The average house in Wilmette sells for around $700,000. People pay those prices not only for the manicured lawns and picturesque cobblestone streets, although there are plenty of those. The families who move to Wilmette tend to be highly educated professionals drawn here because the school system is one of the nation's best. After making their way through elementary and middle school in District 39, Wilmette students take a long yellow school bus to nearby New Trier High School, an institution that prides itself on being one of the top-performing public high schools in the country.

In the spring of 2005, Dr. Glenn "Max" McGee, the new head of District 39—which encompasses the five elementary and two middle schools in Wilmette—realized his schools might have a problem. A lanky man with an athlete's energy, McGee radiates low-key midwestern charm. But make no mistake: He's used to getting things done. Since arriving in Wilmette, he'd been spending at least part of each day popping in and out of classrooms, walking the halls, and talking to teachers. It seemed to him that the boys of Wilmette, like boys in many other communities around the state, simply were not engaging in school to the same degree as the girls.

"You could walk into almost any classroom and see it," says McGee. "Girls with their hands up and boys in the back, checked out."

McGee wasn't entirely surprised. In his old job as the head of the Illinois public schools, he'd seen again and again the ways in which poor and minority boys lagged behind their female counterparts. In the last few years, he'd noticed that the boy problem was spreading into many middle-class communities: "What I had been seeing is that boys were doing worse on standardized tests in reading and writing and not just black boys but all boys, no matter what race and no matter what socioeconomic background."

As Illinois school czar, he had to be realistic: He didn't have the time, the money, or the political capital to address the problem. The reality of public education in low-performing schools, where the boy problem was worst, was that teachers and administrators worked like members of a NASCAR pit crew doing whatever they could, as fast as they could, to help get their underachieving kids over the finish line. Nevertheless, in middle-class communities, many parents, teachers, and school administrators thought it was girls, not boys, who needed all the help.

As school chief in tidy Wilmette, McGee had the perfect petri dish for a radical experiment in education. District 39 has plenty of resources. The schools are well funded by the community. Instead of relying on candy sales or peddling wrapping paper to pay for the extras, fund drives are semiprofessional affairs. Recently, the PTA put together a silent auction that raised a whopping $100,000 for the middle school. With a surfeit of accomplished parents eager to contribute their time and expertise, McGee could launch research projects that in other places might take years to get off the ground. What sealed the deal for McGee, though, were the formidable expectations Wilmette parents have for their kids: They want their children—all their children—to succeed. After walking the halls and observing classrooms, McGee reasoned that if boys were struggling in Wilmette, and if he could come up with some replicable ways to address the problem, he might be able to help children all over the country, not just in Illinois.

McGee asked a high-powered group of parents, experienced teachers, and former school board members to undertake a baseline study to see if there was a difference in how boys and girls were doing. Members of the group were sophisticated enough to know they'd been handed a hot potato. "Some people—including many of the teachers—didn't believe there was any reason to look at the performance differences—and they were insulted and uncomfortable at the suggestion it might be boys—not girls—who were struggling," says committee member Diane Fisher, a clinical psychologist and mother of two boys. "We were taught that boys and girls are the same and if there is a gender difference, it has been deeply ingrained in all of us that this is a code word for the way girls have historically been at a disadvantage."

Despite misgivings, committee members dove in. For four months, they read the data on literacy rates and boys' psychology, and they interviewed teachers, students, and parents. They tabulated scores on standardized tests and classroom grades going back four years. The initial results were startling: Boys did seem to be underachieving in ways that were far more profound and pervasive than any of the committee members expected. They dug deeper. They separated out the performance of the kids who were assigned to special education. They disaggregated the children who were identified as having learning disabilities.

"In order to drive performance, we needed to get information," says parent and committee cochair Jason Weller, who works for a private equity fund and seems to naturally speak in the argot of the corporate boardroom. "The more granular we got, the more we could make people understand the extent of the problem and what we had to do to effect a change."

The final committee report provided irrefutable evidence that upper-middle-class boys were not thriving in school. Although there was no difference in intelligence between boys and girls, boys trailed girls by almost every measure. They were the source of the majority of the discipline problems, and they constituted more than 70 percent of the students receiving special education. In grades 5 through 8, girls had higher grades than boys across all four core subjects—reading, writing, science, and math. The gap was greatest in reading and writing but existed in other subjects, too. For the last four years, at every level of junior high school math, girls outperformed boys. Across all grades, boys were more likely to receive grades of C or lower, and girls were 30 to 35 percent more likely to get an A. The performance gap, the committee found, was wide—and it was getting wider.

The gap was so great that committee members grew uneasy. It was widely accepted that poor boys did worse in school than poor girls. But their study flew smack in the face of conventional wisdom about the new gender gap and wealthy kids. What did this study mean for their community? Was something amiss in Wilmette that caused their boys to lag so far behind? Tentatively, they reached out to sixteen of the most affluent K–8 districts in the state. None of those districts had conducted a comprehensive gender study, but a cursory inspection of their standardized test scores showed that boys in every single district scored 8 to 12 points behind girls in reading and writing. The committee members began to understand more about the boy problem. Those other districts probably had a glaring gender gap, too. They simply didn't have the political will to confront it.

In the spring of 2006, committee members submitted their results to the Wilmette Board of Education and held their breath. If they were expecting fireworks, though, they were pleasantly surprised to receive a sparkler instead. The board found the report cogent and thoroughly convincing. It was clear that something had to be done. The board's only stipulation? None of the "boy-friendly" measures McGee put in place could be at the expense of Wilmette's bright, high-achieving girls. Other than that, McGee's mandate was clear: Do whatever it takes to improve the performance of all children—including boys.

It was then that McGee began to understand the old saying "Be careful what you wish for." He faced one of the biggest hurdles of his career. He knew the roots of boys' underachievement went deep—from the kind of instruction they got in the classroom to what they watched grown men do on television. What changes could McGee make in the seven hours he had the children in class that would effectively reverse an academic trend fifteen years in the making? His boys and girls already attended schools that included plenty of enrichment like music, art, and dance. Teachers already made sure the children got ample recess.

McGee took aim at some of the more subtle dynamics that cause boys to disengage and tried to come up with ways to get them reengaged in school again. He reached out to his teachers. Doing so was risky. He worried that, despite his best intentions, some members of his staff would consider pro-boy initiatives to be anti-girl. Many teachers, McGee realized, have a blind spot when it comes to boys and school. In the past when he'd asked them if boys and girls learn differently, they'd invariably parroted what they'd been told in teachers' college: Boys and girls are equals, and all children regardless of race, ethnicity, or background learn about the same. But when McGee had asked teachers to describe the kids most challenging to teach, they'd launched into a description of kids who couldn't focus, neglected their homework, or failed to follow directions, and nine times out of ten, McGee had seen, the teachers were talking about boys. In addition, teachers seemed to believe that boys were simply oppositional, or that boys' struggles were specific to particular teachers' classes, or that young males who weren't thriving were "catching up" in other grades—ideas that McGee could now demonstrate were untrue.

The Wilmette gender study captured the disconnect perfectly: Of the 265 Wilmette teachers polled, a full 88 percent said they believed that the "curriculum engages both boys and girls equally." Yet for the last four years, those same teachers had given girls far more A's and B's and boys far more C's and D's.

McGee gathered together a group of experienced teachers, took a deep breath, and laid out some of the most salient results from the study. To his surprise, many of his teachers were not resistant but were instead relieved to have a chance to talk constructively about ways to reach hard-to-teach boys. With the can-do attitude that McGee began to see was typical of his faculty, a handful of teachers formed a study group and came up with practical solutions.

Suzanne Goff, a veteran teacher at Central Elementary School, was one of the most enthusiastic members of the group. For years she'd run a Famous Women in History study group for fourth-grade female student leaders. An unapologetic feminist who raised an unapologetic feminist daughter, Goff had long been uncomfortable with ways in which boys were being marginalized in school. "I've watched boys for years," she says. "I know they need something to get them more hooked in." A male teacher, Goff suggested, should provide an enrichment-type class for the boys, and third-grade teacher Kevan Truman accepted the challenge.

Truman pulled his top male students together and gave them a boy-friendly assignment: Figure out how to calculate statistics for star players from the National Football League. The boys' enthusiasm was so overwhelming that Truman quickly hatched another guy-friendly lesson plan for his boys' group: Design and build a play fort.

Second-grade teacher Kate Miller, who was also part of the study group, knew that building forts wasn't her style. But in an effort to get little boys excited about reading, she began offering a greater variety of reading material—including plenty of action stories and nonfiction. Fourth-grade teacher Traci Meziere structured her classroom work so that every 15 to 20 minutes all her kids could get up and move. She also became more relaxed about the noise level. "I realized how much I had imposed a noise standard that was comfortable to me," she says, "but maybe not for the boys. These days, I allow for a little more leeway."

The data-hungry parents of Wilmette have been watching McGee's grand experiment closely. The District 39 teachers say they already are seeing some changes. Some of the hard-to-reach boys are tuning in more frequently. Two charismatic, energetic, and socially dominant boys who in the past simply tolerated lessons have become overtly enthusiastic about doing well in school. That attitude change, in turn, is setting a school-is-cool tone among other young males. Recently, Kevan Truman listened proudly as a boy struggled to articulate a complex response to a social studies question. Before Truman could acknowledge it, another boy unexpectedly chimed in. "Great answer!" he said. At that moment, Truman said, he knew something was changing with the boys in Wilmette elementary school.

"What causes little boys to underachieve is complicated," he says. But maybe "we've figured out one piece of the puzzle."

CHAPTER 10

GOOD-BYE, MR. CHIPS

The Vanishing Male Teacher

In Philip Roth's novel *I Married a Communist,* the main character, Nathan Zuckerman, now an adult, runs into one of the seminal figures in his life: Murray Ringold, a male high school teacher. Zuckerman's/Roth's description of his teacher is deeply rooted in its time—the 1950s—but eloquently conveys the unspoken and often-ineffable effects that male teachers can have on boys:

> Along with brain and conspicuous braininess . . . Mr. Ringold knew very well that what boys like me needed to learn was not only how to express themselves with precision and acquire a more discerning response to words, but how to be rambunctious without being stupid, how not to be too well concealed or too well behaved, how to begin to release the masculine intensities from the institutional rectitude that intimidated the bright kids the most.
>
> You felt, in a sexual sense, the power of a male high school teacher like Murray Ringold—masculine authority uncorrected by piety—and you felt, in the priestly sense, the vocation of a male high school teacher like Murray Ringold

who wasn't lost in the amorphous American aspiration to make it big, who—unlike the school's women teachers—could have chosen to be almost anything else and chose instead, for his life's work, to be ours.

Roth continues:

"In human society," Mr. Ringold taught us, "thinking's the great transgression of all." "Cri-ti-cal thinking," Mr. Ringold said, using his knuckles to rap out each of the syllables on his desktop, "—there is the ultimate subversion." I told Murray that hearing this early from a manly guy like him—seeing it demonstrated by him—provided the most valuable clue to growing up that I had clutched at.

The connection between Roth's fictional stand-in, Zuckerman, and his teacher was a deep one, and it ended up shaping the man that Roth/Zuckerman was to become. These days, many fewer potential authors will have an opportunity to experience a similar connection. Inside our nation's classrooms, male students—especially in the lowest grades—have been all but abandoned by adult males. Females now dominate teaching in a way never before seen in our lifetimes. According to the National Education Association, the biggest teachers' union in the country, the number of male teachers is the lowest it's been in forty years. In 1981, the percentage of male teachers in elementary schools reached 18 percent. Today, it's around 9 percent. The percentage of male teachers in secondary schools stands at about 35 percent, the lowest it has been since the National Education Association started keeping statistics.

So we're faced with two sets of evidence: (1) that the achievement and engagement of boys is failing to keep pace with that of girls and

(2) that fewer men are standing in front of chalkboards. The crucial question is, Does one have anything to do with the other? But before we examine that question, let's take a step back and consider what is keeping men out of the classroom.

The reason is pretty simple: economics. There's a lot of palaver in this country about how being a teacher is one of society's most important jobs. Teachers are sentimental favorites. Most people are happy to reminisce about teachers who changed their lives. We sing their praises to other parents when our children are doing well. We might thank a teacher profusely at graduation or chip in for an end-of-the-year memento after a particularly good year. But we don't pay teachers as if the job they are performing is a vital service to our country. These days, our 3 million full-time teachers earn an average salary of $47,602, and the average starting salary is about $32,000. Teachers are among the lowest-paid public employees in our nation.

Historically, paying teachers less than what they were worth worked out OK for America. Women were barred from most of the professions, and teaching was one of the few careers open to ambitious females. Because there was an almost unlimited supply of smart women who needed or wanted work, school districts could keep salaries low. In the 1970s, it looked as though teachers might finally begin to get their due. The pool of teachers began to shrink as employment opportunities in more sectors of the economy opened up to women. Reflecting the law of supply and demand, teachers' wages began to climb—and with that rise came an influx of men into the profession. The economic slowdown of the early 1980s saw teachers' salaries decline again. Men, who had gotten a toehold in the profession in the 1970s, began to abandon it in droves.

In the last twenty years, two other factors have put even more pressure on teachers focused on the bottom line: the cost of college and the high price of real estate. According to NEA estimates, 42 percent of a teacher's starting salary goes toward school loans and rent. In Seattle,

Oakland, Los Angeles, San Francisco, and many other cities, teachers cannot afford to live near the urban schools in which they teach.

How does this affect the number of male applicants for teaching jobs? People are drawn to teaching for two different but sometimes overlapping reasons: a passion for instructing kids and the perception that teaching provides a low-stakes, family-friendly schedule. Plenty of men love helping kids learn, but, at least until recently, more women than men have been concerned about work-family balance. Even when guys feel called to teach, they often say that they don't see how they can make it a career—teaching doesn't pay enough to buy a home and help support a wife and family. Several states and even the federal government have launched recruitment programs aimed at getting more guys into the profession, but those schemes seem to be having little impact. It boils down to money. Across the country, states that pay the most have the highest percentage of male teachers.

Many of those men who end up standing in front of a chalkboard don't stay there long. Rates of attrition among all teachers are very high. Different researchers have different numbers, but roughly one-third of new teachers leave after five years on the job. Male teachers get promoted more: they are much more likely than their female counterparts to leave the classroom for administrative jobs. (Males make up 9 percent of elementary school teachers but 44 percent of elementary school principals. Males make up 35 percent of secondary school teachers and 74 percent of secondary school principals.) Another factor also may be keeping men out of teaching: Men who stay in the classroom, at least in the early grades, face persistent gender discrimination in the workplace.

When Andrew Ambrose, 36, was hired as a kindergarten teacher in Montgomery County, Maryland, a handful of parents immediately called the principal's office and asked that their kids be assigned to another classroom.

"I know kids. I have two of them. I worked in day care. I subbed all through my undergraduate work," says Ambrose. "I knew I'd be a great kindergarten teacher. But the first thing most parents think is that you are a pedophile or a homosexual."

On the morning of his first day on his new job, his vice principal pulled Ambrose aside to tell him the names of the parents who had tried, without success, to get their kids pulled out of his class. "He said I might have difficulties with these parents," says Ambrose.

The first couple of days at school, Ambrose got "a lot of really weird looks," but he knew what he was dealing with. He printed off some pictures of his wife, a child psychologist with the Air Force, and his son, and had them laminated. Then he hung the photos around his desk. The next day at drop-off, the parents were full of questions. Who was she? How old was his son?

"The parents got a lot more comfortable with me right away," Ambrose reports. By the end of the year, the parents who had complained nominated him for New Teacher of the Year. But his feelings of satisfaction at having overcome anti-male prejudice were short-lived. In the spring, during orientation for the following September, two mothers of incoming kindergartners were standing about six feet away from him, and one said loudly to the other, "Can you believe they allow him in a room alone with a group of kids?"

"I could not believe what I just heard," recalls Ambrose. "I was a wonderful kindergarten teacher. It was such a slap in the face."

There may be another surprising factor that keeps men out of the classroom: Female teachers have been known to practice a very real form of reverse discrimination. Max McGee in Wilmette, Illinois, uncovered it during an investigation into his district's hiring practices. Faced with the gender gap that his research group uncovered, he set out to add males to his staff. Common sense, he felt, dictated that lagging boys would benefit from having male role models in the classroom. But how to hire more men?

He reviewed the hiring practices of the previous few years. Even when Wilmette got a rare male applicant, he found, the would-be teacher never seemed to make it past the initial interview process. Intrigued, McGee asked his human resources director to conduct an experiment, and the human resources director asked the most successful male teachers in District 39 to submit to the interview process again. The well-loved male teachers agreed and, without providing their names, answered the standard set of questions routinely asked of all applicants. Then, as is common practice, a hiring committee reviewed those answers. Committee members—most of them female teachers and administrators—weren't told who they were evaluating.

It turned out that the best male teachers—the ones who connected with kids and were beloved by parents and staff alike—responded to standard interview questions in a way that the largely female hiring committee found unacceptable. For example, the hiring committee frequently asked how a prospective teacher would respond to a difference of opinion in a staff meeting. Acceptable answers, according to the committee, included words like *understanding* and *collaboration*. The best male classroom teachers, though, answered the question by suggesting they were not particularly interested in coalition building. One male teacher said that he "respected other people's right to disagree"— a response that the committee judged to be too confrontational. Prospective guy teachers, it seemed, didn't use the buzzwords that made their potential female colleagues comfortable.

At McGee's urging, the human resources department expanded its definition of *acceptable* in order to encompass answers that qualified male as well as female applicants might supply. Within twelve months, the number of male staffers in Wilmette began to rise.

Does It Help?

WHAT happens when school-age boys are educated almost exclusively by women? Does it impact their achievement or engagement? It makes intuitive sense that teachers, who wield so much authority and play such important roles in children's lives, should reflect, at least to some degree, the ethnic and gender makeup of their students. It would seem at first glance that a boy would have slightly more trouble declaring that school was "too girlie" if his third-grade teacher was, say, a former Marine. But would having more men standing in the front of classrooms be a real solution to the trouble with boys? It's a suggestion worth considering.

A study carried out in Finland with thirteen- and fourteen-year-olds, however, showed that the gender of the teacher had little impact on students' view of the quality of the teaching they received. Similarly, in the United States, researchers looked at the National Educational Longitudinal Study run by the U.S. Department of Education. In 1995, they compared the academic performance of 25,000 eighth- through tenth-grade children and found that boys taught by men and girls taught by women did about the same as boys taught by women and girls taught by men. It *is* a very large study, but the problem with it is this: The kids in that survey were not randomly assigned to teachers. It may have been, for instance, that boys with behavior problems, which often become academic woes, were being assigned to male teachers.

In 2006, economist Thomas Dee, a professor at Swarthmore College, made national headlines when he published a study that was based on the same data as the 1995 study but arrived at a very different conclusion. The NELS data included evaluations of each student by the teachers and evaluations of the teachers by each student as well as students' grades. Instead of comparing the achievement of boys taught by women with the achievement of boys taught by men, Dee looked at the

students who had both male and female teachers in eighth grade—
what their teachers said about the kids' learning and what the students
said about the teachers. Dee determined that the gender of the teacher
mattered very much. His study found that a female teacher raised the
achievement of girls in science and lowered that of boys in social studies and English. When a man led the class, boys did better and girls did
worse. Having a male teacher for a year, he found, could actually narrow the achievement gap between boys and girls by raising the achievement of boys and depressing the achievement of girls.

That seems like a slam-dunk reason to hire male teachers, especially
if we want to get boys on equal footing with girls and remediate the
male literacy gap. But not so fast. Dee warns against drawing easy conclusions from his study. In an interview, he pointed out repeatedly that
he's an economist, not a secondary school educator.

"I don't think people—school boards and principals—should make
policy decisions based on this study," he says emphatically. Rather,
educational researchers need to stop pretending that teachers' gender
doesn't matter—that all teachers treat all kids fairly. Instead, Dee
suggests, his study should prompt other researchers to ask questions
and design more studies to figure out the nature of gender bias in the
classroom.

"I think they should ask, What is going on in that black box we call
a classroom?" says Dee. "What is happening to produce these kinds of
results?"

Parents may not have this luxury. If you're faced with an untried
male teacher for your son instead of an intelligent, compassionate, sensitive female teacher, what should you do? Researcher Laura Sokal from
the University of Winnipeg, one of Canada's leading academics looking
at boys and reading, may have come up with an answer.

Schoolboys in Canada have problems similar to those of schoolboys in the United States. As early as second grade, about a quarter of

Canadian boys feel alienated from school, and almost 30 percent report a negative attitude toward reading. Many describe reading as a "feminine" activity. Sokal wanted to know if all-female elementary school environments might be contributing to the widespread disaffection among young males. So in 2002, she launched a study to see if the gender of the adult who was commanding attention in the classroom really mattered to boys.

Sokal polled librarians, teachers, and school kids to find out what books boys reported liking best. The results? Books with male protagonists and plenty of action. Then she divided eighty second-grade boys into four groups. For a half hour a week for ten weeks, she had two male and two female researchers go into a second-grade classroom and read to the groups of boys. One male and one female researcher read standard schoolbooks, some of which had female protagonists. The other male and female researchers read typical boy books with male protagonists and plenty of action. At the end of ten weeks, Sokal measured the kids' attitudes toward reading—whether they liked school, whether they thought reading was a feminine activity, and whether they liked reading.

She found that the sex of the reading teachers mattered not at all if they were reading standard schoolbooks: Boys were equally turned off. What mattered a great deal to the boys, however, were the kinds of books they were allowed to listen to. Boys who heard a woman read an action book reported liking school more. Boys who heard a man read action stories entertained the idea that reading was not a "feminine" activity after all. Boys were affected more by the book choice. The sex of the reading teacher didn't matter.

Although hiring male teachers makes sense, Sokal's study suggests to me that doing so is not the only way to fix boys' underachievement problem. We don't just need more male teachers; we need more good teachers—both men and women—who understand boys and can advocate for their needs and interests. Thomas Dee, who has a son in first grade, offers parents this advice: "I don't believe the teacher's gender is the most important thing. If [my son] were assigned a female teacher, I wouldn't agitate for change. But I would be attentive to whether or not he feels comfortable with the classroom dynamics, if he feels engaged by his teacher, whether the teacher makes an effort to understand who he is as a boy."

In other words, not gender segregation—boys taught by men and girls taught by women—but just a little extra attentiveness is what makes boys tick.

CHAPTER 11

BOYS AND LITERACY

Why Johnny Can't (or Won't) Read

The uncomfortable realities about boys and underachievement are never more evident than when we discuss young men and literacy. In the forty years in which boys and girls have had equal access to education, boys consistently have scored less well than girls on tests measuring reading and writing. Take another look at the graphs in Chapter 2 that show the NCES scores broken out by gender. There, in black and white, you can see two trends that worry educators. The first trend is that boys do worse in reading and writing the longer they stay in school. They narrow the gap somewhat in third grade, where they are 5 points apart. But by high school the gap has grown to 14 points. The second trend is this: In the last twenty years, the gap between males and females at the end of their schooling has been growing.

This is not a new problem. More than three centuries ago, philosopher and educational thinker John Locke fretted about it in his book *Some Thoughts Concerning Education*. He lamented that male students were not able to write as well as female students, and he marveled at how much more easily girls picked up foreign languages. What *is* new is this: Today, unlike in Locke's day, high-level reading and writing skills are essential not only to economic success but to economic survival.

Until about forty years ago, there were plenty of employment opportunities for boys—and some girls—who didn't read and write well. They could easily find their places in life. They could drop out or squeak by until high school graduation and then find respectable, steady work at livable wages in agriculture, the trades, construction, or manufacturing. For good reasons back then, no one worried too much if some kids—a large portion of them boys—didn't become strong readers. Twenty-five years ago, things began to change. The sectors of the economy that provided jobs for poor readers began to wither. Jobs for unskilled and semiskilled workers were outsourced overseas. As the technological age began to dawn in earnest, the business community and big employers began to urge schools to help students develop high-level skills in math, science, and computer science. There are no illiterate scientists, tech geeks, and engineers. Literacy turns out to be the key. Kids can't do well in math and science unless they have a strong grounding in reading and writing. But as educators have been making these grand discoveries—and creating literacy-soaked curricula in response—boys have been losing ground in the very skills we now know are paramount.

In 1999, Dr. Gary Phillips, acting commissioner of the National Center for Education Statistics, released the 1998 *Nation's Report Card* on writing with this stark appraisal: "Girls had higher average scores than boys in all three grades tested and they outperformed boys in writing in every state and jurisdiction at the eighth-grade level. Girls did so much better in writing that, nationally, there were twice as many scoring in the proficient and advanced categories as boys. And twice as many boys were writing below the basic level at all three grades." Since then, boys' reading and writing scores have actually dropped, and some experts believe that a "male literacy gap" may be spawning a national crisis.

Boys failure to keep pace in reading and writing is already echoing through our culture. In 2004, the National Endowment for the Arts issued a report based on data collected by the U.S. Census Bureau.

Researchers found that between 1992 and 2002 young people of all races, incomes, and education levels were reading less. In overall book reading, young women slipped from 63 to 59 percent, and young men plummeted from 55 to 43 percent. The raw scores indicate that boys now do worse on national reading tests than boys did thirty years ago. Not reading, wrote the report coauthor, Mark Bauerlein, "is fast becoming a decided marker of gender identity: Girls read; boys don't."

We are failing to connect boys to reading and the repercussions are spreading like dry rot through our schools. Right now in this country, 33 percent of male high school seniors score "below basic" in national measures of reading achievement. The male literacy deficit does not solely affect poor boys, either—it affects boys from every walk of life. Psychology professor Judith Kleinfeld, who teaches at the University of Alaska in Fairbanks, runs a consortium called "The Boys Project." For a paper she delivered at the 2006 White House Conference on Helping America's Youth, she broke down the national achievement scores of twelfth-grade males and females by race and parental education. Among white high school seniors who have at least one parent who graduated from college, 23 percent of males and 7 percent of females scored "below basic" on reading. Six percent of white females with one parent who graduated from college scored "below basic" on writing; among males, one in four leaves high school lacking basic competency in writing.

In middle school, state test results tell us that the number of adolescent boys who struggle with literacy is shockingly high. In fifteen states, more than 30 percent of eighth-grade males scored "below basic" on state reading tests. In ten states, 40 percent of eighth-grade boys are barely literate. Those numbers surely include many rural and inner-city lads, but if you think the male literacy gap bedevils only poor boys, consider this: A consortium of administrators from the wealthiest school districts in the country found that the male literacy deficit is alive and well in plush communities such as Wilton, Connecticut; Ladue, Missouri; Oak Park, Illinois; and Austin, Texas.

State education officials know what these numbers mean. Three decades of research is unequivocal: The better a child reads, the greater is the probability that the child will succeed in school. To help build skills, kids now experience a literacy-centered curriculum from the first day of kindergarten to the last day of high school. In an effort to provide plenty of instructional hours in reading and comprehension and to give budding readers and writers plenty of practice, almost every aspect of school—sometimes even gym and recess—are tied to some kind of literacy activity. As a result, reading scores have moved up slightly for elementary school boys, but by high school, those slender gains have disappeared.

Success in reading sets the stage for success at school. Unfortunately, the inverse is also true: Reading failure breeds school failure. Kids need to get and stay at grade level; those who fall more than two grade levels behind in reading rarely catch up. If your son is a struggling reader at the end of elementary school, know this: State education authorities frequently use middle school reading scores as a rough measure of future graduation rates. If a student is not reading at grade level by eighth grade, teachers and administrators are already assuming that he (or she) is unlikely to ever wear a cap and gown.

Given the magnitude and significance of the problem, you might assume that a host of research projects, government-funded studies, experimental pilot programs, academic consortiums, and private foundations are trying to come up with innovative ways to address the male reading deficit. You might think that public service announcements (PSAs) would be calling the public's attention to this thorny problem— urging parents to get their kids, particularly their sons, to read. You'd be wrong. There are a few outstanding researchers on boys and literacy— in particular, Thomas Newkirk at the University of New Hampshire, as well as William Brozo, Jeffrey Wilhelm, and Michael Smith, who have done some fascinating work on boys and reading. Lately, a handful of other academics and researchers have begun looking at the issue. But knowledge of their work remains, for the most part, within the Ivory Tower; it has not reached the Teacher's Lounge. Beyond that, very little research is being conducted in this country on why boys aren't reading and writing well. There are a few closely watched pilot programs but, astonishingly, no big government studies. Needless to say, there are no PSAs.

In 2004, the people who design the tests for *The Nation's Report Card* decided that the federal government needed to take a hard look at the male literacy deficit. A big national survey of that sort would be invaluable. By providing a massive amount of data on the problem, it would kick-start microanalysis by educational researchers around the country. But the project is not on the fast track. Since the study was proposed, exactly nothing has happened. As of this writing, it is unclear if the reading-and-gender research will ever be funded.

Before entering the private sector in 2005, Dr. G. Reid Lyon headed up the National Institute of Child Health and Development, which is part of the National Institutes of Health, the government's research arm. He was one of the primary architects of the federal Reading First program, the administration of which later became mired in controversy. But at its inception the program was one of the first to rely on evidence instead of tradition to teach reading. Like anyone who is familiar with the data, Lyon acknowledges that the male literacy deficit is a serious and complicated problem. NIH scientists might well have spent the last ten years examining whether there were any biomedical dimensions to the problem, he says.

"At the NIH, we looked at all kinds of specific topics [related to learning] *except* gender," he says ruefully. With the gaps so clearly tied to gender—boys from all races and all walks of life lagging behind their female counterparts—why not? Misguided sensitivity toward women's issues kept the discussion of boys and literacy at the margins, Lyon explains. Grant proposals go through a peer-review process. The idea that a particular project was pro-boy and not anti-girl was too complicated and too risky for most peer-review panels to absorb. What would overcome the resistance to conducting potentially important research on this issue? According to Lyon, an adviser on literacy issues to both a Democratic and a Republican White House, the massive bureaucracy at the NIH needs leadership, but neither the Clinton nor the Bush administration had the appetite for it: "There just wasn't the political will to take it on." Lyon predicts, however, that as the problem gets worse, doctors and researchers from the NIH will eventually step in to fill the void. They almost have to: "When you look at the downstream effects of boys not doing well in literacy and reading, it is not just an education problem, but a public health problem."

What does he mean? Lyon is using the same kind of shorthand used by state education officials who calculate dropout rates from eighth-grade reading scores. Reading and writing are make-or-break skills in today's economy. Males who fail to earn a high school diploma are less likely to have a steady job, less likely to get married, and more likely to get divorced if they do marry. They are more likely to have contact with prison and the welfare system and to live in poverty. Not surprisingly, those negative experiences undermine a person's health and longevity. Men who aren't well educated and are single are far more prone to chronic ailments such as heart disease and cancer. Men who are unmarried high school dropouts don't live as long as educated married men.

When pressed, even the most passionate reading advocates don't want to talk about what's wrong with our boys. Bob Wise is the head of the Alliance for Excellent Education, a Washington think tank that focuses on adolescent literacy issues. The Alliance for Excellent Education is an impressive organization. Members are tireless advocates for important legislation in Washington aimed at supporting middle and high school readers and writers. Wise is happy to talk about the problems that adolescent readers face and the wave of reform in middle and high school that his organization believes is needed to build on the success of No Child Left Behind. Wise, a former governor of West Virginia, clearly knows his subject inside and out. Since boys from every socioeconomic background and every racial group underperform their female counterparts, I asked him what steps the Alliance advocates for addressing this problem; then I listened to a long silence on the other end of the telephone.

"Boys," he said finally. "It may be something to look at." Then Wise resumed his discussion of high school reform. A savvy politician, Bob Wise knows that to look at literacy through the prism of gender is to enter a political minefield.

"For a long time, if you ever mentioned the boy problem, lots of people would act shocked and offended," says Timothy Shanahan, a professor of urban education at the University of Illinois at Chicago, who is one of the few literacy researchers who is happy to have a candid discussion about the politics of gender and reading. "It was almost like, 'How dare you notice that we are missing all these people at the bottom?' There are some women, not all, but a small minority of women, who are just scared to death that if we put attention on these male literacy issues we will be taking oxygen away from what they need for the women's movement. They see looking at the issues of boys and reading as taking away from the discussion about the glass ceiling."

The Male Reading Deficit

WHY do boys start out a little behind girls in language? Can we blame biology? Can we blame culture? The data isn't clear. What is clear, though, is that those small differences get amplified by the careless, and

sometimes crushing, messages that boys often get about the importance of reading from their parents, teachers, and communities. Let's
take a look at how that happens.

We know that children who hear and speak plenty of words tend to
learn to read more readily. We also know that in the home most little
boys speak fewer words and get read to slightly less than girls. It would
stand to reason, then, that kindergarten—which is designed to be a
language-rich environment—would enable the boys to catch up. Kindergarten, however, seems to make things worse. In the fall term of
kindergarten, girls outperform boys by 0.9 points in reading. By the
spring semester, the difference has nearly doubled to 1.7 points.

Early in elementary school, classes divide—sometimes formally,
sometimes informally—into good readers and not-so-good readers.
Too often, the gap between them widens every year in what reading
researchers call the "Matthew effect," after a New Testament parable
about the rich getting richer and the poor getting poorer. In first grade,
a child in the not-so-good reading group reads an average of 16 words
in a week, and a skilled reader reads an average of 1,933 words. As any
primary school teacher will tell you, the more kids read, the better they
read. The inverse is also true. By the end of fifth grade, boys who are
poor readers are at a disadvantage from which they will never recover.
By middle school, a poor reader reads 100,000 words a year, an average
reader 1 million words, and a voracious reader 10 million words.

Around fourth and fifth grade, another factor comes into play as
well. Good readers take a leap forward as they move from learning to
read to reading to learn. The curriculum demands it. It's no longer
enough to be able to "sound out" words. Children have to comprehend
sentences and paragraphs from history and science books and make in-
ferences from those texts. Kids who don't make that jump fall into what
experts have dubbed the "fourth-grade slump." They are stuck trying to
figure out how to decode the word *everglades*, for instance, while other

kids are learning about the kinds of animals that live in those Florida swamps. It's an important cognitive leap.

By every measure, the fourth-grade slump hits boys harder than it hits girls. This is reflected in boys' engagement in school and in reading. In 2006, Scholastic, a publisher of materials for children, commissioned one of the nation's top polling firms, Yankelovitch, to do a study of the attitudes of nine-year-old boys and girls toward reading. Children were asked if they like to read. More girls than boys were reading enthusiasts (49 percent of boys, 57 percent of girls). More boys than girls said that they didn't like it (10 percent of boys answered "not at all," 6 percent of girls). Those little boys become what Thomas Newkirk, professor of English at the University of New Hampshire and author of the seminal book *Misreading Masculinity: Boys, Literacy and Popular Culture*, calls "reluctant readers." "Boys don't like reading," he says, "so they don't read." It's a disastrous decision. When they turn off reading so young, says Newkirk, "they can't build up enough stamina to read in a sustained way."

The fourth-grade slump draws those boys inexorably toward the "eighth-grade cliff." Because girls read so much better than boys, struggling boy readers, perhaps defensively looking for reasons why they're not succeeding, begin to express the opinion that reading is "feminine." Then they go out of their way to avoid things that they classify as "girlie" activities. It's a silly, self-defeating pattern, but boys find plenty of support for this attitude in their families and their culture. Mom is the person who usually reads them a bedtime story. Mom is the person who makes up the grocery list or follows the recipe. Mom is the person who is most likely to buy books, read magazines, and take books out of the library. She's the person they're most likely to barge in on reading a novel.

What do boys conclude about the world of reading? Men don't read. So boys begin to check out, and the consequences are almost inevitable.

"Unless you're reading fluently in late elementary school, getting an assignment to read a two-hundred-page book will just defeat you," says Newkirk.

Is there anything we can do to help boys overcome their early deficits and to raise them to be passionate readers? It turns out that the answer may be yes.

Boy-Friendly Reading Instruction

As WE'VE discussed, on average, boys from all socioeconomic strata and every ethnicity learn to read less well than their female counterparts. Those results are so consistent and seemingly immutable that parents, teachers, and schools now simply take them for granted. They blame the boys themselves: Poor boys don't read well because of their impoverished backgrounds, middle-class boys because they are "wired" that way, affluent boys because they have "too many distractions." In the last five years, though, the idea that boys are predestined not to read as well as girls has been coming under fire. No one has done more to fuel that discussion than Joyce Watson, a seventy-six-year-old woman from the east coast of Scotland.

Watson found that if kids were taught to read in a certain way, boys—especially poor boys—did every bit as well as and often even better than, their female counterparts. Because her findings flew smack in the face of conventional wisdom, for a time her ideas were dismissed by critics and ignored by most school administrators. Recently, though, her method has become the foundation of a reading reform movement taking place all over the United Kingdom aimed at improving the reading scores of all children, and of boys and poor boys in particular.

As Watson tells it, she arrived at her astonishing findings completely by accident. "One thing," she says, speaking with a Scottish brogue so thick you could spread it on toast, "just led to another." It's easy to be fooled by her self-effacing manner. What Watson brings to the question of boys and reading are qualities any high-level research team would pay good money to find: a lifetime of teaching experience, acute sensitivity toward classroom dynamics, a wellspring of empathy toward teachers and students, a rigorously scientific mind, and massive doses of both patience and common sense.

After working as a primary school teacher for ten years, Watson became a lecturer at a teachers' college in remote Dundee, Scotland. For twenty-five years she taught there and raised her daughter. As was the custom, she taught teachers how to teach kids to read using the whole-language approach—the "see and say" method, as it is also known. Instead of receiving top-down, rote instruction on decoding and sounding out, children memorized words (sight words) and learned to use cues from pictures and from familiar words in a sentence to figure out the rest.

The whole-language method is considered more child-friendly, less authoritarian, and less boring than old-style phonics.

But Watson never felt completely comfortable with the "see and say" approach. It seemed to the ever-practical instructor that it assumed the existence of skills that kids didn't necessarily have. "It seems to me that you need to know how to read before you can read," she says today. Also, the "see and say" method called for a lot of guessing, which is fine for some kids but frustrating for others.

At age sixty-four, with her daughter grown, Watson "retired" from the teachers' college. Good teachers, though, never stop learning. "I thought it would be nice to round off everything to get a Ph.D.," she says simply. She enrolled as a self-paying student at the School of Education at prestigious University of Saint Andrews and began working with Dr. Rhona Johnston, who did research in reading development. "I didn't know what I wanted to study exactly," Watson says. So she began visiting schools, sitting in classrooms, and trying to decide what the most important educational question of the day might be. "It took me a long time to figure out what I wanted to research," she says. A year went by, then two. Then, gradually, a question began to form in her mind—one that could potentially touch upon the experiences of all students in all schools.

Reading instruction is more an art than a science, and it varies widely from place to place. What, Watson asked herself, was the best way to teach children to read? From her observations in the classroom, she'd noted that her long-held hunch was right: Teachers who emphasized phonics instead of the whole-language approach seem to get better results out of the children. But that was hardly a scientific conclusion.

Watson set up an experiment in a tiny Scottish county called Clackmannanshire. It's Scotland at its best—heather-topped hills, crumbling castles, and cold, crystal clear lochs. The area enjoys some fame among American tourists who visit the fourteenth-century Campbell family seat there. But unlike tourism, the other industries in Clackmannanshire—mining, textiles, and brewing—were in wholesale retreat, and many of the children attending public school were poor. Here's the question she wanted to answer: What would happen if children were taught to sound out words with phonics from the start?

Watson divided three hundred kids from different schools into three groups. The first group was taught reading with a smattering of phonics but mostly using the whole-language approach—the "see and say" method. The second group was taught with a blend of whole language and phonics. The third group was taught with an all amped-up phonics program that Watson devised and dubbed "Synthetic Phonics." The experiment would follow the children from primary 1, the Scottish equivalent of kindergarten, straight through to primary 7, the equivalent of fifth grade.

Synthetic Phonics worked like this: From the outset, the primary 1 teachers operated on the assumption that their students, who were between 4.5 and 5 years old, had no previous reading knowledge. Watson wanted to make sure that classroom instruction supplied each student with every tool he or she would need. Teachers dispensed with the traditional sight-vocabulary instruction that is part of the "see and say" method. Instead, for 20 minutes, starting on the first day of school and continuing for 16 weeks, children began to learn letter sounds. After they memorized a few—for instance, the sounds for T, A, and P—they were given magnetic letters and asked to move the letters around on a magnetic board and make words. When they could fluidly manipulate sixteen different letters into forty or more different words, they were given books, and they began the laborious process of reading.

Watson's approach was simple. It was direct. It was unadulterated phonics—but taught in a way that engaged the students. By the end of the second year, all the children were seven months ahead of their chronological age in reading ability and nine months ahead in spelling. By the end of year three, they were eighteen months ahead. "We were quite surprised," says Watson mildly. Then Watson and her partner broke their results out by gender and socioeconomic background. "We were surprised again. Many of our children came from backgrounds that were quite deprived. We didn't expect our approach would give disadvantaged children such a big advantage."

By the time her subjects were in second grade, the girls who learned to read by using Synthetic Phonics were still well ahead of the national mean, and the boys significantly outperformed the girls instead of scoring well below them. "I thought I had made a mistake," recalls Watson, "so I went through the numbers again looking for where I had gone wrong."

But her results were solid. Right into primary 7, children who were taught to read with Synthetic Phonics continued to flourish. In the same years in which many boys in the United States get mired in the fourth-grade slump, the boys in Clackmannanshire were about eleven months ahead of girls in reading ability.

What about attitudes and engagement? Boys in Clackmannanshire still regarded reading as "girlie." At age ten, girls in Clackmannanshire reported a more positive attitude toward reading and made greater use of the public library. But bucking the international trends, there was no difference between the amount of fiction that boys and girls read.

As the study progressed, word of Watson's Clackmannanshire experiment became the talk of educational circles in the United Kingdom. There were plenty of naysayers, especially among whole-language devotees. Who was this Joyce Watson? And where in the world was Clackmannanshire? What, asked the critics, could reading scores in a tiny backwater of Scotland say about reading instruction in the rest of Britain? The study group was too small, grumbled others. The program left too little room for teacher discretion.

But the answer was in the reading scores. In February 2005, a report issued by the Scottish government's educational authorities validated Watson and Johnston's extraordinary findings. In 2006, authorities for the English government did the same and advised that schools around England begin using some variation of Synthetic Phonics to teach all British children to read.

How does it feel to have single-handedly changed reading instruction in the United Kingdom? Joyce Watson gives a self-conscious little laugh. "Honestly, I try not to think about it," she replies.

What gives the boys of Clackmannanshire the edge? Watson isn't sure, but, relieved not to be talking about herself and her own success, she's happy to share her ideas: "We ask ourselves this question all the time." Watson has her theories. "I think boys like using the magnetic letters," she says. "They can see the letters and a representation of the sound, which for many children is very abstract. For boys, the magnetic letters are a little like Legos. The method also plays on their interest in building things. They are building words, after all. And giving them the tools to build words means they don't have to guess. They can work it out on their own. They don't have to be wrong and corrected by the teacher." She pauses, draws a deep breath, and allows herself a moment of satisfaction. "Whatever is happening with them," she adds, "I think it's brilliant."

The Clackmannanshire experiment is only one study. And although the Scottish government found it convincing, it is far from conclusive. But it does suggest something very important: The male literacy deficit is not something that is immutable and hardwired in boys. It turns out that schools may be teaching them wrong.

Less Brontë, More Bond

VIVIAN Gussin Paley, who taught kindergarten and nursery school for thirty-seven years at the University of Chicago's renowned Laboratory School, is a keen and sensitive observer of classroom dynamics. In the 1984 book about early education *Boys and Girls: Superheroes in the Doll Corner*, Gussin Paley, who is the only early childhood teacher to win a MacArthur Award, contrasts the natural, unaffected ways in which little boys and little girls tell stories.

Here's the girls' story: "Once there were four kittens and they found a pretty bunny. Then they went to buy the bunny some food and they fed the baby bunny and then they went on a picnic."

Here's the boys' story: "We sneaked up in a the house. Then we put the good guys in jail. Then we killed some of the good guys. Then the four bad guys got some money and some jewels."

"Kindergarten," Gussin Paley writes, "is a triumph of sexual stereotyping. No amount of adult subterfuge or propaganda deflects the five-year-olds' passion for segregation by sex. They think they have invented the difference between boys and girls and, as with any new invention, must prove that it works."

What is true of storytelling is also true of what kind of stories girls and boys like to read. All children use the same simple books to learn to read. Once they are fluent enough to take their first tentative steps toward independent reading, they are at an important crossroads: They need to read material that jibes with their natural penchant for telling stories. Unfortunately for our boys, many young men tend to gravitate toward material that many teachers find unacceptable—comic books, books that are goofy and irreverent, and magazines. And rather than encourage their attempts to tackle a new work of literature, their teachers often advise them to leave their copy of *Captain Underpants*, their latest installment of *Spider-Man*, or their new edition of *PC Gamer* at home.

What should teachers do instead? Jon Scieszka, elementary school teacher turned children's book author, is happy to tell you. In fact, he'd like to tell the whole world. An exuberant man with a shaved head and a wide smile, he has made it his mission to encourage primary school teachers to give boys the kinds of books they like.

"Boys," he says, "like books that are about stuff—science books about pyramids and grasshoppers. And book that are just facts, random facts, like the *Guinness Book of World Records*. They like books that have plenty of action. Books that are about men acting courageously in the face of danger. Or showing their loyalty. They like sports books and some biographies. Comic books. Graphic novels. They like funny books, too. Especially irreverent humor or books that mention bodily functions. Especially farting!"

He laughs out loud. Then he gets serious for a moment. "Not every book is right for reading out loud in class. I get that. But that's what boys like! We shouldn't make them wrong for liking to read what they like to read."

Why do boys like these kinds of books? Don't blame the parents. In this arena, nature wins out handily over nurture. In 2001, a Canadian researcher polled boys on their reading preferences, then investigated the children's families to see if there was a relationship between types of books and whether or not the child's parents expressed traditional ideas about gender. There wasn't a connection. Mormon families in Salt Lake City and lesbian couples in Cambridge, Massachusetts, are equally likely to produce a *Captain Underpants* fan. There's no link between how a boy is raised and the kind of books he likes.

Some teachers don't know how to handle it. Too often, writes English education researcher Elaine Millard, teachers of young boys "experience the change in boys' reading habits as a kind of denial of their own interests and values." It's an awkward moment when a teacher suggests *Little House in the Big Woods* by Laura Ingalls Wilder and her little male student opts instead for *The Day My Butt Went Psycho.* The latter choice can seem to signify the triumph of trash culture over literature or to exemplify the kind of loutish behavior that teachers know stands in opposition to good learning. So the teacher makes a face, in a chiding tone tells the boy, "That's at-home reading," and then helpfully suggests that he leave his book in his backpack, where he can retrieve it after school. Boys, forced to read a book they perceive to be "girlie" (girls love Laura Ingalls Wilder books for their attention to household details, their descriptions of relationships, and the challenges faced by individual characters and their families), make a decision. At what may be the most crucial turning point in their educational lives, they decide they don't like to read. And they won't do it.

I'm not suggesting that boys should get a dumbed-down literary curriculum—that little guys should read comic books while little girls slog through *Middlemarch,* or that a reading curriculum should begin and end with *The Gas We Pass: The Story of Farts.* Not every book should highlight bodily functions, and not every character should be a hypermasculine sports figure, soldier, or secret agent. Let's not forget that one of the chief purposes of literature is to stretch your imagination beyond the limits of your own circumstances. And remember, too, that educated women have always had to bend their minds around über-male books such as *Moby Dick* and *Heart of Darkness,* which certainly weren't written with a female audience in mind. But reading experts believe that in these tender years of early schooling, teachers who champion the kind of books that girls like and ignore or marginalize the kind of reading that boys like may be hurting boys far more than they ever could realize.

Elementary school administrators need to be on the watch for female members of their staff who put together a classroom library consisting of the kinds of books they liked when they were growing up and, maybe, as an afterthought, two or three titles for boys. Teachers need to have boy books on hand and know a fair bit about them, too. Experts have found that boys can be poor judges of their own abilities, often selecting books that are too hard or too easy. Teachers need to help boys make a selection at the right level of difficulty that will appeal to their interests. Books written in a series are often crowd pleasers for little boys. Why? Unlike girls, who discover good books by word of mouth, boys almost never recommend books to each other.

Veteran principal Mary Kay Sommers from Shepardson Elementary school in Fort Collins, Colorado, is well acquainted with the male literacy gap. It's been a constant concern of hers. Ever since the district became so focused on state achievement test scores, she and her staff have been trying to figure out how to get boys to read more. "We noticed right away that many of our teachers were not tied into what boys are into," says Sommers. "Boys just don't get [the stories of] Junie B. Jones, which are about children and such. They get tired of it. Boys want to hear factual things. Nonfiction for them is huge."

Besides having a broader choice of books, boys need to see men reading. The association between femininity and reading, which grows stronger every year, has to be rolled back. Doing this will take some concerted effort. In a 1993 study, two Canadian researchers, John

Willinsky and Mark Hunniford, found that in English-speaking countries reading is represented as an activity preferred by girls. Girls are more likely to be portrayed as readers in illustrations in children's books and to be given books as presents for birthdays and Christmas. Dads need to take the lead in bedtime stories, reading out loud to their children from the newspaper or off the Web. As boys get older, fathers or uncles need to engage them in discussions about the kinds of things that adults read—and to gradually initiate boys into the world of literate men.

Three years ago, Principal Theresa Bollinger decided that the boys at Ridge Central Elementary, a public school outside Chicago, needed some positive macho role models for reading. Now, every day, one male officer from the local police department enters the school in full uniform complete with holster, peaked cap, and shiny badge. He walks into the classroom, settles himself on a small chair, and pulls a children's book out from under his arm. For forty minutes, that officer reads to the children. The police rotate the duty every day. The kids love it. And boys—who, for the most part, live in a world of simple sexual stereotypes—get to see a man with a gun in his holster and a book in his hand.

Justin's Bloodthirsty World

THE public school in an affluent area of Southern California where Justin Johnson now attends fifth grade maintains high standards. And that's a blessing for his parents—Mark, a personal assistant, and Melissa, a banker. In third grade, though, something happened that made Mark and Melissa begin to worry, not that the school's standards were too high but that the school's ideas about acceptable ways of writing might be too narrow.

Since he was a very little boy, Justin has seen himself as a hybrid of

Luke Skywalker, General Douglas MacArthur, and the swashbuckling pirate Captain Kidd. He's transfixed by *Star Wars*. He's fascinated by all things military. He has dragged his parents to repeated showings of *Pirates of the Caribbean*. In his hands, a tree branch, a broomstick, or even a pencil can be transformed into a sword, a bayonet, or a light saber.

Mark used to apologize for his son's passions. "I'm not that centered on those kinds of things myself," he says with a little shrug. "Living in a liberal section of California," he adds, "I've certainly never owned a gun. But this is what my son loves."

After spending the last five or six years observing children on the playground, Mark has gradually become less self-conscious about his son's obsession with fighting and what sometimes seem like blood-thirsty fantasies. "It seems to me that a lot of little boys are like that," he says.

So Mark was surprised when Justin's third-grade teacher called him in to discuss Justin's early attempts at writing a fictional story. "I'm very concerned about your son's journal," began Justin's teacher, getting out the marble composition books where the children drew pictures and described them in short captions. Mark wracked his brain. Justin had made major gains in the last year or so. His handwriting, which had been large and uneven, was almost passable now. His spelling was definitely improving. Besides, Justin loved telling stories, the wilder the better. What could have gone wrong?

"Look here," the teacher said, as she opened Justin's notebook.

The journal page was crowded with an animated drawing and a neat (for Justin) caption. So far so good. Justin had clearly followed the directions. From the amount of crayon on the paper, Mark noted proudly, it was obvious Justin had worked very hard on his story.

"What am I looking at?" Mark asked tentatively.

"Look closer," the teacher directed.

Mark saw that Justin's illustration was a carefully rendered massacre. Swords were drawn. The air was thick with arrows. Several figures were in the process of getting decapitated. In short, Justin had taken great pains to vividly share with his teacher and his class one of his favorite narratives.

Mark started to laugh but bit it back. He could see from the teacher's face that she wasn't in a joking mood.

"Is there anything that he's done here that violates school policy?"

"No," the teacher replied. "I'm simply concerned about the subject matter."

There was a long pause. Mark couldn't think of what to say.

"I have other children in the class, and I have to be concerned about how they view his work," the teacher said, starting to sound defensive.

Mark tried to consider her point of view. She did have a big class. "Did any of the students have a negative reaction to his work?" he asked.

"No," she admitted.

Mark felt his face flush. The teacher was judging his son—not just his work but what he loved. He felt a rush of protectiveness toward Justin.

The teacher tried another approach. "I'm a parent," she told him, "and if my son brought home work like this, I would tell him that it didn't represent our family values."

Mark's protective feelings quickly sharpened into concern. He and Melissa had encouraged Justin to pour his heart and soul into school. What was it doing to his young son to be in a classroom and try to win approval from someone who could barely conceal her repugnance for the things he loved best? How could he learn to write fiction from someone who disapproved of the workings of his imagination?

Later, Mark raged to his wife: How dare she talk about family values, he said. What about the value inherent in letting boys be their authentic selves?

Five Tips for Teaching Boys to Write

How do we help boys catch up in writing? Children's book author Ralph Fletcher has a few ideas. Fletcher, who spends a lot of time teaching elementary and middle school teachers how to teach writing, has been fretting about the male writing gap for years.

"What you hear from teachers is that when it comes to writing," he says, "boys are not engaged. And when you go into the classroom, what do you see? They're exactly right. Boys are not engaged."

Fletcher set out to find out why. His goal was to give teachers some strategies to get boys over their writers' block. But first he had to answer this question: What keeps boys from putting pen to paper? What's getting in the way? To find out, he handed out a complete-the-sentence questionnaire to school-age males. This is how boys responded:

"When we write at school, I wish we were able to . . ." The majority responded with some variation of "Write what I want."
"The worst thing about writing is . . . ?" A common response was "My hand hurts."
"The best thing about writing is . . . ?" "Letting my ideas flow." "Creating a different world."

From those responses and many others, Fletcher crafted the writing program described in his book *Boy Writers: Reclaiming Their Voices*. His guidance is both practical and theoretical.

First, identify the kids—most will be boys—with what teachers call "poor grapho-motor skills" but what we know as bad handwriting. More boys than you realize have this problem. Then find a way for them to use keyboards. Handwriting is not taught much in school anymore (although that may be changing because of the new SAT requirement). Kids are supposed to pick it up on their own, but many boys don't. You can't write, points out Fletcher sensibly, if you can't write.

Second, allow boys plenty of choices when it comes to what they want to write about. Doing this can be a challenge. "There are so many curriculum mandates that writing has become so much more content driven and less about choice. Kids are moved quickly through genre studies—the five-point essay, a magazine article, crafting a persuasive argument. Boys rarely get a chance to write what they want."

Third, allow students to use visual cues—drawings, arrows, and signs—when they are making the transition from drawing to prose. "We let kids draw in the first and second grade and then, cold turkey, they have to write stories. Without visual stuff, some boys are left high and dry."

Fletcher's fourth suggestion is for teachers to develop appreciation of the way in which boys write: "It's different than girls. For starters, girls write for the teacher, boys write for each other. Boys use kid language not classroom language. Their stories are goofy, fanciful, sarcastic, funny and designed for the amusement of their peers. Teachers have a way of looking at this, not as a virtue but as a problem. They complain that boys are always grandstanding in their writing, that they are showing off to get attention and to see who can yuck it up the most. Teachers might say, 'it's disruptive.' But I'd challenge them to look at it a different way. We have a personal agenda in the classroom: we champion the kind of writing that is sincere, poignant, personal and full of telling detail. Maybe boy writers aren't exhibiting those qualities but they are exhibiting others—they are particularly good at connecting. Boys are good at knowing who their audience is and playing to it. Instead of sanctioning the boy who writes a wacky story, we need to let [him] share it."

Fletcher's fifth suggestion is about tolerance. If you want boys to write, be prepared for them to tackle dangerous topics replete with violence, mayhem, and gore: "We need to redefine our goals in teaching reading so that we champion the great energy boys can bring to a project and their willingness to take risks." Too often, teachers look at boys' writing as if it were a problem to be managed.

Kindergarten teacher James St. Clair works hard to give boys a positive first impression of writing. For the past thirty years, he has been one of the only three male kindergarten teachers in the public school system of Cambridge, Massachusetts, outside Boston. His reputation as a boy-friendly teacher is no secret to parents. In the twenty years he's worked at the bilingual Amigos School in Cambridge, he's been sent more than his share of what he affectionately calls "wild boys."

"Parents send them to me because I understand boys," he says.

St. Clair makes a special effort with all the boys—in part, because he grew up a boy. Plus, he explains, he has four sons of his own. He devotes a lot of energy to finding ways to make them feel that they are valued members of the school community. His concern shows in his language. Here's how he describes some of the high-energy, exquisitely curious, and wildly kinetic males in his classroom: "I have some real little boys in my class," he says, laughingly. "Real little boys."

Unlike some experienced teachers, who fondly recall the days when kindergarten was reserved for social and emotional development, St. Clair thinks teaching kids to read and write early is good. But he's seen for himself that girls and boys don't respond to the same lessons in the same way. Not long ago, he attended an early reading seminar. The specialist told the gathered teachers that to teach reading, they should start with personal narratives.

"When it comes to boys," St. Clair says, "I just don't think that's so."

He has observed that boys and girls have different writing processes.

He lets all his kids choose their own topics, and he is careful not to judge them—even if they are writing about massacres or that old favorite, *Star Wars.* Experience has taught him that children need to feel strongly about what they are writing. To illustrate his point, he tells me about a magical moment he shared not long ago with a student named Ben.

This five-year-old was a reluctant writer. For some reason, he got distracted when it came time to put pencil on paper. Then, in the middle of the school year, Ben came to him during a writing assignment and asked how to spell *Wookiee.* St. Clair and Ben spent a transformative five or six minutes figuring out the letter sounds that make up the word that represents the hairy extraterrestrial.

"He just wouldn't have been that excited about writing about something more traditional," St. Clair says.

Once his boys get engaged in writing, and begin to master the laborious mechanics of it, St. Clair gently nudges them toward different topics. *Star Wars* stories can get boring, too. "By the third *Star Wars* story I usually ask them to give it a rest and write about something else," he says with a smile.

Sometimes, he gets a boy to write by making him see what a practical life skill writing can be. A boy who was struggling with writing created a pizza parlor in the dramatic play area of the classroom. "I suggested that he make a sign," says St. Clair. After much deliberation, the boy wrote PIZZA in big red letters—his first successful attempt to make a word.

"Instead of being an abstract activity, writing was part and parcel of pretending to be a pizza man. It was a beautiful thing," says St. Clair with evident pride. "We left it up for days." To St. Clair, that sign was writing at its finest.

Although the male literacy gap is being ignored at the top, awareness of the problem at the grassroots level is beginning to grow. School librarians across the country are starting to carve out sections for books that are of special interest to boys. Getting boys to write is moving higher on the priority list.

"When we talk about the problems boys have with reading," says Ralph Fletcher, "the teachers I'm working with—and they are 90 percent female—are getting it. They're looking at what I'm saying and responding with 'Maybe you're right. What I'm doing with boys is just not clicking.' For the most part, teachers don't look at this as political." Fletcher adds that most teachers are simply looking for strategies that work.

Because reading and writing are so important, let's recap ways in which we can help boys succeed. First, parents and teachers need to banish the notion that boys are somehow predestined to become second-class citizens when it comes to reading and writing. Parents may need to take the lead.

Lay down plenty of preliteracy experiences (talking, singing, story time) before your son starts school. Then, to misquote Mark Twain, make sure your son's education doesn't get in the way of his learning. Pay close attention to how your son is being taught to read. Some boys (and girls) seem to read almost spontaneously. Some need direct instruction and scaffolding. If your son is not one of the spontaneous readers, his reading instruction should include a healthy dose of phonics.

Once your son starts to sound words out, get busy finding the right books to match his interest. Better yet, make your husband or your father, or your father-in-law, find books that they and your son can share. Boys need to see men reading, so turn off the TV. Moms, don't do what I did and hand your son a book that you loved from your girlhood and expect him to have the same reaction to it that you did. Comic books, newspapers, sports biographies, and graphic novels are all good. Look for irreverent, funny, exciting, scary books. And, yes, sometimes bloody ones.

Pay close attention to the messages teachers give your son about reading and writing. If the teacher has a narrow idea of what is appropriate, make it clear to your son that you don't share her (or his) vision.

Teachers, you have a huge role to play here, too. Make sure that you are supplying boys with plenty of boy-friendly reading material. It's important for all writers to connect with their readers, but writing about feelings isn't the only way to do it. Humor can be effective, too. So can battle scenes.

Parents, buy a copy of Ralph Fletcher's book to take to your next teacher-parent conference. Teachers, get a copy of Ralph Fletcher's book and share it with your fellow professionals. Let's allow our boys to become the readers and writers they are meant to be.

CHAPTER 12

THINKING WITH A BOY BRAIN

What Brain Science Tells Us

I'm lying in a cold empty room with my head in the hole of a giant doughnut-shaped magnet trying to figure out if there really is such a thing as a boy brain and a girl brain. A rigid brace immobilizes my skull. I am wearing headgear not unlike the old holiday viewfinders, but instead of looking at pictures of Niagara Falls, I'll be looking at words flashed on a small white screen. I'm visiting a group of neuroscientists at the Kennedy Krieger Institute, a medical research facility affiliated with Johns Hopkins University in Baltimore. The scientists will be watching as the functional magnetic resonance imaging (fMRI) machine—which now surrounds me Jonah-and-the-whale-style—maps the blood flow to various parts of my brain as I try to make letters into words. The procedure is totally painless and noninvasive, but nevertheless I'm feeling apprehensive.

"Are you OK in there?" asks researcher Amy Clements. Her voice, which is warm and reassuring, sounds muffled coming through the earphones clapped to my head. These scientists usually administer this test to nine-year-olds, I remind myself. How bad can it be? Clements and her boss, Dr. Laura Cutting, are part of a loose confederacy of scientists around the country who have received big government grants to become literary neuro-cartographers of sorts—coming up with a road map of the brain as we read. By figuring out what part of the brain normal people use to decipher and decode letters, the federal government hopes scientists will be able to pinpoint the seat of learning disabilities—in particular the biological basis of dyslexia—and come up with effective strategies to identify reading problems and treat them more effectively.

For the past few months, Cutting has watched the brain function of a group of seven- to fifteen-year-olds as they perform simple reading tasks, such figuring out if nonsense words (for instance, *leat* and *jete*) rhyme. Quite by accident, she made what seems at first glance to be an extraordinary discovery: Using her high-powered fMRI machine, she found that boys and girls use different neural pathways to decipher simple words. Inside the "black box" of their skulls, boys and girls use different parts of their brains to read.

The implications seem obvious and full of possibilities for the classroom—at least to a layperson like me. Boys are lagging behind girls in reading. If boys and girls use different parts of the brain, maybe we can tailor different kinds of instruction to boys and girls to eliminate the male literacy gap. It seems like a half step—or maybe a half step and a hop—from Cutting's discovery to a solid solution for a problem plaguing the country's educators.

Back in the laboratory, I'm learning a different kind of lesson. Getting an fMRI is a lonely business. The machine creates a strong magnetic field around my skull and then "reads" the tiny disruptions in the field caused by the minute electrical impulses reflected off the oxygen-rich blood inside my brain. Stray magnetic impulses would give a false reading, so the researchers, who are kind and quietly encouraging, stay behind a thick pane of glass, thick steel-reinforced walls, and a door sealed with a thick rubber gasket.

Clements repeats herself. "OK in there?"

"Fine," I say shortly. I'm flashing on that old movie *The Man with the X-Ray Eyes,* in which a mad scientist attends a cocktail party and uses his power to ogle women wearing torpedo-style bras. I can't help but think that the researchers at Kennedy Krieger are going to be looking at something a hundred times more intimate than the make of my undergarments. They're going to watch something that no one has seen before and will probably never see again—the flow of my blood in my brain.

"Remember, push the button if you see a word. Don't push the button if it's not a word."

"Right," I gulp, fingering the red trigger I'm holding in my right hand.

"OK, we're going to start."

There is a long pause, then a loud throat clearing, like the tractor engine starting but failing to turn over; then a jackhammer blast of white noise wipes out any other sound. I feel an uncomfortable sensation in my jaw. I check myself to see if I'm grinding my teeth. No. Is this giant magnet going to suck out my fillings?

The first word is on my screen.

Size. I depress my thumb. *Rate.* I do it again. *Skib.* Mistake. I realize my error immediately, and I flush.

More jackhammer noises.

Soon, the test is over. A technician helps me up and I rub my jaw. I feel a rush of Woody Allen–level hypochondria. What if my brain is riddled with mad cow disease and looks like Swiss cheese? What if while I was struggling to wring meaning out of *skib*, the researchers were staring at my giant brain tumor and are now holding a hushed but urgent debate on how best to break the news to me? I walk through the door with the thick rubber gasket, my eyes wide with fear. But the researchers are smiling.

"You did very well," Clements says. She hands me a printout of the cross section of my brain. I'm fascinated and repulsed. My tongue, which I usually notice only on the roof of my mouth, appears to start somewhere around my shirt collar. My eyes actually look as though they're on stalks. I notice with some relief that my brain looks tumor-free.

Then one of the researchers pays me a compliment that stands in its own category for unique: "You have," she says, looking at the cross section of my brain admiringly, "remarkably clear sinuses."

Teaching to the Brain

LATER, over lunch, Cutting and I discuss what brain science can and cannot tell us about the way we educate our children. On the face of it, you'd think the two fields—teaching and neuroscience—should be having a fruitful cross-pollination. They share some goals—figuring out how the brain absorbs, maintains, and synthesizes information. It's an urgent quest for scientists who hope to unravel many of the mysteries of learning with the newest generation of high-tech scanning equipment. It's an even more urgent question for every second-grade teacher trying to make sure that twenty-eight restless students meet or surpass state standards. So far, though, classroom innovations backed by solid neuroscience remain frustratingly elusive. After fifteen years and hundreds of millions of dollars' worth of studies, scientists can only conclusively tell teachers pretty much what their grandmothers told them: In order to provide optimum conditions for learning, you have to make sure kids get plenty of sleep, eat well, and don't get too stressed. You have to read to them early and often. The rest, scientists say reflexively, "has to be studied more."

That hasn't stopped educators from appropriating science—especially brain science—often with poor results. These days, with the gender gap fast becoming a national concern, the temptation has proven irresistible. The mismatch between boys and school stems from cognitive differences between the genders, the thinking goes. Boys and girls learn differently. On an intuitive level, the appeal of this idea is obvious. Any mother who has sat unblinking while her sons split their sides laughing at the Three Stooges suspects there are things about a boy's brain that are unlike her own. Family physician and psychologist Leonard Sax, founder of the National Association for Single-Sex Public Education, catalogs biologically based differences in the way boys and girls learn in his book *Why Gender Matters: What Parents and Teachers Need to Know About the Emerging Science of Sex Differences.* He concludes that biological differences between boys and girls lead to learning differences that are so significant that teachers should adopt different strategies to teach them in the classroom and that many kids would do better in all-boy and all-girl classes or in single-sex schools.

Some advocates for boys argue that by popularizing biological differences between boys and girls, teachers can customize instruction in order to help boys learn better. Michael Gurian and Kathy Stevens, authors of the best-selling *The Minds of Boys: Saving Our Sons from Falling Behind in School and Life,* make their living training teachers how to provide what they call "brain based, boy friendly instruction." "There's all this great brain research out there about gender difference, and I believe teachers need to be made aware of it," says Gurian. He and his staff have delivered talks about what brain science tells us about learning to about twenty thousand teachers around the country. "We need to do it now because boys really need the help. All over the country, they're in trouble!"

The essentialist idea has spread like wildfire in public and private schools. "I know boys and girls learn differently," one teacher told me after listening to a Gurian trainer. "I've seen the brain scans that show it!"

But neurobiologists who study the brain say talk about gender-specific ways of thinking and about customized instruction for boys and girls shows a fundamental misunderstanding of brain science. "When people talk about the brain, they talk about it as if there is a one-to-one jump from neuron to behavior," says Kurt W. Fisher, director of the Mind, Brain and Education Program at Harvard University's Graduate School of Education. Human neuroscience—and how we learn—is much more complicated than most people grasp.

About fifteen minutes into my lunch with Cutting, it becomes clear that her fascinating discovery about gender and reading certainly isn't going to become the basis for any boy-friendly reading program anytime soon. In fact, Cutting herself remains maddeningly neutral when I ask her to describe the implications of her discovery about reading. It seems obvious to me—a nonscientist—that her findings are nothing short of the Holy Grail. Doesn't this prove that boys and girls read differently? She pauses, then answers carefully: "It piques the interest."

I'm flabbergasted and not a little baffled at what seems to be her false modesty. Couldn't her research be used as evidence that teachers should instruct boys and girls to read in different ways? She struggles to answer my question. "Could there be a downstream effect of brain activation difference?" she asks rhetorically. "Possibly," she says.

I'm thoroughly confused. I sputter something about how important her findings will be to classroom teachers. Cutting doesn't blink: "It's something that needs to be studied more."

The Ugly History of Gender and Brain Science

WHY are scientists so cautious? Blame history. For centuries, science has been used to bolster what turned out to be nothing more than prejudices, pure and simple. For millennia, historians and writers—most of them male—regarded women as inferior: mentally and spiritually closer to beasts than to men. Until fairly recently, men of science pretty much backed that view. Medical textbooks brim with the names of physicians, anthropologists, craniologists, and psychiatrists who cloaked themselves in scientific "objectivity" and interpreted data as "proof" of women's inferiority. In 1861, French surgeon and anthropologist Paul Broca autopsied 432 men and women at four Paris hospitals, then weighed their brains and concluded that, because the brains of women, on average, were 14 percent lighter than men's brains, women were innately less intelligent than men. Size mattered to his student Gustave Le Bon, physician and social psychologist, who in 1879 wrote that "there are a large number of women whose brains are closer in size to those of gorillas than to the most developed male brains. This inferiority is so obvious that no one can contest it for a moment: only its degree is worth discussion. All psychologists who have studied the intelligence of women . . . recognize today that they represented the most inferior forms of human evolution and that they are closer to children and savages than to an adult, civilized man." Le Bon then listed female characteristics, drawing on his observations—purely scientific ones, of course. Women, he wrote, "excel in fickleness, inconstancy, absence of thought and logic and incapacity to reason."

In 1884, scientists located the seat of women's intellectual inferiority in the frontal lobe of the brain, which scientists assumed was smaller in women than in men. As dissection became more commonplace, however, male scientists discovered that women's frontal lobes were generally larger than men's. And in a classic exhibition of fickleness, inconstancy, and the absence of logic, they revised their theory: The parietal lobes at the back of the brain, scientists determined, not the frontal lobes, were the seat of intelligence.

The history of brain-based learning is shorter but no less flawed. One hundred years ago, education pioneer Maria Montessori was measuring the circumference of children's heads and inferring that her best prospects had the biggest brains. As scientists begin to unravel some of the mysteries of brain function, our best guess about how the brain controls behavior and learning seems, at least on one level, to have become more sophisticated. Twenty years ago, after Robert Sperry's pioneering research with monkeys and epileptics seemed to show separate capacities for the right and left hemispheres of the brain, teachers jumped right in. Hard-to-reach students and their instructors, they concluded, must not be using the same brain hemispheres. Soon, enthusiastic teacher trainers were holding seminars providing instructional techniques for right and left brain learners. They were administering diagnostic tests to schoolchildren to determine whether the left or right hemisphere of their brains was dominant. Within a few years, though, neuroscientists discovered that although the left and right hemispheres do seem to have different functions, each hemisphere depends on interaction with other parts of the brain. Quietly, teaching to the right brain and to the left brain disappeared from our nation's schools.

That setback didn't slow down proponents of brain-based instruction—especially when it comes to gender differences. They seize on every tendril of gender difference that emerges in animal or human studies as "evidence" that can be used in the classroom. The brains of laboratory rats, however, may or may not indicate anything about how humans behave. Brain scans may show activation patterns or glucose consumption levels, but they don't show boys and girls thinking differently.

"There's a trend in the educational world to take a little brain-based science and run with it," says Jay Giedd, an adolescent psychiatrist at the National Institute of Mental Health and one of the country's foremost authorities on brain-based gender difference. "It sounds great. And it's fun—men are from Mars and women are from Venus—but there is a danger that it can get taken too far."

Mars and Venus

BEFORE we jump into a discussion of those dangers, let's take a step back and briefly consider what we know, or think we know, about the interplay of biology, behavior, and gender.

In most Western cultures for most of recorded time, gender, like eye color, has been considered an immutable human characteristic. God made boys and girls to act in certain ways and to fulfill specific roles, the conventional wisdom went, and that, pretty much, was the end of the story.

As women struggled for equal rights, feminist intellectuals began shining a light on the concept of gender: What is it? Where does it come from? Who says what is "girl" and "boy" behavior? Around 1970, feminist psychologists gave the whole concept of gender a jolt by suggesting that gender is not innate but is largely a social construct. Boys and girls, they argued, were spiritually, emotionally, behaviorally, and intellectually more similar than different, despite their different reproductive organs. Babies were, for the most part, androgynous at birth. Why did girls end up acting in one way and boys in another? Their behavior resulted from subtle and overt socialization mostly aimed at perpetuating the oppression of women.

The radical and arresting notion that babies are, at least initially, unisex gripped the culture with a strength that is hard to overestimate. It was one of those ideas that shook the Western world and gave rise to a decade of public and private soul searching. If women and men were biological equals, then to perpetuate—deliberately or unconsciously—a world order in which females were at a disadvantage flew in the face of democratic ideals. As a society, we began to revisit long-accepted limitations placed on women and to recalibrate goals for young girls.

The idea of the unisex baby also ushered in some interesting child-rearing trends and educational practices. In an effort to unshackle children from the constraints of a sexist society, earnest young mothers and fathers in the 1980s and 1990s dressed their baby girls in yellow, for example, instead of pink, or they gave their six-year-old boy a doll for his birthday and their daughter a truck. Conscientious preschool teachers reminded children that during pretend play every child should get a turn to be the pilot and no one should serve drinks. Even the most sanctimonious lefty parents, though, sheepishly reported what Gussin Paley had observed as well. Most kids not only reflexively expressed their gender but did so in the most traditional of ways. One set of parents reported finding their daughter tucking her "truckies" into her toy baby carriage for a nap, while their sons in the next room were using their dolls as weapons.

In the last twenty years or so, the notion of the unisex child—born a clean slate and socialized for Wisteria Lane or for the NASCAR bleachers—has loosened its hold on the culture. In part, the evolution in thinking was ushered in by scientists who began to conclude that although all children are indeed subject to socialization, there are significant differences between males and females and we ignore them at our peril. In research and clinical practices, female physicians noted, for instance, that women process some medicines more slowly than men. When women have heart attacks, they tend to have different symptoms than men, too. In the name of promoting equal health care for women, major medical centers began opening women's clinics that offered not only reproductive medicine but women-focused cardiac care, stroke rehabilitation, internal medicine, and mental health services.

Around that time, researchers began concluding that many of the most profound behavioral differences between boys and girls were influenced by nurture but had a taproot in nature, and that many were laid down by the time a baby was born. How can this be? It turns out, all fetuses begin as females. About ten weeks after gestation, when the soon-to-be-baby is about the size of a large lime, the chromosomal encoding of the fetus signals to the thymus gland to begin producing androgens. Those androgens, in turn, cause the brain to form in ways that control—at least initially—some of the most obvious expressions of gender. In other words, prenatal hormones, not whether you buy blue or pink bunting for the crib, are responsible for your daughter cradling her truck.

How do we know? Because girls who get a super dose of boy-type hormones end up acting a lot like little boys. Sheri Berenbaum, a professor of psychology at Pennsylvania State University, has been studying the prenatal hormones of a group of about seventy females with a condition called congenital adrenal hyperplasia (CAH). These girls have an enzyme abnormality that leads to excess production of androgens—mostly testosterone—before birth. The CAH girls identify themselves as female, but in early childhood they showed a pronounced preference for trucks and Lincoln Logs while their non-CAH sisters played with kitchen toys and dolls. In adolescence, the CAH girls were more interested in becoming engineers, architects, or airline pilots. Other studies have found that CAH girls have better spatial ability than non-CAH girls.

The fetal brain, it seems, is exquisitely sensitive to testosterone. Prenatal exposure has wide-ranging effects on many aspects of a baby's life. Melissa Hines, professor of psychology at the City University, London, drew on an enormous database called the Avon Longitudinal Study of Parents and Children, which includes medical information on 14,000 English mothers and their offspring. Hines sent a questionnaire to all the moms in the study when their children were 3.5 years old asking them to describe their children's play preferences. She asked them to specify which toys, games, and activities they liked. When they played make-believe, she asked, do they pretend to be a fairy princess or a soldier? Do they like snakes? Rough-and-tumble play? She separated the girls out, sorted the answers into a continuum ranging from "girly-girls" to "tomboys," then picked 337 girls from both extremes of the continuum. Personal circum-stances—the presence of older brothers or sisters in the home, whether a girl's parents had traditional gender roles, whether the mom had a male partner in the home, and level of maternal education—did not seem to affect gender role behavior. But androgens did. Hines went back and cor-related the 337 girls' play preferences with maternal levels of testosterone taken from a blood sample during pregnancy. The results were striking. Hines found a direct correlation between maternal testosterone and play preferences in preschool girls. The daughters of moms with the highest levels of testosterone were tomboys—less interested in dolls and more interested in cars, trucks, and swords.

"People assumed that boys' and girls' interest in different types of toys was a result of socialization," Hines said. "But I have to say, No, I don't think it is."

When it comes to biology, behavior, and gender, these days most scientists believe that nurture rides shotgun with nature. But what should this mean for classroom teachers?

Teaching to the Boy Brain

In *The Minds of Boys,* Michael Gurian says he knows. The solution for underachieving boys, as he sees it, is a program of boy-friendly learning-based strategies tailored to the hardwired differences in male neurobiology. "New nature-based gender science," he writes, "can arm teachers and parents with successful methodologies to teach boys."

Learning that's boy-friendly? It sounded like a smart solution to me. And after interviewing a few school administrators who had enthu-siastically adopted Gurian's brain-based methods, I wrote a mostly pos-itive article about his book. But as time went on and I read more deeply in the subject, my thinking evolved. A year or so later, I had a chance to catch Gurian in action—in Salt Lake City, where he was one of the keynote speakers at a conference for a thousand or so public school teachers from Utah—and many of my misgivings about his work blossomed into full flower.

A handsome man with a full beard and salt and pepper hair, Gurian knows how to command an audience. He's a very confident speaker, but then he gets a lot of practice. His best-selling book *The Wonder of Boys: What Parents, Mentors, and Educators Can Do to Shape Boys into Exceptional Men* transformed him from a part-time family therapist and adjunct professor of English at Gonzaga University, in Spokane, Washington, to a well-paid and highly sought-after lecturer on the teacher education circuit. His partner in the boys' business, Kathy Stevens, whose résumé mentions her experience in the nonprofit sector, runs fifty or so in-school "trainers" who take slides of brain scans around to schools and talk to teachers about biological differences affecting the ways boys and girls learn. Every summer, Gurian and Stevens hold a series of seminars at what they call the Gurian Institute, on a university campus in Colorado Springs, Colorado.

At the Salt Palace convention center in Salt Lake City, Gurian launches into his talk. Dwarfed by two giant screens in the vast hall, he quickly introduces himself as a "social philosopher." His mission, he tells the assembled teachers, is to provide a "revolutionary new framework—neurobiology—in order to improve their understanding of boys." For the next hour and 45 minutes, the audience sees giant projections of multicolored PET scans that Gurian says prove how different boys and girls are, and he makes suggestions on how teachers can teach boys. Testosterone, he says, formats the right side of a boy's brain for spatial and mechanical tasks. "The further you are on the male spectrum," he says, "the more you will be visuo-spatially inclined. And the more you'll have to move your body. You'll also be less verbal. The visuo-spatial centers take over the verbal-emotive centers," and that's why boys tend to supply less detail in their writing.

Gurian continually throws out neuro-factoids—for example, "Male brains tend to compartmentalize their learning." He projects another slide showing brain scans: The female brain shows more activation patterns than the male brain. "Girl brains," Gurian tells his audience, "are on alert. They're better at multitasking. When boy brains rest, they can't pay attention. In fact, a boy brain at rest shows almost no functioning beyond digestion and breathing. I'm sure you've seen this at home." There are a few appreciative titters.

From time to time, when he senses he might be losing some members of the audience, Gurian suggests that he's not only an interpreter of science but also a researcher. "At the Gurian Institute, we have ten years of action research," he says. "And these things work. They can work in your classroom, too."

Afterward, over lunch, I press Gurian about his credentials for interpreting complicated neuroscience. With an M.F.A. in creative writing, Gurian scraped by for years, teaching English and psychology and publishing fiction (*An American Mystic*), poetry, and books on Jungian psychology (*The Prince and the King*). In the 1990s, he took an eight-hour course in psychotherapy and began seeing clients. While still teaching as an adjunct professor, he moved from being fascinated with Jungian archetypes to brain science, and he perfected his "brain-based" theories. His book *The Wonder of Boys*, a bestseller in 2000, led quickly to *The Minds of Boys*, which capitalized on people's fascination with all things neurological.

Gurian is a likable man. And having spoken to him, I believe that he believes he is correct. But here's my problem: Since initially writing favorably about his ideas, I've yet to find a well-regarded neuroscientist who believes we know enough about gender and learning to come up with brain-based gender-specific instruction. Take, for example, Ruben

Gur, a professor at the Institute of Biological Sciences at the University of Pennsylvania and one of the foremost authorities on brain science and gender difference. Gurian, in *The Minds of Boys* and in his talks, draws heavily from Gur's pioneering work, which shows, among other things, that when girls and boys are at rest, girls experience more blood flow to the brain than boys. This is how Gurian, in his book, extrapolates from Gur's findings: "As Gur . . . has proven, the female brain is not structurally and bio-chemically set up for the same quality or frequency of rest state as the male." He continues, "Even when a female brain goes into a state of rest, it does not shut down the way the male brain does: a large portion of its brain blood flow 'rests' in the cingulated gyrus, a central brain stimulator and motivator. Hence, even when a female student is bored by a lesson, her brain is more actively able and willing to keep her eyes open, continue taking notes, and process information before her."

Ruben Gur says that Gurian's conclusions are nonsense: "If you ask me, does higher base line activity result in a lower likelihood of zoning out, I'd have to say, it's possible. But is there any evidence for that? Not a shred."

But doesn't it make intuitive sense? Not to people who study the brain, Gur assures me.

"More blood flow," he says, "may indicate that the brain is more active at rest. But maybe not. It could be that there is blood flow for other reasons and the activity is not higher. What does it mean to have a brain that is more active when it idles? We don't know. It can be tested but it hasn't been tested yet. This part of science has not been done yet. There are pitifully few studies that correlate resting activity with any type of behavior."

I tell Gurian that Gur, and several other prominent neuroscientists who have reviewed his work on gender-specific learning styles, complain that he repeatedly oversteps the research.

"They have to say that," Gurian quickly fires back. "They're scientists. But what I do is I take it and I say, let's apply this to learning. Let's see what or how we might use it."

Gurian's can-do attitude is infectious. But people who are in a position to know about this stuff claim that what Gurian is doing is not only wrong but worrisome. The questions that Gurian answers so neatly have no pat answers. Brain scans aren't proof. Our brains do not turn red and blue when we are multitasking, for instance. The colors represent increases (or decreases) in blood flow beyond a preestablished baseline. What we see on a brain scan is complex data after considerable statistical processing—and the data is subject to different interpretations by different scientists. No one is sure whether certain patterns reflect innate behavior or learned behavior.

According to Gur, people like Gurian who make up theories of behavior based on a scattershot perusal of neuroscientific papers do the science a disservice. "The danger in making these kinds of leaps—deriving incorrect theories from scientific evidence," warns Gur, "is that when you try and apply them, they don't work. And people don't say, 'He doesn't understand the science.' They say, we are applying the science and it isn't working. They blame science." Or maybe they blame the boy.

Does Gurian agree that we need to unravel some of the fundamental questions about the brain before we base teaching strategy in the classroom on "brain-based gender difference"? Gurian says he doesn't have much time for doubters. "I don't need to have ten years of study before I say, this application works. Everything I'm saying now, all its applications will be common in ten years. It's working. Besides," he points out, "what I suggest is just common sense. It's not harming kids."

Perhaps. But the more scientists study the brain, the more intertwined function, structure, and experience seem to be. Genes, hormones, and the environment are locked into a far more dynamic relationship than anyone ever anticipated. While genetics and hormones affect brain activation patterns, which in turn influence the impact of experiences, experiences can influence the "expression," or activity levels, of genes. Prenatal testosterone may compel a boy to prefer G.I. Joe to Barbie. But the boy's brain is also astonishingly plastic and is shaped by the experiences and attitudes that he's immersed in. Gurian's books are popular because they supply a much-needed corrective to the outdated notion of the unisex child. His lectures give parents and teachers a chance to safely acknowledge what has been in front of our faces all along—that, yes, boys and girls are different. But when Gurian lards his discussion of gender difference with his opinions about what gender difference in the brain should mean in the classroom, I grow uneasy.

There are broad distinctions that we can draw between boys and girls. For example, William Eaton, whom you met in Chapter 4, using those jury-rigged Timex watches, was able to show that the most active kids tend to be boys. He arrived at this conclusion after formulating a hypothesis and devising a series of experiments to see if the hypothesis was correct. Paul Broca and Gustave Le Bon, in contrast, had certain preconceptions about gender, shaped by the society in which they lived, and they found characteristics of the brain—size, structure, and weight—that they could interpret to support their preconceptions. I don't want to suggest that Gurian is a misogynist like Le Bon. He genuinely seems to mean well. But it seems to me that Gurian falls into the same trap as Le Bon and Broca. He cloaks himself in the mantle of scientific objectivity to interpret snippets of information about brain function, not as a way to generate new ideas but to illustrate his own preconceptions about gender.

Is that harmful? Some teachers in the audience at the Salt Palace might use Gurian's ideas to develop greater tolerance for different kinds of learners. That would seem to me to be a very good outcome. But other teachers, I fear, might be emboldened to classify students on the basis of what Gurian tells them are innate differences in the abilities and proclivities of males and females and might end up reinforcing old gender stereotypes.

In follow-up conversations with school administrators and visits to schools that hosted Gurian and Stevens, I saw that I was right to worry. One principal who had his teachers "trained" by a Gurian presenter told me the following: "Our kindergarten girls like to sit on the rug and talk in the morning. Because of their oxytocin levels, they want to bond. But boys, because of their testosterone, like to run around. They just do. It's their biology." For educators to spout those gender stereotypes—all the while claiming that they're backed by the "hard evidence" they saw on Gurian's brain scans—seems to me to be a giant step backward.

We are taking a big risk when we introduce any kind of pseudo-science into our schools. By broadcasting our cultural expectations about children, we risk conditioning boys and girls to favor certain activities and accept certain limitations. We make them vulnerable to a phenomenon known to scientists as the "stereotype threat."

Over and over, scientists have observed that the human brain is uniquely sensitive to external values—especially values cloaked with the mantle of scientific objectivity. The stereotype threat has been shown in about fifty different studies in about fifty different ways, but a study published in the journal *Science* provides a neat illustration of how it works. In 2005, two psychologists from the University of British Columbia gave four groups of women a peculiarly designed test. It consisted of two sets of math questions separated by one of four essay questions. Three of the essay topics contained information—some bogus—about women and math. The topics: (1) that there is no difference in math ability between boys and girls, (2) that gender stereotyping and different experiences affect how girls score in math, (3) that there are genetic reasons why girls aren't good in math, and a fourth about women and art.

All the women scored about the same in the first math section. Differences in performance were evident in the second math section. After reading and responding to the essay question, women who had read in the essay question that boys and girls scored the same in math did well. Those who had read that gender stereotypes accounted for females' poor performance in math did slightly less well. Women who had read that females were genetically predisposed not to do well in math did worse than the other two.

The brain, it seems, responds to its environment. Because education—lessons delivered to a child by a widely recognized authority figure—is laden with values and expectations, we need to make sure that teachers understand exactly what they are communicating. Teachers who adopt the Gurian model must do so with care. I don't believe for one second—and you shouldn't either—that boys are hardwired to pay less attention to teachers or to provide less detail in their writing than girls. And if we're not careful, we may find out that so-called gender-based learning differences become for students a self-fulfilling prophecy.

Having written all that, I admit that there is one bit of brain science that I think teachers, parents, and boys themselves need to be aware of. Boys' and girls' brains develop at different rates, and sometimes the difference is dramatic. Dr. Francine Benes, who heads up a brain-tissue bank at Boston's McLean Hospital, has seen this difference up close. Examining samples obtained from 165 children autopsied at Boston Children's Hospital, she found gender differences in levels of myelin—the waxy coating on neurons that allows for faster and more efficient transmission of signals and therefore information—in the part of the brain dedicated to forming memories. From around the age of six, girls show about 25 percent more myelination than boys in the hippocampal formation. Boys and girls show equal levels of myelination until boys reach their early twenties.

"The male brain is not at its full size until approximately age 30," Benes says. "The female brain attains optimal size during the teenage period."

Most fourteen- and fifteen-year-old boys are not able to make judgments like adults. This developmental difference is so well established that most car insurance companies charge higher premiums for sixteen-year-old boys than they charge for sixteen-year-old girls. It has even been mentioned in state court proceedings by criminal defense lawyers who want to convince the jury that their young male defendants should get a lenient sentence. We don't need to do any fancy interpreting to figure out the implications of this developmental difference in the classroom. Boys, on the whole, are likely to reach optimum cognitive efficiency later in life than girls.

If we want to create the best learning environments for both sexes, we might allow families greater flexibility so that they can delay certain subjects for some children, especially boys. We might find a way to discuss this vital bit of brain science with boys themselves—to help them see, for example, that the pattern of school failure they encountered in sixth grade doesn't necessarily spell doom for the rest of middle school and high school. The same kind of growth spurt that is making their feet grow, their legs get hairy, and their Adam's apple swell is likely to hit their brains a few years down the line. They need to keep trying— go to class, hand in homework, study for tests—and stay in the academic game until their brains catch up. We might encourage teachers to monitor some of their lowest-performing boys and be ready to embrace dramatic academic improvement if and when it occurs—even if it occurs only a few months before high school graduation. If there is one thing that brain science tells us, it is this: While girls are busy collecting their A+ papers, for boys, the light upstairs may just be flickering on.

Note to parents: Be wary of "brain-based" learning. It's a fad and it will pass. And be patient with your son. His maturation may take longer than you expect.

CHAPTER 13

[VIDEO] GAMES BOYS PLAY

The World of Electronic Distraction

It's a few minutes before midnight on a cold night in November, and about forty-five young men are lined up behind police barricades outside a Best Buy store in midtown Manhattan. Most sit on coolers. Fast-food wrappers litter the ground. Some of the young men huddle under tentlike structures to protect themselves from the cold wind and freezing downpours. All of them wear parkas and heavy boots. Their pockets bulge with cash. They smell damp and unwashed, as indeed they are, and they faintly reek of stale pizza. They're restless. They have been lined up on a small grim patch of pavement in the freezing rain for three days and nights so that they can be among the very first to purchase the latest video game console, PlayStation 3.

For the past few weeks, the hype about the machines has been intense. Sony Corporation, claiming production problems, heightened demand for the product by warning that they may not be able to ship many more of the consoles before the holidays. The PlayStation 3, which costs between $500 and $600, is expected to be sold out in less than a day.

All around the country, little Gamervilles like this one in Manhattan have sprung up outside the big-box stores—Wal-Mart, Circuit City,

Best Buy. There have been reports of violence. In Putnam, Connecticut, two gunmen tried to rob people waiting in line and shot one would-be customer when he refused to surrender his cash. In Fresno, California, police arrested two people and threatened to use Taser stun guns after the crowd rushed the store and trampled people in the parking lot. In Henrico, Virginia, police fired a paintball gun at the ground outside a Target store to capture the attention of 350 unruly gamers waiting for the consoles to go on sale.

In Manhattan, Best Buy is taking no chances. Inside the store, sales associates warily eye the hard-core gamers through the floor-to-ceiling windows. When the crowd grows more impatient, the home office sends out a handful of private security guards, and members of the New York Police Department are on hand to keep the peace.

J. Gustavo Sanchez, 19, a college sophomore from Long Island, has been standing in the same section of sidewalk for thirty-six hours. He is a small man with an elfin face, and his knit cap pulled low over his brow gives him a slightly thuggish look—a calculated effect by a skinny guy with a great deal of cash in his pocket who plans to sleep on a Manhattan street. When Sanchez speaks, though, he's an open book. His innocence, enthusiasm, and some deep-seated ambivalence are on full display. He's here, he explains, for the same reason the pioneers went west—to strike it rich. The limit on consoles is two per customer, and Sanchez, like every other young man in line, wants to buy one for himself and sell the other on eBay. Rumors fly through the crowd that bidding on eBay has risen to $5,000 or more.

Sanchez is also standing here because he's obsessed with gaming. He's a smart kid. He knows that he should know better. He graduated from a selective high school in the Bronx and attends the State University of New York at Stony Brook. His mother, he volunteers, raised him right. Early on, she figured out that the lure of electronics would be too great for him so she banned them outright. "No Game Boy, no Xbox. No nothing," he recalls. He always found a way to get some gaming time in, though. His dad helped—he'd buy Sanchez video games as a reward for getting good grades in school. Once Sanchez got a little older and out of his mother's reach, he began to play more regularly. There were times in high school, he says, when he started to think his mother might have been right. His enjoyment of *Halo* became a compulsion.

"Five, six hours at a time," he recalls. "I was addicted."

At college he found himself in a gaming-friendly culture. Students were separated from their families and their hometown friends, and LAN (local area network) parties, where participants set up multiple consoles and screens, became a comforting ritual. They provided a good way to get to know guys in the dorm without going through that embarrassing where-are-you-from, what's-your-major small talk. "Plus, they were fun," recalls Sanchez.

As the semester went on, Sanchez noticed that the guys who spent a lot of time playing video games were having academic troubles. Sanchez was feeling the strain himself. Knowing he'd have a hard time explaining any failing grades to his parents, he cut back to one hour of gaming a day. But as we talk, it seems to become clear to Sanchez that he's not in control of his gaming habit quite yet, that he is, in fact, living out his mother's nightmare: He blew off important classes, traveled almost two hours from campus to New York City, and stood outside in line in the early winter cold for three days—all for his love of gaming.

It's for a good reason, he says, suddenly a bit defensive. He wants the new console, and the money he makes by selling his spare is earmarked for a flat-screen TV.

"I want to enhance my gaming experience," he says. But as he spouts his justification, you can almost see his mind split. He is still his mother's son. He switches from gung-ho gamer to self-conscious nerd, fretting about the classes he is missing and the work he'll have to make up. There's his sculpture studio class, for starters. "There's a big block of cherry wood back in my dorm that is untouched," he says, sounding confused and a little ashamed.

The rain stops, and as the clock moves closer to midnight, sales associates from Best Buy, wearing blue polo shirts, spill out of the store and form a sort of cheering section near the weary, smelly men. "B-E-S-T-B-U-Y," they shout out, while others scream "PS3." The gamers give them tight smiles, and it's clear that they just want to get the goods and go home.

"Looking forward to sleeping in your own bed?" Sanchez is asked.

"Eager to try out some games!" he snorts. He's back to being an indefatigable enthusiast.

More security guards materialize at the front of the store. A TV camera crew sets up quickly before the doors open—the craze for PS3 will be a big story on the evening news for a few nights to come. Then the glass doors swing open, and in groups of seven or eight, the young men are allowed to file in. They walk through the aisle of accessories quickly. As flashbulbs pop and cameras record the moment, they make their purchases. Sanchez saunters in, looking exhausted and relieved, grabs and pays for two big boxes, and heads out into the night.

On Killing

ALMOST nothing about the lives of boys these days concerns parents and teachers quite as much as our sons' seemingly boundless appetite for video games. Many parents of an underachieving boy are sure there's a link between their son's obsession with *Madden* and the C's and D's on his report card.

"I fear that every hour my son plays video games is one point off his IQ," a father told me recently. "And he plays a lot!"

Parents worry that computer games—with their fast-paced graphics, finely calibrated system of challenges, and glorification of extreme violence—are hurting our sons in ways we only dimly understand. Part of our worry is that the games are everywhere. The video game industry, which has its roots in the clunky arcade games of the 1940s and 1950s, is now a slick $10 billion industry with tentacles reaching into nearly every household. Over one-third of all households have some kind of game console. And kids, especially boys, love them. Many boys now report that they prefer video game play to television, movies, reading, and playing real-life sports.

Boys start playing them young, too. The official line from the gaming industry is that the average gamer is a twenty-nine-year-old male. But parents know better. Even a casual visitor to a store like GameStop can see gaming's powerful allure for young boys. A closer look at the industry's own research shows that a substantial portion—maybe even a majority—of committed gamers are not grown men but impressionable young boys. In a 2006 study, NPD Group, a retail marketing firm that supplies data to the gaming industry, polled over sixteen thousand respondents between the ages of six and forty-four. Between one-third and one-half of the most obsessive users—"Heavy Gamers" and "Avid Console Gamers" in industry parlance—were males between the ages of six and seventeen.

What are video games doing to our sons? Some psychologists who work with school-age boys think that video games are so harmful they should be severely limited and that certain games should be banned outright. Senator Hillary Clinton spoke for many parents when she said, "the disturbing material in [the video game *Grand Theft Auto*] and other games like it is stealing the innocence of our children and making the difficult job of being a parent harder." In 2005, she proposed legislation limiting the sales of violent games to kids.

Just how bad are video games—violent or otherwise—for our

children? Will playing video games affect their IQs? Could it be contributing to the underachievement of boys in school?

What we see with our own eyes in our own living rooms is not much comfort. Boys who are gaming sit motionless on the couch for hours, their hands over the controller, often oblivious to the world around them. What enthralls them? When we join them on the couch, our unease can quickly morph into alarm. Video games, especially the most popular ones, are a veritable smorgasbord of hyperaggression and blood-spattered violence.

Plenty of experts say we've got good reason to be very concerned. In his influential book *On Killing: The Psychological Cost of Learning to Kill in War and Society,* Daved Grossman, a former West Point psychology instructor, argues that violent video games—especially the subgenre known as First Person Shooters—condition players to become more violent in real life. First Person Shooters work on the human psyche, Grossman says, in much the same way that boot camp does—turning peaceful citizens into soldiers. By repeatedly participating in virtual violence, video games disable a kid's innate "safety" device—overcoming his natural inhibitions against firing on others, hurting, or killing. According to Grossman, "The important distinction between the killing-enabling process that occurs in video arcades and that of the military is that the military's is focused on enemy soldiers. . . . The video games that our children conduct their combat training on have no real sanctions for firing at the wrong target."

When Grossman's book was published in 1995, it caused a sensation. Crime rates of all kinds, including juvenile crime, were at an all-time high. The nation was groping for a way to explain the high school killings dominating the headlines. Authoritative and well informed, Grossman provided a plausible explanation for the unexplainable.

Since that time, though, violent video games—especially First Person Shooters—have become more popular, not less. But a funny thing happened: As hyperviolent video games have become ubiquitous, crime rates and especially the juvenile crime rate have fallen. High-profile aberrations like the April 2007 shootings at Virginia Tech by a mentally ill undergraduate who gunned down 57 people, killing 32 of them, still occur. But in the last fifteen years, during the time video gaming has become the dominant form of entertainment for young boys, violent crime among juveniles has plummeted. Murders are down 68 percent, rape is down 25 percent, robbery is down 43 percent, and assaults are down 26 percent.

Video games do indeed have effects on the boys who play them. But the effects are not the same ones or of the same magnitude as Grossman predicted. Douglas A. Gentile, a developmental psychologist at Iowa State University and director of research at the National Institute on Media and the Family, a media education group, has been trying to figure out exactly what those effects are. Between 2000 and 2003, he followed 430 third-, fourth-, and fifth-graders from rural and suburban public and private schools in Minnesota who played video games during the school year. He charted their gaming habits and got feedback from teachers, peers, and other students about their behavior. He found that kids played a lot. Over-all, the girls averaged about six hours of play a week, and the boys aver-aged about thirteen hours. Some of the children—boys and girls—played mostly violent video games; others played nonviolent games like *Sims* or *Madden*. During the school year, the teachers, peers, and students them-selves reported that the violent-video-game-playing cohorts became more aggressive on the playground and in the classroom than their nonviolent-video-game-playing peers. Gentile reported that the level of video-game-induced aggression did not appear to be different for boys and girls. Sig-nificantly, though—and we'll return to this idea later—he found that the effects were "dose related." Boys who, on average, played video games twice as long as girls were twice as aggressive as girls.

Video Addiction

GAMING becomes a habit that some kids can't kick. When your son plays an exciting or violent video game, his heart rate increases, his breathing quickens, and his blood pressure goes up. In some cases, particularly when games offer surprising or disturbing scenarios, players' brains release the hormone cortisol, making it more likely that the players will remember what they've seen or heard.

For some people, the physical changes the body undergoes during the playing of video games can lead to full-blown addiction. In 1998, a group of researchers in Britain using positron-emission tomography (PET) scans identified the neurochemical foundation of what can become a debilitating and uncontrollable compulsion to game. They charted the brain chemistry of gamers as they maneuvered convoys through a battlefield and destroyed enemy tanks. The scientists found that the brains of these players released massive amounts of dopamine. This is the same neurochemical response that occurs in the brains of cocaine addicts when they snort their drug of choice. Just like classic addicts, problem video gamers develop "triggers" that lead them to play more and more.

In a small study at Charité University Medicine Berlin in Germany, researchers assembled a group of fifteen men in their twenties who were problem gamers and a group of fifteen casual game-playing but otherwise healthy control subjects. They showed the members of both groups a variety of visual cues and asked them to rate how they felt about each image. All had normal reactions to neutral images such as chairs and tables. But the problem gamers showed classic signs of craving when they were presented with freeze frames from some of their favorite games. They desperately wanted to play, expected to feel better when they played, and after seeing the freeze frames reported that they fully intended to play as soon as possible.

Insurance companies remain unconvinced about the addictive qualities of video games and rarely agree to cover costs that families incur trying to get treatment for their video-gaming addict sons. But members of the therapeutic community around the world have begun to respond to what they see as a growing problem. In South Korea, the government is sponsoring a massive public health campaign and has opened publicly funded treatment centers to get problem gamers the help they need. In the United States, residential treatment programs that deal with alcohol, drug, and sex addictions have begun admitting problem gamers. There are also websites that offer online support to help obsessive gamers break the chains of their addiction. A loose confederacy of social workers and psychologists offer individual treatment for youngsters—nearly always young males—who play too much.

To meet addicts and their families, I traveled to an affluent suburb of Seattle. There, in the shadow of the Microsoft complex, I sat with a group of middle-aged parents who meet in a nondescript office building Al-Anon style. Their sons aren't addicted to alcohol, though. They're addicted to their computers.

Most of the parents seem exhausted. They talk with some bitterness about the early warning signs. Several recall being pleased when their sons started playing video games.

"We took it as a sign of intelligence—he had good motor skills, it gave him a sense of accomplishment," say Nancy and Steve, who ask that their last names not be used. But gradually, their son's fascination with gaming—in his case, *EverQuest*—replaced his interest in school, social life, and family. Their son decided not to go away to college, then dropped out of the local community college because he couldn't find a way to balance gaming and his studies. Eventually, their son stayed in his room around the clock—eating irregularly, sleeping at the computer. When his parents forced him to leave his room, he took his laptop with him.

"My daughter said we should throw him out," says Steve, the pain breaking through his voice. He shakes his head. Where would he go? How would he live?

Not long ago, Nancy and Steve contacted Elaine Duncan, a therapist, who did a classic AA-style intervention. The ultimatum? Unplug or leave home. The boy attended a three-week Outward Bound program without his computer, but since he's been home, he's been gaming uncontrollably again.

"I just don't know where it's going to end," says Nancy, with a heavy sigh.

It's a difficult addiction to tackle, says gaming addiction specialist Hillarie Cash, who also practices in suburban Seattle. Unlike alcoholics, who can abstain from drinking, most gamers continue to use a computer, and some continue to game at least a little bit.

Aaron Dona walks that line. A pale, skinny guy with a broad forehead and deeply set eyes, he's been spending the summer of his twenty-first year figuring out how to get his life back. When we meet at a sushi restaurant in a strip mall near his home in an upscale section of suburban Seattle, he seems young and naive. He wears a Japanese anime T-shirt that is more suitable for a middle-schooler than for a college dropout. But when we talk about computer addiction, he sounds older than his years. The child of an architect and a learning specialist, he grew up gaming.

"The year of my birth, 1985, was also the year that the first Atari console was available," he says with a little wry smile. He got his first PC when he was ten years old and his first Game Boy soon followed. He dabbled in a few games, including *Dune* and *EverQuest,* but not until he found the Massively Multiplayer Online Role Playing Game (MMORPG) *Lineage* in high school did his virtual life came into conflict with reality. In school, he skimmed along under the radar with B's and enjoyed a small network of friends. Online, he was a leader, creating different avatars, transforming himself into a knight, a wizard, an elf, or a prince.

"It was a power trip. As the prince, I was at the social center of a bunch of people I didn't know. They called me 'my liege' and it felt good," he says.

Gradually, he began to feel that his avatars reflected the person he was and wanted to be more accurately than his flesh-and-blood existence as an unremarkable high school student. "Other people respect a prince because they know he's worked five times as hard to get there. But at the same time, if you're not charismatic and likable in the game, they don't follow you."

To hold on to that respect, Dona had to participate in virtual activities with other gaming buffs online. "My allied prince had a siege at 2 a.m., for example, and I didn't want to lose my reputation as a reputable Lord," he says, seriously. "I started losing sleep to the game."

As his gaming increased, he began staying up all night to play. His parents saw their son starting to disappear. Cathy Dona, his mother, recalls that she'd come home from her job at three o'clock and find him still in bed. "He'd get up, eat dinner, and play all night. It was crazy. At the weekend, if we go out to eat, we have to rush back so he can play. All weekend, that's what he'd do." His behavior—and his emotional life—suffered. "I'd ask him, did you do your homework and he'd lie to my face," she says. When he was winning, he was elated, but when he lost, his mother noticed, he seemed unreasonably upset. "To him, it was more than just a game. He was living in a pretend world."

Aaron Dona graduated from high school with a B average and enrolled at Rochester Institute of Technology to study film and animation. Around that time, he also began playing *World of Warcraft*, another popular MMORPG. "I was a warrior, a warlock, a paladin, and a mage," he says. But while he was amassing power and influence in his virtual world, he was running into big trouble in real life.

"You can't really make films yourself," he says glumly. "You need a director, soundman, and other people as well. I helped other people with their films, but they wouldn't help me." The boy who was so adept at making alliances online was baffled about how to make them in real life.

He couldn't get his homework done. His video addiction, his mother says, was behind his problems. "He says it wasn't the computers, but it was," she says tartly. By spring of his sophomore year, Dona was on academic probation and also playing *World of Warcraft* about forty hours a week. He was in anguish. "I was playing and I knew I shouldn't be. My thinking at the time was 'Why bother to work hard and fail when I can do what I want and fail?'"

Finally, a college health services adviser told him point-blank to log off and take real-life steps to stop his academic free fall, but it was too late. Dona left college and returned home.

These days, Dona says, he's forcing himself to experience things that don't offer immediate gratification. Willpower and self-control are like muscles, he quotes his dad as saying. The more you exercise them, the stronger they are. To that end, Dona has taken a job working the night shift building window frames in a nearby factory. He gets cut often. At one point, he sliced the sensitive tips of two fingers. But he's hanging on to the job as proof that there's more to him than his online life.

"If I can do this job, maybe I will be able to do schoolwork," he says.

He sees a counselor who specializes in gaming addiction. He attends a 12-step program aimed at helping fellow gaming addicts. He limits himself to two hours of *Warcraft* a day—a limit he is rarely able to keep. He loves gaming, but he's been betrayed by it, too. "The thing is, when you rescue people in a quest and they are grateful, they don't stay rescued. The next person comes along and they still have to be rescued. You never really accomplish anything." And despite the toll gaming has taken on his life, he's still at least partially in denial. "Plenty of people play more," he says. "I don't think I'm really an addict."

Gaming for Knowledge

TEACHERS say that even boys who aren't addicted but who game in the normal-to-heavy range often become progressively harder to teach. Mary Pat McCartney, vice president of the American School Counselor Association and a school counselor in Bristow, Virginia, says she sees this all the time. The attention spans of boys who game seem to grow shorter and weaker: "When I talk to some of the boys about why they're having trouble paying attention in class, it's because they're thinking about it. Games are something that just kind of grabs their attention and demands such a concentration. When they're trying to beat those games, it's all-absorbing. It takes every part of them." Traditional schooling involves transitioning from one subject to the next, but gamers are most comfortable when they are zeroed in on a task. They are not particularly interested in receiving verbal directions. They are not inclined to pretend to be interested in something they find boring. Gamers, some teachers say, seem to get more impatient than other students with the pace of traditional chalk-and-talk lessons.

"It's frustrating," says Betty Will, a veteran teacher who now works as a media director in a middle-class parochial school in San Antonio, Florida. "The boys who are playing games want more instant gratification at school."

Although teachers complain bitterly about kids who game, David Williamson Shaffer, associate professor of learning science at the University of Wisconsin at Madison and author of *How Computer Games Help Children Learn*, says they should be embracing it. Gamers, he believes, are actually developing a different—and in some ways superior—pattern of learning. He predicts that boys will not stop gaming but rather that schools will begin to adapt what's good about games into their curricula. He sees the time coming soon when teachers will use games that teach the fundamentals of mathematics, review science concepts, and help students practice reading and writing.

That's not such a pie-in-the-sky prediction. There seems to be an almost unlimited supply of grant money available from private foundations to find ways to harness gaming for learning. In response, educators at nearly every major university center in the country are working on coming up with new technology for the students of tomorrow.

To help you understand the coming trend, I'm going to ask you to do some fieldwork. Play a video game with your son for a half an hour. Whether you are playing *Sims, Fable, Counter-Strike,* or *Halo,* all games have roughly the same elements:

You can begin without any previous training.
You spend a large chunk of time acquiring knowledge and skills.
You figure out new ways to problem-solve and apply those skills
    (getting to a new level; killing a bad guy).
Your knowledge base is continually tested until you achieve
    competency.
Once you achieve competencies you are rewarded with another set
    of challenges.

You may not love spending 30 minutes as a hulking warrior wearing body armor and carrying a high-powered weapon. Rescuing a big-breasted woman from a fire-breathing dragon may not be your idea of a good time, but you can see the way in which gaming condenses and distills the learning experience. Games teach rules, use formulas, and introduce ideas in a way that most teenage boys find wholly engaging. Still not sure what I'm getting at? Suppose your son needed to use algebra formulas to rescue Lara Croft. He'd probably have them memorized and be trading them with his friends. Now are you starting to see how this might work?

The U.S. Department of Defense recognizes the instructional value of gaming. Building on the rich history of military war games, the U.S. Army began using video games about a decade ago, first to train soldiers how to use sophisticated machinery and then to practice battle strategies. In the last two or three years, some corporations have begun using video games to train employees. Medical schools are doing it, too—for example, teaching doctors how to do laparoscopic surgery through video games rather than using real cadavers.

Teaching kids, however, is a little different from teaching medical students. So I'm wary. It's not unusual for early enthusiasts for new technologies—from the motion picture, to television, to laptop computers—to oversell their potential and overlook their limitations.

On a warm February morning, I paid a visit to Edgewater High School in Orlando, Florida, where some teachers are using video games to encourage reluctant-to-read boys to brush up on their literacy skills. Edgewater is no suburban Valhalla. Although it's located in a nice section of Orlando, the school has its share of problems. Just this year, the principal took three handguns away from students on campus.

"Every kind of problem, we have," says principal Rob Anderson.

Anderson's staff struggles to keep test scores up. Like teachers at many high schools, Edgewater instructors are particularly focused on a subsection of kids who fall well below grade level in reading and math. This year, Anderson is hoping a new video game course will help them. The class is billed as "game design instruction"—an irresistible lure for the two dozen or so teenage boys who signed up. Once enrolled, the boys learn to design rudimentary games—and they also do plenty of reading and writing.

For the last nine weeks, the students have logged on, then traveled to a virtual office building, taken the elevator to their offices, and entered their cubicles. Once they get to "work," they run through tasks that are typical for most wage slaves but novel for high-schoolers—responding to a virtual "boss," answering e-mail, and reading and writing memos. Then they get down to designing, using *DarkBASIC* to come up with a computer game that advertises a fictional product, a soda called CarbonAde. They write the introduction to and directions for their game.

I seat myself next to a boy who I've been told is several grades behind his classmates in reading and writing. For 45 minutes, though, he plows through the simulation, deciphering directions, writing memos, and working on his game design. His end product will probably not be featured in *PC Gamer* anytime soon. But engagement, says his teacher, Paul Ackerman, is half the battle: "You can't teach unless kids are paying attention, and they are paying attention. Engagement in my class is almost 100 percent."

I agree with Ackerman—to a point: Game-based learning might aid rote learning. It might be useful for drilling and review. It's an interesting way to provide remedial instruction, too. But nothing I saw at Edgewater convinces me that gaming would be an effective tool to promote thoughtful discourse in the classroom—which is fundamental to learning in its purest sense. Even the most avid cheerleaders for technology admit that not every classroom lesson can or should be taught with a console. There is no way to use video games to discuss the impact of current events, for example, or to do a meaningful analysis of *Catcher in the Rye*. But upstairs at Edgewater, veteran English teacher Scott Bowen says that practicing basic technical writing—memos, directions, instructions—by means of video games has his blessing.

Bowen tries to help me put this new development—games in the classroom—in context. "Teachers need to stop resisting and use what's working for kids," he says. There have always been naysayers, he points out. "When I was a student," he recalls, "teachers said graphic novels and popular writers like Stephen King had no place in the classroom. Now graphic novels are front-and-center, and King is a worthy writer—a popular bridge to dustier classics. Kids are learning from video games, and teachers resist it. The next generation—they will have it."

Before I leave Bowen's classroom, I notice that one of the books his ninth-grade honors students are reading is the novel *Speaker for the Dead*, by Orson Scott Card, who has also authored several popular video games. Bowen catches me looking at the title and gives a knowing nod. "You're already seeing the cross-pollination between literacy and video games. We're wondering if it's going to happen, but in fact, it's already begun."

So perhaps gaming has its place. But in our enthusiasm to embrace the Next Big Thing, let's not forget that as gaming becomes the dominant form of entertainment for our sons—and, increasingly, part of their classroom experience—the lives of our sons may be growing poorer, not richer. Sure, crime rates have dropped. But so has boys' involvement in out-of-school activities that support learning, improve socialization, and promote community. In the last twenty years, the amount of time that teenage boys report spending reading; attending a concert, a dance performance, or the theater; or wandering into a museum has plummeted. So has the amount of time they spend outdoors. Gaming is a tricky pasttime to keep under control—even by kids who don't appear to be problem gamers. About 15 percent of children surveyed in a recent National Institute on Media and the Family (NIMF) study said they feel they spend too much time playing video games. One in ten admit playing so much that gaming sometimes hurts their homework. Over half the kids surveyed said they sometimes try to stop playing video games.

What do experts say parents need to remember? Douglas Gentile's research at NIMF clearly shows that the negative effects of gaming are "dose related." That means your son needs to have his game time limited and to mix his gaming with hearty doses of other—real-life—experiences. Aaron Dona said it best when he unself-consciously told me, "Some people just can't gauge when enough is enough." Often, the responsibility falls on parents to create those limits. For better or worse, the average American boyhood these days includes gaming and, yes, some virtual bloodshed. If your son is spending more than two hours a day at it, it's time to pull the plug. It's almost a certainty that a gaming habit exceeding two hours a day is undermining his social or scholastic life. He needs your help to grasp the difference between fascination and obsession. He needs guidance on how to balance gaming with eating, sleeping, homework, interacting with friends, and active play. If your attempt at limit setting goes nowhere and your son's problem with video gaming grows bigger, it may be time to seek professional advice.

CHAPTER 14

SINGLE-SEX SCHOOLING

Could It Be the Answer?

A Wrestler and Baritone

WHEN we talk about single-sex schools, the Montgomery Bell Academy, an all-boys day school in Nashville, Tennessee, is the kind of place that comes to mind for most people. The movie *Dead Poets Society* could have been filmed here—in fact, the screenwriter is a Montgomery Bell alum. The boys at Montgomery Bell, founded in 1867, receive the kind of instruction that will smooth the way for their admission to the top colleges in the country. On any given day, 680 boys, ages twelve through eighteen, attend school in the brick, white-columned buildings. In the shadow of the 3,500-seat football stadium, boys scrimmage on beautifully maintained sports fields. Some run on the eight-lane, all-weather track. Some work in the well-equipped science laboratories. Others crack their books in the newly refurbished library.

Education at Montgomery Bell doesn't come cheap. Annual tuition is $17,000, and annual giving—the money that parents are asked to pay in addition to tuition—topped $2 million last year. But parents aren't complaining. Most could afford to send their sons anywhere—there are fine public, parochial, and private schools in the area—but they choose Montgomery Bell, whose motto is "Gentleman, Scholar,

Athlete," because they believe the teachers and administrators at boys' schools know best how to educate young men.

It's easy to find parents eager to rave about Montgomery Bell. Bill Bellet, a clinical psychologist, is a true believer. He has four sons—a junior, a freshman, and two eighth-graders—enrolled there because he wants them to be educated in a boy-friendly world.

"An all-boys school," he says, "tends to attract teachers who genuinely have a feeling for how to teach boys. And they shape the material in a way to keep boys engaged." In what way? "For instance, in history, they don't focus on the emotional impact of history, and they don't ask boys about their feelings in relation to history. As a clinical psychologist, I know that most boys are just not going to be interested in a history class like that. Yes, you want all kids to learn to think critically. But how people might have felt, well, you need to intersperse that with a lot of attention on more concrete information like the facts, the dates, and the names."

The school environment at Montgomery Bell puts a premium on competition, too. Bellet continues: "In the classroom, competition helps boys stay focused. My boys are wrestlers, and I've seen that through athletics they've been challenged to master themselves physically."

And there's another benefit. Far from enforcing a rigid expression of masculinity, Bellet says, the single-sex environment allows his boys the latitude to try many different kinds of activities that boys in coed schools would often consider "too girlie." The all-boy environment pushes boys to participate in activities that defy gender stereotypes. Bellet says that his sons are "less inhibited" than some of their friends who attend coeducational schools. "They're more willing to take risks. They are more willing to get involved in the arts and music, without fear of embarrassment. Sometimes it's not cool for boys to be in the chorus, but at Montgomery Bell it's only boys. And if they want to have a chorus, it's going to be boys. It turns out that one of my sons was not just a good wrestler—he was also very good in art. It was his best subject. Another of my sons wrestled, just like his brother, but he is also a wonderful baritone."

Single-Sex Revival

IF YOUR son is struggling at school, chances are good that you've already begun to consider alternatives. Maybe you've tried to weigh the benefits of an all-boys school. What you may have found is this: It's tricky to tease out the benefits and deficits of single-sex education. Plenty of people have opinions, but few flash points burn quite as hot as opinions about whether single-sex schools are a good thing or a bad thing for our children.

For decades, how a person regarded all-boys schools depended on his or her political orientation. For conservatives, there was always something comforting about all-boys schools. They are, after all, part of a long and august tradition, especially for the wealthy. They hold out the promise of education "the way it used to be"—a curriculum grounded in classics and taught with plenty of competition and rigor. For some people on the right, all-boys schools seem to be places where unreconstructed masculinity shines, where boys can unashamedly be boys, and where notions such as women's rights and diversity won't cast a shadow.

For lefties, all-boys schools are by their very nature elitist. They exude more than a whiff of the kind of crushing patriarchy that forty years ago sent smart boys to Yale and smart girls to finishing schools where they were prepared for lives as contented wives and practical mothers. They enforce a narrow version of masculinity, too. Sure, strapping scholar-athletes do fine, but boys who are less traditionally macho find that the much-heralded competitive environment feels a lot like bullying. Homophobia is rampant. Despite all the talk about boys' schools turning out "gentlemen," there's the sneaking suspicion on the left that they have damp pockets of unexamined misogyny.

The debate over coeducation at Virginia Military Institute, which made national headlines in the mid-1990s, fanned those anti-boys-school ideas. A publicly funded military-type college, VMI for years fought a bitter battle against granting admission to women. The school has a long history. In 1864, the cadet corps marched to New Market to help Confederate forces defeat the advancing Union army. It makes much of its strict honor code, its ritual hazing, the lack of personal privacy it afford its students, and its emphasis on hierarchy and chain of command.

When the state legislature demanded that VMI admit women, the administration responded in horror. Admitting women, claimed a school spokesman, would erode VMI's "tradition and discipline." VMI, as it was constituted, could not exist as a coed school, he claimed. When the Supreme Court of the United States finally demanded that VMI admit women or forfeit public money, VMI's legal counsel Robert Patterson, a VMI alum, told the *Virginian-Pilot*, "It's a sad day for VMI, it's a sad day for the state, and a sad day for the nation."

Somehow, both Virginia and the nation managed to contain their grief. In 1997, VMI became coed—but it's been an ugly process. Women students reported incidents of sexual harassment. In 1999, the highest-ranking male cadet was dismissed from the school for demanding sex from three female cadets.

VMI aside, though, single-sex education for boys has begun to gain popular support, not from hidebound traditionalists but from concerned parents who believe that boys' schools may be better able than coed schools to meet the academic, psychological, and social needs of their sons. An all-boy class, the thinking goes, allows teachers to tailor instruction to the specific pace, interests, and needs of boys. At the same time, in many parts of the country, single-sex education, which has been simply too expensive for most American families, is fast becoming a real option. In the last five years or so, two new controversial trends have been sweeping across public schools: using tax dollars to convert public schools to single-sex academies—all-boys and all-girls schools; and launching single-sex classes within coeducational public schools.

Some people are skeptical that this back-to-the-future innovation really offers a solution to the problem of underachieving males. Does it really work? More important, is it right for your son and your community? To distinguish the facts from the hype, let's take a brief look at the history of single-sex schools and single-sex classes within mixed-gender schools. Let's see what we know, not just what we think we know, about whether single-sex schooling will help boys succeed.

The Melting Pot

As I've mentioned, until the early twentieth century, when America was still a largely agrarian society, the education of middle-class and poor children tended to be a haphazard affair. Most children had little access to formal education beyond basic literacy instruction that took place in the winter months between harvesting and planting. Farmwork took precedence over algebra. Wealthy families educated their sons in a more consistent and deliberate fashion, sending them to all-male schools and colleges that went heavy on the classics—mathematics, ancient languages, and rhetoric. The goal of education for those boys was clear: to prepare them for life as gentlemen.

In the early part of the twentieth century, educational opportunities began to expand. Wealthy families began to educate young girls—often in all-girl environments. The primacy of these single-sex academies was challenged by the rise in public education, which tended to be coed. In

New York, Boston, and other cities, skyrocketing immigration rates intensified the need for public education to help the children of immigrants find their way in the New World. Publicly funded coed schools were opened to help the male and female children of newly arrived Europeans learn the English language and American customs. Immigrants continued to arrive, the public school system continued to grow, and single-sex education gradually became the exception rather than the rule.

At that time, the goals of the public school system reflected the national ideal of the great melting pot. Teachers were prepared to teach children from different regions of the globe how to act and think like Americans. The day-to-day experience of the classroom, though, reflected the national reality: Public schools were as economically stratified and racially divided as the society they served. Children from poor, black, rural, and newly immigrated families attended overcrowded, underfunded, hardscrabble schools. Children from more affluent families attended schools that were better run and better equipped. In even the most troubled cities, though, almost every public school system had a few single-sex academies—usually highly regarded, well equipped, and reserved for the highest-achieving kids.

In 1954, public education was dramatically changed by a landmark decision by the U.S. Supreme Court—*Brown v. Board of Education*—which struck down racially segregated public schools, saying "separate is inherently unequal." The court battle highlighted the nation's growing unease with segregated public schools. The *Brown* decision—that different tracks in education would only worsen divisions and inequities in society—became a guiding principle for schooling in the next four decades. *Brown v. Board of Education* was about racial equality, but the doctrine that separate is inherently unequal was, in the years that followed, interpreted to apply to gender equality. Private single-sex schools were untouched by the ruling, but it sounded the death knell for elite, public, single-sex schools. Single-sex public schools might be committed to offering a high-quality academic environment for each sex, but women's groups argued that it was impossible to monitor whether boys and girls were having comparable experiences or whether girls were being relegated to an educational ghetto as they so often had been in the past.

By the 1980s, feminist legal organizations, which had successfully used the courts to open up better-paying jobs to women, were using the principle laid down by *Brown v. Board of Education* to compel city governments to get public all-boys schools to admit girls. Back then, many boys' schools admitted women without a fight. All-boys schools seemed anachronistic. Improved methods of birth control meant that girls could control their reproductive lives. Segregating adolescent boys and girls, at least for the obvious reasons, became unnecessary. Colleges, prompted by Title IX, were welcoming women, and in order to pursue those educational opportunities, girls needed access to the top-drawer college preparation that was available to boys. As women entered the workforce in record numbers, the conventional wisdom about single-gender schools went something like this: If ambitious young professional men are going to share office space with equally ambitious young women, they might as well learn cooperation in grade school. Coeducation was the best preparation for the employees of the future. In that era, sending a boy to an all-boys school was seen as a conservative gesture—indicating discomfort with the titanic societal changes brought about by the women's movement. Most single-sex private schools hit on extremely hard times, and many boys' schools either accepted young women or closed their doors.

It was feminism that nearly put boys' schools out of business, and it was also feminism that put them back on the map again. In 1992, three decades after Title IX began to revolutionize education, the American Association of University Women published the report *How Schools Shortchange Girls,* which was intended to refocus attention on how girls were fairing in public, co-educational schools. As I mentioned in Chapter 3, the picture the report painted was grim. The report was intended to galvanize educators to address the rampant and institutional sexism in coed schools, which, the authors of the report claimed, was actively hurting young females. But parents took away a different message: Your son may be OK, may even thrive in a coed school, but if you want to do what's best for your daughter—and help her take advantage of the new wider horizons—an all-girl environment would be best. The AAUW report, and other scholarship of the day, suggested that girls have a highly gender-specific learning style and undergo a unique kind of psychological development, and that unless girls were encouraged and supported in specific girl-friendly ways, families, schools, and society would be placing a crushingly heavy burden on them. Enrollment at all-girls schools went through the roof. Women's colleges, which had seen the cream skimmed off their applicant pools when Ivy League schools were forced by Title IX to begin admitting more women, saw their applications soar. All-girls schools were suddenly considered cutting-edge.

All-boys schools, however, continued to decline. "Inherent in the idea that girls were shortchanged was that boys were privileged. And nowhere were they more privileged than at boys' schools," says Bradley Adams, of the International Boys' Schools Coalition, a consortium of all-male schools. A girls-only education was judged to build strength and to reinforce a positive identity, but "boys' schools," says Adams, "were seen as toxic."

By the late 1990s, more data began to emerge that compared the relative successes of boys and girls—and girls, rather than being part of a disadvantaged class, were soaring. Very soon, psychologists, educators, and parents began to propose that the flip side of the Grrrl Power paradigm might also be true: Boys had their own needs and learning style, which were often ignored. In a series of books, boy psychologists William Pollack and Michael Thompson acknowledged the unique makeup of girls but forcefully suggested that boys received conflicting, limited, and often damaging messages about their own passage to adulthood.

There was a cultural reversal. Suddenly, administrators at private boys' schools found themselves identified not as standard-bearers for bygone days but as innovators of a boy-centered education. Bradley Adams saw the transformation: "We began to realize that what we did—educate boys—we did very well indeed." All-boys schools took it as a starting point that boys were different from girls—they were more active, messier, less organized, more energetic, noisier, and funny. "And," continues Adams, "we had institutions that were set up around the learning styles that best suited them," which included a large measure of accountability, competition, and a strong sense of consequences. "Many of us had been teaching boys by tradition. In the last ten years or so, we've begun teaching boys out of conviction."

Even Montgomery Bell, which enjoyed a strong academic reputation, a rich tradition, and enthusiastic and generous alumni, was whipsawed by the gender politics of the last forty years. In the early 1980s, along with administrators at many other private boys' schools, Montgomery Bell administrators found the enrollment was dwindling. Hoping to save the ailing institution, a wealthy donor offered Montgomery Bell "seven figures" if the school would admit girls. Montgomery Bell's board of trustees considered the offer, says headmaster Brad Gioia, but decided the student body would remain all-male.

These days, business at Montgomery Bell has never been better, in part because the school markets itself to parents who are eager to hear the boy-centered message. The school offers plenty of organizational support for boys who struggle to keep their backpacks neat and to hand homework in on time. The school boasts a boy-friendly schedule—one offering plenty of opportunities to eat and lots of physical activity throughout the day. Central to the Montgomery Bell mission, though, is the presence of teachers who like instructing boys. The school's promotional material, naturally, doesn't address sticky issues of bullying, homophobia, or misogyny, but it does throw a wide frame around masculine identity. The material makes it clear that well-regarded Montgomery Bell boys participate in the arts and sports in equal numbers. Parents get the message.

"I think consciousness has been raised," says headmaster Gioia, unself-consciously borrowing the terminology that feminism appropriated from the civil rights movement. "Parents feel boys' schools are a safe place where their sons can get more complete exposure—they see them as schools that teach to the whole boy."

Can Separate Be Equal?

ALTHOUGH single-sex schools for boys have become an attractive option for families who can afford private school tuition, the notion of single-sex public education remains divisive. In the 1990s, while members of the general public were wringing their hands about all kinds of girls, public school administrators were noting that poor, African American, and Hispanic boys were rapidly losing ground. Boys of color were performing much worse than white boys, for instance, but they also were performing much less well than girls in their own cohort. There was something about being poor and black and male in the United States, educators suggested, that was getting in the way of academic success. Educators in the poorest neighborhoods in some of the most troubled school districts in the country began looking to successful male-centered learning environments like Montgomery Bell and tried to re-create modest equivalents for disadvantaged boys. Some of those public school experiments, most notably in California, collapsed quickly—victims of poor planning and lame execution. Public all-boys schools that opened in underserved areas such as Detroit and Chicago came under attack almost immediately from feminist legal groups. The courts backed the women's groups, declaring that public money could not be spent on all-boys schools. Most of those fledgling institutions were forced to close.

In 1996, Ann Rubinstein Tisch, a wealthy independent-minded Manhattan woman, broke the deadlock and made single-sex schooling available for middle-class and poor kids by launching a single-sex public school for girls. Like many people, Tisch was shaken by the AAUW report and deeply concerned about the fate of adolescent females. So she came up with a plan. Why not start a public school that offered poor girls everything that a private girls' school would offer: small classes, uniforms, college prep, high expectations, and a cohesive, caring learning community?

With plenty of behind-the-scenes drama but not much public notice, Tisch got the New York City Board of Education to open the Young Women's Leadership School of East Harlem with the aim of educating poor black and Latina high school girls in a supportive all-girl environment. Poor families lined up around the block to get their daughters a desk in the well-funded, well-organized school.

The New York Civil Liberties Union and the New York Civil Rights Coalition filed a complaint with the U.S. Department of Education charging that the school discriminated against boys. The National Organization for Women joined the complaint. Anne Conners, president of NOW's New York chapters invoked *Brown v. Board of Education* when she declared that the Young Women's Leadership School should be closed because "separate but equal is not OK."

While those complaints were percolating at the Department of Education, the school was having a big impact on the lives of its students. Every girl who graduated in the class of 2001 went on to attend college—exclusive colleges such as Smith, New York University, and Mount

Holyoke. As the school's reputation grew, the school began to pick up political support. In 2001, Texas Republican senator Kay Bailey Hutchison and New York Democratic senator Hillary Clinton, a grateful graduate of an all-girls school, successfully cosponsored an amendment to an education bill to make single-sex public education possible, legal, and eligible for $450 million a year in federal funding. The Young Women's Leadership School of East Harlem, said Clinton on the floor of the U.S. Senate, is "one of the premier public schools for girls in our nation . . . we could use more schools such as this."

Once the bill became law, the rush to open single-sex public schools was on—and not just for poor kids and for kids of color in underserved communities. Dr. Leonard Sax, a Maryland family practitioner who founded the National Association for Single-Sex Public Education, has been a cheerleader for that movement. He argues that we need to separate girls and boys in order to create optimum learning conditions for both. In his book *Why Gender Matters: What Parents and Teachers Need to Know About the Emerging Science of Sex Differences*, Sax cites studies that show young girls and boys draw differently. Girls use a larger variety of colors and more objects while boys draw action scenes in blue, gray, silver, and black. Because of innate gender-based hearing differences, teachers need to speak louder to boys than to girls. He argues that both boys and girls are short-changed by a gender-neutral education and that "today we know that innate differences between girls and boys are profound." He writes, "Of course, not all girls are alike and not all boys are alike. But girls and boys do differ from one another in systematic ways that should be understood and made use of, not covered up or ignored." Sax's critics bristle at the notion of discernible biologically based differences in learning style and say an environment that purports to be boy-friendly might end up suiting almost no one because there is almost as much variety among boys as there is between boys and girls. (Confused? Look at it this way: You can say that boys are on average generally taller than girls, for instance, but if you adapt the furniture in the classroom for boys by making the seats higher, there are plenty of shorter-than-average boys who will be ill suited for it.)

School administrators, faced with pervasive underachievement by young males, began seizing on single-sex education as a cure-all. Some saw a chance to establish a different kind of learning environment and foster different kinds of attitudes toward learning among boys. Some single-sex schools, like the hastily remade Thomas E. FitzSimons High School in North Philadelphia, got off to a shaky start.

When FitzSimons opened its doors in September 2005, one of the toughest schools in the city was reborn as an all-male academy. But FitzSimons was a recipe for disaster. The school had a long history of instability, with a new principal every year. Much of the staff was inexperienced when it came to teaching inner-city kids in general and boys specifically. Seven hundred middle school and high school boys from two rival neighborhoods had been randomly assigned to the all-male school. In the first four months, assaults on teachers and students doubled over the previous year. FitzSimons went from being one of the lowest-performing schools in Philadelphia to one of the most violent. Teachers fled, and administrators called for Social Services backup. "It's been pretty rough," principal Richard Jenkins told the *Philadelphia Inquirer.* "We're working hard to correct things."

Many school districts developed plans for single-sex academies but left them on the drawing board until the U.S. Department of Education clarified exactly what the 2001 law really meant. In the fall of 2006, that clarification arrived: The Department of Education declared once and for all that single-sex public schools were legal.

Academic feminists rattled their sabers. "Single-sex schools are a giant step backward in the struggle for girls' and women's equality," Kim Gandy, president of the National Organization for Women, proclaimed in *USA Today.* "It's ironic and discouraging that the Bush administration has chosen to use its regulatory power to encourage sex discrimination by promoting single-sex education," wrote Leslie Wolf, president of the Center for Women Policy Studies, in a letter to the *New York Times,* conveniently forgetting that it was prominent female politicians who, in the name of empowering girls, had gotten the law passed. Between 1995 and 2007, the number of single-gender public schools jumped from 3 to 52, and about 150 new single-sex schools are slated to open in Arizona, Connecticut, Florida, Pennsylvania, California, and Maine in the next two years.

Gryffindor for Harry, Hufflepuff for Hermione

WHILE support for a new wave of single-sex public schools is building, another, even more experimental variety of single-sex education is emerging around the country. Administrators in over two hundred public schools are reorganizing schedules so that kids are taught core subjects in all-boys and all-girls classrooms. Roncalli Middle School in Pueblo, Colorado, a former steel-mining town, is giving it a try. Boys at the school, which is about half white and half Latino, have been lagging badly behind the girls. The principal's motivation was simple. "Our biggest concern," says principal Peter Farbo, "is improving the boys' performance." So in the fall of 2005, he launched single-sex classes in social studies, science, math, language arts, and reading for about one-fifth of his 220 sixth-graders. The children were selected more or less at random. The chief criterion was that each student's parent had to buy into the program. Farbo is pleased with the results so far. At the end of the first semester, the all-girls class was the best performer in the grade, but to the surprise of the administration, the all-boys class came in a strong second, comfortably ahead of the six coed sections of the sixth grade.

The kids at Roncalli seem to like the single-sex classes. Student Taylor Voss, who spent a year in an all-male math class, says he found it easier to speak up when he wasn't around girls. "The girls in the fifth grade would talk about what kind of answer you write," says Voss. Boys, he finds, are less confrontational. "If you answer something funny, with an all-boys class, they don't say anything." Being in an all-boys class, he says, is "less distracting."

The teachers noticed right away that boys and girls, once separated, seem to go about tackling their work in different ways. Science teacher Pat Farrell says he can count on the girls to approach the assignments in a methodical and directed way. When it comes to chemistry or physics lab assignments, "they follow the directions and go from the beginning to end without asking questions." Boys, however, go in two directions at once. They also cut up more. Faced with lab supplies, "it is only the boys who will raise their hands and ask, 'Can I eat this?'" But they also ask more penetrating questions. "They want to know how it works and then some," Farrell says. "They want to go beyond just what the lab asks them to do."

Math teacher Amy Goehl also saw differences almost immediately between her all-male and all-female classes. Last year, instead of simply reviewing problems from a book for test prep, she had each kid write a review problem on a 3-by-5-inch card. When she shouted "go," the kids scooted around the room to exchange and solve problems in the allotted 30 seconds. When she shouted "go" again, the students raced for another problem. "It was a little chaotic," she admits. At the end of the day, Goehl was surprised by the feedback.

"The girls hated it," she says. "They said it was too much noise and they'd rather work by themselves." The all-male sixth-grade class, though, was riveted. "The boys said, 'This is great, I learned so much.' It drove home to me the differences," she says.

Goehl is trying to figure out how to tailor her classroom techniques to suit different learning styles. With girls, she says, "I can go out and get coffee and show up ten minutes later, and they'll still be busy, doing the work. They want to do it by themselves, and everything's nice and neat and turned in." With boys, long explanations cause them to zone out, and firm classroom management is key. "The boys need activities," Goehl says, "but also structure. They get to roughhousing and pushing and shoving. It's easy for them to get off task." All the teachers at Roncalli agreed that the all-boy classes were the most challenging ones.

No one knows if these kinds of programs will be successful in the long term. When it comes to single-sex classrooms in coeducational schools, Cornelius Riordan, a sociology professor at Providence College, in Rhode Island, and an authority on single-sex education, points out that "there is virtually no research on those except anecdotal research, which is to say, no research at all."

Roncalli's Farbo says the idea for single-sex classes is evolving. For scheduling reasons, the school no longer offers single-sex social studies. But next year, the program will expand to other grades. Single-sex math and science and reading and English-language courses will be offered to sixth-, seventh-, and eighth-graders. "We think the program is helping them," says Farbo. The boys in single-sex classes score better than the boys in coeducational ones.

Some Benefits, Sometimes

But is it worth it? Is there any hard evidence to suggest that single-sex instruction is more or less effective than coed instruction? Does it have any impact at all? Let's look at what we know.

The best studies show that the academic advantages that many parents hope to gain by sending their kids to single-sex schools are mostly illusory. Kids who attend single-sex schools perform only modestly better than those in coed schools. Alan Smithers, a professor at Buckingham University, twenty miles north of Oxford, England, conducted a cross-cultural examination of single-sex education. He found that in Hong Kong, where 10 percent of schools are single-sex, girls appear to do better, but in Belgium, boys and girls who study together get the best results. In general, Smithers found private boys' schools have greater success than public coeducational schools in college admission because the former draw from a largely affluent, well-educated population—children who tend to dominate the upper echelons of educational achievement anyway.

Researchers in the United States have found that there is some positive impact from sending your child to a single-sex school. In the early 1980s, Cornelius Riordan evaluated the experiences of students at single-sex Catholic high schools by a variety of criteria—from test scores, to engagement, to positive self-esteem. He found that, above all, kids who attend single-sex schools seem to like school more, have better self-esteem, score better on tests, and are more likely to go to college. "And while it's true that boys in single-sex schools did better than boys in coed schools, the difference was most pronounced among at-risk African American and Hispanic students of both sexes," says Riordan. Bottom line: Single-sex schools "don't make a lot of difference for middle-class boys."

In 2006, U.S. Department of Education guidelines on single-sex public education reflected, at least in part, the equivocal nature of the research on single-sex education. Although the U.S. Department of Education was supporting it in principle, Stephanie Monroe, who heads the Education Department's office for civil rights, hardly championed it as the Next New Thing. She wrote: "Educational research, though it's ongoing and shows some mixed results, does suggest that single-sex education can provide some benefits to some students, under certain circumstances."

That is not to say that it has no impact on middle-class kids at all. One of the biggest and most comprehensive studies on the long-term effects of single-sex schooling was carried out in England and showed that all-boys and all-girls schools had a significant and far-reaching impact on students, though probably not in the way that you imagine. Researchers at the Centre for Longitudinal Studies at the University of London, have been following thirteen thousand individuals born in 1958 throughout their lives with the aim of determining the lifelong consequences of different types of schooling. The study subjects, now in their forties, were varied across economic background and geography. Researchers found that the academic advantages of a single-sex school were negligible: Single-sex education did not make students any more likely to get a four-year degree or to enter a high-status occupation. What their data did reflect, though, was intriguing. People who went to single-sex schools were more likely to study subjects not traditionally associated with their gender than were those who went to coeducational schools.

"Girls were more likely to pursue math and science. Boys were more likely to pursue English and languages. Single-sex schools seem more likely to encourage students to pursue academic paths according to their talents rather than their gender," says researcher Dr. Alice Sullivan.

Getting the Message

SOME of the benefits of a single-sex education for African American boys are apparent at the Eagle Academy for Young Men, an all-male public high school in the South Bronx. The neighborhood around Eagle defines mean streets. The boys who attend Eagle come from an assortment of rough neighborhoods in the South Bronx and Upper Manhattan that are the primary feeders for the string of state prisons that stretches across much of the northern part of the state. The school building itself, a 1970s-style pale brick structure, sits almost in the shadow of the Bronx criminal courthouse, and it's no exaggeration to say that the courthouse is a stark reminder of the life that awaits Eagle students if they drop out.

The founders of Eagle watched the legal skirmishing over the Young Women's Leadership School of East Harlem with their breaths held. When female politicians moved to keep civil liberties and feminist legal groups from closing the girls' school, says Eagle principal David Banks, One Hundred Black Men of New York, a regional branch of the African American professional association, activated plans for a school for at-risk African American and Latino boys. They didn't wait for the federal government's seal of approval before launching their grand experiment. "We couldn't wait," says Banks. "Our boys are going off a cliff." Eagle Academy opened its doors in 2004.

The guiding principle at Eagle is similar to that at Montgomery Bell: Boys have particular needs—academic, social, and emotional—that their school environment should address. Yet what Eagle boys and Montgomery Bell boys require could not be more different. When it comes to college, few Eagle boys will feel torn between applying for early admission to mommy's or to daddy's alma mater. Most of the boys who attend Eagle moved through substandard neighborhood elementary schools. They come from families in which receiving a high school diploma is a major educational achievement and paying the rent is of higher priority than securing entrance to a competitive college. The families of most Eagle boys are headed by women. Almost no one in the lives of these students, and certainly very few men, are able to demonstrate the lifelong social and economic benefits that come from staying in school.

Like Montgomery Bell, Eagle aims to graduate "gentlemen, athletes, and scholars." Instead of wearing jeans, gold jewelry, or hip-hop-style trucker hats, Eagle students are required to wear pressed blue shirts, blue ties, and gray slacks. Like the Montgomery Bell curriculum, the Eagle curriculum emphasizes college preparation, but the social skills that

Montgomery Bell boys pick up around the dinner table or at the country club—how to speak well, act courteously, and move smoothly in the adult world—are the subject of explicit instruction at Eagle. Many young men are assigned mentors from the community—professional working men who can remind Eagle students that, for instance, a good grade in algebra can lead to a strong SAT score, which in turn can lead to college admission and maybe even a scholarship. Students are held accountable for their assignments and homework and receive a wide variety of tools, including after-school reviews and Saturday classes, to help them succeed in spite of the difficult circumstances of their lives.

On a recent visit, it's clear that the school is a work-in-progress. The boys are more self-conscious than most teenagers and work very deliberately against the negative stereotypes of young, black, urban males. No thuggish behavior is on display here. The boys greet a visitor with great formality and gravity by standing and shaking hands, and bidding the guest "good day." The fault lines of the school, however, are immediately evident. Admissions criteria are low. The thirty-three young men in an English class discussing William Golding's novel *Lord of the Flies* have different levels of proficiency in reading comprehension. Keeping peace in the classroom is an ongoing challenge. During an examination of the opening pages of the book, there's much high-fiving and scraping of chairs and even some impromptu wrestling. About half the kids seem genuinely eager to learn. A quarter of the kids seem to be stealth students, tossing paper back and forth and clowning around, but when asked a question contribute to the discussion in ways that make it clear they've been following along. The final quarter of boys seem checked out.

How does Eagle differ from other tough urban schools? In some ways it's better. The strong culture of the school provides an anchor for the students. Statistically, some students show strong achievement once they arrive at Eagle. But about 25 percent of students drop out or leave. Evidence that Eagle boys can perform well on the all-important standardized tests is hard to come by. Seventy-one percent passed the statewide math test—the state average is 79 percent—which is hardly stellar performance. The all-male environment makes some aspects of education easier, others harder. Female staff members have difficulty winning the boys' respect. Rigid male stereotypes abound. Openly gay students have been the targets of hazing and even violence. But there is a positive attitude toward learning that is hard to miss. Unlike boys in many inner-city schools, who actively discourage one another from participating in school, students at Eagle clearly consider learning a good thing. They are quick to praise one another for strong work, or for a sensitive observation, with calls of "well put" or "I agree one hundred percent." Their enthusiasm for one another's achievement is touching.

After a year at Eagle, veteran educator Joel Heckethorn, who teaches tenth-grade English, reflects on what makes Eagle unique: "Unlike other places I've taught in my ten years as a teacher, the boys at Eagle know that they need the benefits of the education that we are offering them. As poor young men, as young men of color, they may not understand exactly why they need it, but they've gotten the message that they need it."

Because Heckethorn teaches some kids who are far above grade level and others who are far below, adapting lessons for individual abilities is challenging. "I received a lot of guidance about how to teach to multiple intelligences," he says. "Some kids remember and comprehend better if they read silently, some if they are read to out loud. Some hear words better when they are part of a song." That last notion led Heckethorn and his class to create a rap version of an SAT study guide. (For perhaps the first time in hip-hop history, boys in the South Bronx sang rap lyrics that made liberal use of the words *celerity, panache,* and *calamity.*) He also draws from his own experience as a boy: "I try to remember what it was like when I was younger—when I got bored. When having to do one more example would push me over the edge. And what kept me from getting antsy." Heckethorn keeps the boys active by switching chalkboards, using an overhead projector, asking kids to do their work on the chalkboard, and, from time to time, calling on kids to lead the class.

It's not clear whether the courts will continue to back the use of taxpayer dollars to support a single-sex school. The American Civil Liberties Union is preparing a lawsuit over the new single-gender public school programs. And it's not clear to what degree the boys themselves are profiting. Still, school districts have been encouraged by the success of all-male public schools like Eagle, and all-male public academies have opened or are slated to open in Florida, Georgia, Louisiana, Pennsylvania, Texas, and Illinois.

Even proponents of single-sex education have begun to wonder if boys' schools, especially in inner cities, might become victims of their own success. Bradley Adams, of the International Boys' Schools Coalition, says that his organization has been flooded with inquiries about how best to set up all-boys schools. Adams's response is circumspect: "We tell them that there is no magic curriculum. You build a faculty and they build a curriculum and then you build a school." Leonard Sax cautions that single-sex public schooling may not turn out to be the easy fix that people want: "In the past five years, there has been an extraordinary surge of interest in single-sex public education," writes Sax. "Unfortunately, this exuberance has led some schools to plunge into experimentation with this format without grounding in the complexities of gender difference in how girls and boys learn."

Boy-Centered Instruction

WHAT do all-boys schools have to teach us? Is it possible to transplant what they do well—teach boys—into a coed institution? That may be easier than we think. Research suggests that what works with boys is less about biology and more about thoughtful pedagogy and common sense.

In Britain, where the debate about boys began about a decade ago, the government has launched several initiatives aimed at underachieving males—including, in the mid-1990s, opening single-sex schools and single-sex classes in coed schools. In 2006, Michael Robert Younger and Molly Warrington, two professors from the University of Cambridge who originated some of the best early research about boys and girls in the United Kingdom, took a hard look at the most successful single-sex schools to tease out what the good ones were doing right. In general, they found the single-sex schools that did the best with boys had a strong mission and clearly articulated purpose. School administrators supported the single-gender idea and promoted it vigorously. Teachers were trained, evaluated, and encouraged to take advantage of opportunities for ongoing development. What specifically did they do to get the best from their boys? Younger and Warrington reprinted a list of goals from the Sovereign School, a top all-boys school about sixty miles west of London. Teachers there were instructed to provide the following:

- classes with a coherent structure that is clearly explained
- vibrant and fast teacher-pupil interaction
- high levels of teacher input
- constant reinforcement of high expectations
- well-established baseline rules with known and enforced sanctions when the rules are broken
- short-term targets, public praise, the use of humor, informality, and topics that the students could relate to
- an environment in which sexist comments and stereotypical behavior are challenged and not condoned

The researchers found that many teachers started off focusing on what they thought would be the best way to teach boys. And, yes, they found that they needed to pay more attention to classroom management.

They needed greater tolerance for noise and disruption. They needed to quickly put the kibosh on boorish behavior. In classroom discussions, the teachers found it helpful to refer to sports, technology, and music. But over time, the classroom techniques that they used to get boys to achieve turned out to look more familiar—yet be more elusive—than anyone could have anticipated. Good teaching for boys turned out to look a lot like good teaching.

Are you considering a single-sex education for your son? Let's recap what we know. Wealthy families have long exercised the option of sending their kids to separate boys' and girls' academies, and lots of those schools are feeder schools for some of the best colleges and universities in the country. But it's not entirely clear that single-sex education is a key component of their success. Boys from very wealthy families have the early enrichment, means, support, and scaffolding to do well no matter what kind of school they go to. Objective research on single-sex education that controls for the wealth advantage is not conclusive. What we know is that all-boys and all-girls schools seem to provide academic benefits for girls and poor African American boys.

Should you rush to enroll your son in a single-sex public school if one opens in your neighborhood? I'd proceed with caution. Separating kids by gender goes a long way toward creating a certain kind of school culture that, in the best of circumstances, can help bring out the best in boys. But it's not a silver bullet. Single-sex education is not a pedagogy unto itself. To be successful, public schools for boys—like all schools— have to attract good students and good teachers. Those teachers must be given the right kinds of training, materials, and ongoing support. The schools must be well funded, well organized, and well run. If you enroll your son in a hastily-put-together, poorly run boys' school, you're going to trade one set of problems for another.

CHAPTER 15

NOTES FROM THE FRONT

Project Earthquake

Ossining High School sits on the eastern bank of the majestic Hudson River. Standing in the school tower, you can see the mossy green hills that cradle the U.S. Military Academy at West Point, home of some of the finest and most disciplined minds in the country. From the same tower you can also see the thick stone walls of Sing Sing, the notorious and storied maximum security prison that houses murderers, rapists, and other violent criminals. Over the years, there have been alumni from OHS at both institutions.

As you might imagine, Ossining High School is not a lily-white suburban school. The kids who attend it are 50 percent white and Asian, 20 percent black, and 30 percent Latino. Their socioeconomic backgrounds are far from homogenous. Kids with dual-income professional parents sit next to kids who are being raised by their grandmothers on public assistance. The school has the kind of gender imbalance found almost everywhere—boys get more C's and D's than girls and take fewer AP courses.

Not long ago, the principal, Joshua Mandel, realized that African American boys were doing worst of all. So he consulted with Martin

McDonald, who is African American, an OHS graduate, and currently the cable television station manager for the school.

"I wanted some ideas of how to get black boys more engaged in school," says Mandel. "McDonald discussed the problem with several other African American male staff members. Then the men said, 'Let us talk to them.'"

What transpired was a session of tough love that may have changed the school community forever. The boys, McDonald and the two other administrators decided, needed to be held accountable. So they created slides showing the grades and test scores of all the students, of the boys, and of the African American boys. Then in November 2005, they called a mandatory assembly in the spacious auditorium for every African American male in the school. After closing the swinging wood doors on the curious white and Latino boys and girls lingering in the hallway, McDonald, a lanky man with an easy smile, drew in a big breath, motioned for the house lights be to turned off, and snapped on the overhead projector.

"We let them have it," he says. "We showed them the sad facts." The three men quickly ran the kids through the data they had collected, pointing to the red line that ran along the bottom of the graph. "We said to them, 'This is who you are! This is what you do here! And as adult black men we want to tell you young black men that these grades are unacceptable!'"

That day, a small African American boys' empowerment movement, which McDonald dubbed "Project Earthquake," was born. Every week since then, McDonald, who operates on a tiny $2,500 budget, holds a meeting with twenty-five or so young black OHS boys. In the early winter of 2006, I returned to my old alma mater to sit in on one of the meetings. McDonald faced the class and began a process of questioning, lecturing, taunting, motivating, praising, and badgering. One goal is to get the boys to publicly acknowledge what most adults know: African American boys are lagging badly behind white kids and African

American girls in school. Another goal is to get them to figure out what to do about it.

"What kind of house are you going to live in?" McDonald asks the twenty or so boys who attend the after-school session.

"A nice house," replies one. There's some talk of neighborhoods and three- and four-car garages.

"Are you going to live in it by yourself?"

Some of the boys nod yes, but the others shake their heads. "Nah, I'm gonna have a girlfriend," says one.

"A wife," volunteers another.

"What's she going to be like? Is she going to be well spoken? Well dressed?"

The boys all nod.

"Is she going to be educated and have a good job?" McDonald persists. Now all the boys are nodding, ready to sign on to this rosy view of the future.

McDonald's voice thunders: "Well, how are you going to attract and hold on to a well-spoken, well-dressed, educated woman if you yourself are not well spoken and well dressed and you don't even make it through high school? What you are is what you will attract!"

Some of the boys look shocked at this brutal formulation of cause and effect. Others are amused, some baffled. But all of them are riveted.

McDonald doesn't sugarcoat the message: "Who does better in this school, boys or girls?"

"GIRLS!" the boys shout back.

"Who does better, white girls or African American girls?"

"Depends on the girl," some say. But others point out that white girls do better on the whole.

"Who does better—African American boys or girls?"

There is an uncomfortable silence. Then someone says, "Girls!" and the boys nod.

"What do you think their average is in school?" asks McDonald.

"B, B minus," the boys call out.

"How many of you have B-minus averages?"

About half the boys raise their hands. McDonald counts the hands; then his eyebrows shoot up. "Nine of you are lying! You. You. You. I've seen your report cards. Put your hands down!" He points to the high achievers. "You. You and you. You are the ones who are best representing our community. You are the ones whom the rest aspire to be."

It's astonishing, but the poorer-performing boys actually smile and congratulate the higher-performing boys, who are beaming.

"And we respect you because we know that you will be helping your brothers in any way you can to get to where you are today!" He goes on. "I have a daughter in college. She is going to get a degree. She is going to be dating. She'll be dating a college man. Her chances of dating a black man are shrinking because not as many black men as white men are going to college."

McDonald backs up his megadoses of reality with some uplifting messages. He encourages his boys to practice self-discipline, to be responsible, and to own up to their failures. That, he tells them, is the essence of being a man. On the side, he does some informal counseling, speaking with parents, intervening with a teacher, championing his boys every time they study for a test, complete a project, or boost their grades. "Men can't live without success," he's fond of reminding Earthquake boys. "But you have to see the small successes that lead up to the big ones." He also dogs his boys to dress correctly, address adults respectfully, and treat each other with respect.

McDonald invites speakers—mostly successful African American men from the business community—to attend Earthquake meetings and tell the boys how they themselves made the leap from high school to the world beyond. McDonald never wavers in his main message: You must go to college. To that end, he arranged for the Earthquake boys to go on a trip to historically black colleges. Last year, he took them to Harvard to visit a former Earthquaker who's enrolled as a freshman there. Who goes on the college trips? Every African American boy McDonald can get to sign on. "Even the freshmen," he says, with energy. "Because they need to see it. They need to know that if they put in the effort, this is where they will end up. Not on the unemployment line. Not working in construction. But on a beautiful campus."

Are the Earthquakers doing better in school since the program started? In these days of quantifiable pedagogy, McDonald wishes he had rising red lines on a graph to prove that what he's doing is succeeding, but he doesn't. In the 2005–2006 school year, a substantial portion of Earthquakers saw their school performance, as measured by their GPAs, improve. but some GPAs dropped back again. "And I'm talking to them about that," says McDonald. Nevertheless, there are signs that the culture he is creating among his group is having an impact. Attendance and, more important, engagement in school are on the rise.

Fortunately, everyone involved knows that turning the life of a young man around is not going to be easy. And everyone knows that what McDonald is doing is as important as any statewide test. McDonald is standing against a tsunami of popular culture that glamorizes the thug life for black male adolescents. By the time boys get to Ossining High School, many are far behind grade level in math or reading or sometimes both. But there are signs that small positive steps are being taken to help the younger boys. The middle school has started its own Project Earthquake–type program. Not long ago, elementary schools in the district began assigning mentors to African American boys. Civil liberties groups protested that black boys were being "profiled" as poor students. McDonald isn't going to argue. Small successes lead to bigger ones. McDonald knows he's reaching the Earthquakers. And for him, doing that has become something of a calling.

CHAPTER 16

SMART BOYS WHO GET BAD GRADES

Are Schools Biased Against Boys?

In 2006, high school senior Doug Anglin, who attended public school in Milton, an affluent community outside Boston, filed a federal civil rights complaint with the U.S. Department of Education. Milton High School, he charged, was biased against boys. Anglin pointed to the gender breakdown of the honor roll, where girls outnumbered boys by almost two to one. He pointed to Advanced Placement classes that were almost 60 percent female. Girls, he charged, were outperforming boys because the school system favors them. Exactly how are females given the advantage? His lawsuit laid it out. Girls faced fewer restrictions—for example, being able to wander the halls without a pass. Grading on homework sometimes included points for decorating a notebook, which also favored girls. School administrators, he said, needed to get teachers to change their attitudes toward male students, look past boys' poor work habits and rule breaking, and find ways to encourage boys academically.

As soon as word of the lawsuit became public, the outcry was intense. Anglin, a white, middle-class soccer and baseball player with a 2.88 grade point average, found himself in a firestorm. There is no such thing as bias against boys in school, his critics claimed. "The reason girls do better at Milton High School than boys is that girls work harder," sneered one community member in a letter to the *Boston Globe.*

Anglin tried to defend himself. "I'm not here to try to lower the rights of women or interfere with the rights of minorities," he told the *Globe.* "We just want to fix this one problem that we think is a big deal."

Although he garnered plenty of scorn from people who read about his lawsuit, it turned out that many of his male and female classmates, the ones who walked the halls and studied for tests with him, agreed with his complaint. From their perspective, the school did favor girls.

Is Anglin right? Are middle and high schools biased against boys? It's a provocative question and a counterintuitive one. So much of the world has, for so long, been biased against women. Yet, looking at the national data and at the academic experiences of boys and girls, you may conclude the answer is yes. As I've mentioned, we know that boys and girls score about the same on intelligence tests, but by the time your son gets to middle school and then high school, you need only count the number of boys on the high honor roll, see who's inducted into the National Honors Society, or compare the number of boys and girls in Advanced Placement classes to see who's thriving in school. If you look at a list of the lowest-performing students, you will find boys invariably overrepresented in the lowest quartile. Check it out at your own school. The results, you will find, are sobering.

Something is depressing the achievement of boys in middle and high school—and is doing so dramatically. Is it purposeful bias? I doubt it. There is evidence, though, that for a lot of reasons middle and high schools have created programs that may inadvertently put boys at a disadvantage. Let's take a closer look.

Stay Organized

FOR twenty years, Susan Mulcaire was a hard-working lawyer for the FDIC; then she switched professions and became a teacher in California. She quickly discovered that to thrive in a middle school today you have to possess the same level of organizational ability as the average corporate attorney.

"It's crazy," she says. "Eleven-year-olds go from having a single nurturing teacher to having six teachers with different personalities and different expectations. Then there's the paperwork. Every teacher gives handouts, requires you to bring certain textbooks or workbooks to class. Each one assigns homework, and each assignment has a deadline." Then there's the sheer breadth of content: "Part of it has to do with our attention to test scores. There's just more material to go over. It has to do with the competitive college admission scene, too. Parents and teachers worry more about whether their kids are getting it."

Mulcaire is not sure when eleven-year-olds entered the rat race. "I never had a day planner in sixth grade, that's for sure," she says with a little laugh. "But I can tell you, the load and the pace of middle school have really changed."

All kids are affected by the growing demands, but boys suffer more than girls. In a 2002 study conducted by New York University's Child Study Center, Dr. Richard Gallagher, head of the Parenting Institute, identified nine hundred children who attended third through eighth grade in the metropolitan area. His researchers asked the kids' teachers to answer a forty-question survey rating each child's organizational skills. Boys, teachers reported, were less organized than girls at all grades. "The difference between boys and girls is significant," says Gallagher.

Mulcaire sees it, too. For the last two years, she's been teaching a popular after-school class in the Newport Beach and Irvine schools aimed at helping disorganized kids get organized. Parents pay $110 for a six-week class in hopes that their kids will absorb a few strategies for staying on top of the information flow. The gender ratio in Mulcaire's classes is three boys to every girl.

Most middle and high school administrators are aware of the information overload and try to embed some basic study skills lessons in their curricula. At the same time, they remain completely oblivious to the natural learning curve that many kids and most boys experience when it comes to organization. Recall from Chapter 12 that neurologists believe that boys' brains develop more slowly than girls' brains. In the brains of many boys and some girls, the neurological connections that make possible the millions of tiny judgments that help a person stay organized—by remembering to bring a sharpened pencil to school, finish a homework assignment on time, or save a handout—may still have a few bugs in them. Schools, however, don't separate out a show of solid organizational skills from actual learning. And they are quick to mete out poor grades in response to poor organization—hurting boys' chances for interesting electives, accelerated course work, and, later, admission to a good college.

Mulcaire tries to impress her boys with this message. "I tell them a D is a D is a D, whether you got it because you didn't understand the material or because you handed the assignment in late. Nobody—parents, teachers, or college admission people—is going to make a distinction."

So poor organization—which may be rooted in neurological maturity—becomes synonymous with underachievement. "Then, in boys this age, underachievement starts to harden into a personality trait," says Mulcaire. "You begin to think of yourself as a loser or an underachiever or not smart."

She pauses. "It's not that any school or teacher would set up boys to fail but under the current systems, boys are more prone to fail."

Write Neatly

BETH Rosenstein, the mother of a teenage boy and girl, saw how much the emphasis on fine motor skills can hurt boys. Not long ago, her son, then a ninth-grader at a public high school in Marin County, California, was required to take a semester of world geography.

"They had five assignments during that semester—to draw a map of the world freehand. No tracing was allowed," says Rosenstein. "They had to label the countries and capitals and color it in. Accuracy counted. So did neatness."

A few of the girls were able to draw a map freehand, but none of the boys in the class could do it. "This happened five times. A friend of mine was so fed up by the last assignment that she colored her son's map for him. That's the only one he got on A on." Rosenstein shakes her head as she recounts the story. "The assignments were so blatantly skewed toward the artistic skills of girls . . . my son got a B in this class that brought down his GPA for college applications. Sadly, when he looks back on that class, he says he wishes they had discussed politics and culture during that class instead."

Many boys, who tend to have poor grapho-motor skills compared to girls', are not going to be able to successfully draw maps freehand. Clearly expressing ideas is important. But when it comes to gluing, drawing, and handwriting, how much should neatness count?

Collaborate, Don't Compete

IN THE last couple of decades, competition has become something of a dirty word in the classroom. Competition alienates some kids, critics of competition say, and it highlights distinctions between kids who get things right and kids who don't. These days, teachers are often instructed very specifically to replace competition between students with collaboration among students.

"Collaboration, rather than individual competition, is a social norm for many groups including African Americans, Native Americans and females," writes educational researcher David Sadker in *Teachers, Schools, and Society,* managing to pull off a prodigious feat of both gender and ethnic stereotyping in a single sentence. He continues: "When cooperation is less valued . . . inequities emerge."

Whatever your own position is about African Americans' propensity for collaboration, research shows that collaboration can *limit* the engagement of boys. When boys and girls work together on a project, boys tend to take a passive role. During a laboratory experiment, boys might fiddle with the equipment, but they are likely to let girls draw the conclusions and write up the report.

That is not to say that teachers should avoid collaborative approaches. Not every class is tailor-made for every student. But instead of faulting the boys when collaboration doesn't work out—assuming that boys are lazy and deserve lower grades than girls—teachers might acknowledge that even though collaboration avoids distinctions between kids who are getting it right and kids who are not, it might highlight a distinction of another kind: between kids who are engaged (females) and kids who are tuned out (males). Collaboration might be disadvantageous for some boys.

Writing About Your Feelings

ENGLISH teachers started it. In the late 1960s and 1970s, English teachers saw themselves in a struggle for relevancy. The country was on the cusp of a new era, and schools were reexamining their goals. Assimilation, so important earlier in the twentieth century, when immigration rates were high, seemed less important. Public consciousness was shifting, too. The media seemed transfixed with the population bulge known as the "baby boom." Cultural mores were loosening. The study of the writings of dead white men was starting to seem increasingly out of step with the times.

In 1966, the National Council of Teachers of English, and NCTE's British counterpart, the National Association for the Teaching of English, began meeting in a series of conferences, first on the leafy campus at Dartmouth College and later in York, England. Intoxicated by the headiness of the times, the teachers of English decided to throw off their tweedy blazers once and for all. The goal of English instruction would no longer be acquiring skills or amassing knowledge of the Western cultural heritage but instead would be personal growth. English instruction, declared the teachers, should be about self-discovery.

"Response to literary experience of many kinds, not only the study of the best that is known and is thought in the world, is again a major concern in planning the literary education," reads the foreword to *Growth Through English*, which functioned as a manifesto for English teachers and later for teachers in the humanities. In practical terms, this meant that English classes became less about reading and understanding the classics and more about creative dramatics, informal classroom talk, journal writing, and creative experiences involving drawing, art, film, and music. *Growth Through English* also opened the door for books from other cultures—and for literary works with less well-established reputations that had something to say about the female or ethnic experience—to become a legitimate part of the English curriculum.

Your reaction to the personal growth model in the humanities probably depends on your political orientation. Putting politics aside, though, let's take a look at the new English curriculum in a different way. Is it working? For some students, the answer is yes. We know that some kids—boys and girls—learn best through visual representations, want to discuss their feelings about certain novels, and are much better off for having drawn maps instead of having a geopolitical discussion. But a look at standardized test scores and GPAs indicates that for plenty of kids—many of them boys—this approach has been an abysmal failure.

Rewarding Risk

So what can we do? Some schools have begun to take a hard look at how teachers evaluate students, with an eye toward improving the GPAs of boys and helping teachers realign their use of assessments with the real goals of education. In 1997, when the (mostly male) attrition rate reached 17 percent at the elite Episcopal High School, an independent boarding school in Alexandria, Virginia, administrators began to investigate to find out what was going wrong with their boys. Back then, girls dominated the honor roll, and the academic prizewinners were a sorority.

"We found that boys have less academic maturation. Planning, steady work habits, organizing their desk or room, keeping an assignment book," says Episcopal headmaster F. Robertson Hershey, "those were the accoutrements of learning, and girls seem to get them earlier." But what looked like success for girls, Hershey noticed, didn't necessarily add up to solid learning. Yes, girls were neater and more organized. They were able to hand in homework and hand it in on time. But weren't Episcopal teachers simply rewarding compliance at the expense of creativity and risk taking?

Jackie Maher, Episcopal's assistant head for academics, challenged her teachers to expand their criteria for success in the classroom: "We opened up a conversation. How do you judge students? Whether their notes are in four colors or whether they are engaged and passionate about the material? Yes, they still need to do their history homework, but are they thinking like a historian or are they regurgitating the textbook? We needed to expand our criteria for successful learning."

The discussion, coupled with a few other innovative programs, had a huge effect on the school. The attrition rate at Episcopal has dropped to 4 percent. Girls still dominate the high honors, but there are a few more boys on the list. Boys now win some of the academic prizes, too.

There are good ways to ensure that both boys and girls thrive in school. But prizing organization, handwriting, collaboration, and rule following over intellectual growth is not going to help, in the end, either gender. If your son is getting hung up on one of these issues, know that you are not alone. Other parents may not be expressing their dismay, but there are other boys who are struggling as well. Begin networking with other parents of boys, and see how widespread some of these problems are. Remember the lessons that principals are taught early and often: One complaining parent is a fruitcake; three parents are a fruitcake with friends; seven parents are a force to be reckoned with.

Parents: Be prepared to work with teachers to develop flexibility around issues that historically hang boys up. These days, most teachers recognize that there are many kinds of intelligence and many ways to learn. Be prepared to discuss how your son works best and how his teacher might vary or adapt assignments to suit him and other boys.

Principals: Talk to your teachers. Begin a discussion in your school about how to turn classrooms into places where all kids can learn.

CHAPTER 17

BOYS ALONE

How We Devalue What Boys Need

If you've spent any time with an adolescent girl, you easily figured out that relationships are an important part of her life. Why? Because she talks about them. Girls are happy to tell you about their friends, their former friends, the boys they have a crush on, their favorite teachers. They talk about their values, their friends' values. They form alliances around shared tastes in music and fashion, attitudes toward boys, and their dreams for the future. Talking about relationships is a way to spawn new relationships. Although the cell phone bill can be high, most parents of adolescent girls conclude that it's a small price to pay. A rich variety of connections, they've been told, are central to girls' self-image, happiness, and mental health. As a society, we champion friendships between women—from the wide-eyed virgins in *Sisterhood of the Traveling Pants* right up to the bawdy cosmopolitan-swilling babes in *Sex and the City*. We admire girls who know how to knit together networks of friends. And for good reason: Psychologists tell us—and popular media confirm—that girls insulate themselves from the ups and downs of adolescence with a protective web of strong, interlocking social connections.

Not so for boys. Cultural stereotypes dictate that adolescent boys couldn't care less about relationships. When a group of boys get together, parents don't validate their connection but instead assume that the boys might be up to no good. Individually, boys echo the culture's ambivalence about seeing boys together. Boys who get close to each other, physically or emotionally, seem compelled to clarify that they are "not gay"—as if a relationship with another boy, for its own sake, is somehow suspect. As a society, we encourage boys in a million different ways to be physically tough, independent, self-sufficient, and stoic.

Good studies suggest that we may have it wrong—that the ways in which we isolate boys undermine their ability to become resilient students and productive men. Researchers who look at the emotional lives of boys suggest that young males are every bit as wired for relationships—with each other and especially with adults—as their female counterparts. Researcher Judy Chu, who teaches a class on boys' psychosocial development at Stanford University in California, spent a year studying the relationships of adolescent boys who attended a school outside Boston. What she found flies in the face of a large body of literature on boys that suggests they aren't hardwired for relationships. What she found, says Chu, is that "boys are profoundly affected by and oriented to relationships with peers and other adults."

So why doesn't the Marlboro Man have a cell phone in his holster? How did we miss this so completely? It turns out that when it comes to relationships, the difference between boys and girls is not that boys need relationships less but that boys tend to talk about them less. "They say they aren't going to spill their guts to just anyone. They learn to be selective about what they reveal about themselves or be what researchers call self-disclosing," says Chu. But rich, deep relationships with peers and adults are vital for boys' well-being. "For boys, having at least one close confiding relationship was the single best predictor of psychological health and well being."

Do schools and communities support this crucial need of adolescent boys? No, they don't. Boys are herded into huge industrial-size middle schools and taught in large, impersonal classes. Rather than supplying them with adults with whom they may forge a connection, we seem committed to reducing, rather than enhancing, the roles of teachers in their lives. Curricula are becoming more standardized. Administrators focus on what has become the scholastic equivalent of the corporate bottom line: test scores. One side effect of these developments is that teachers are increasingly seen not as guides or mentors but as interchangeable parts in the process that transfers information from a textbook to our children. Inexperienced teachers in some schools are given not only curriculum guidelines and preplanned lessons but actual scripts to be read during the class period. This kind of instruction is not good for girls, but for boys, who are already struggling against personal and cultural tides to establish and maintain connection, it can be disastrous.

Boys are isolated at home, too. More and more boys are growing up with no men in their lives. According to the U.S. Census Bureau, about 30 percent of boys don't live with their biological fathers. In many poor African American communities, female heads of households are the norm, not the exception. Boys may grow up without ever spending time living with a man who works a regular job to earn money. In well-off communities in the suburbs—in the families that are often held up as the societal ideal—mothers run the households and manage their kids' increasingly complicated schedules while fathers put in long hours on the job. In the lives of those boys, a father is only a dim presence.

Does it matter? Researchers who study poor boys who grow up without a father find that those boys have higher rates of drug addiction, drop out at higher rates, and are more likely to spend time in jail and to end up on welfare. But are those negative social effects attributable to fatherlessness, to poverty, or to both? It would be unreasonable to suggest that fatherlessness has no impact at all. It's fashionable in some circles to suggest that fatherhood is a social construct left over from an earlier time and that fathers' roles are easily duplicated by smart, capable, economically empowered moms. But it seems to me that those attitudes have more to do with cultural stereotypes of boys than with boys themselves. If 30 percent of our girls were growing up in households without their biological mothers, it would probably be declared a national emergency. Boy psychologist Michael Thompson, who has thought deeply about boys and their dads, says it best: "A boy growing up without a male role model is like an explorer without a map." Boys need to see how men act on the job and at home, how they handle stress, how they balance obligations, how they get along with family members, and, most important of all, how they plan for the future.

"Somehow," says Thompson, "we just assume that boys will be able to figure all these things out on their own, but it's not true. We act like they can handle it. Because we want them to be able to handle it. But many can't."

Isolated in the Community

THE message that girls receive, at least while they are in school, is very loud and very direct. As a community and as a country, we are unequivocal: We want girls to reach their full potential. In the last three decades, the U.S. Department of Education has spent about $100 million running conferences and seminars for teachers, providing PowerPoint presentations in schools, and disseminating textbooks and pamphlets that tell teachers how to stamp out sexual harassment, eliminate overt and subtle forms of sexism, rewrite textbooks, and revamp classes to help girls do well in school. Women lawyers sued for equal opportunities for girls in the classroom and on the playing field. Private foundations and corporate philanthropy have funneled even more money into schools—encouraging girls to work hard, dream big, and go to college. In the early 1990s, the National Science Foundation began to focus on getting more girls into science. Today, parents from every economic background urge their daughters to pursue their dreams and obtain the credentials they'll need to ensure their lifelong economic independence. (Once a woman enters the workplace, the messages we give her about society's expectations are much more cloudy. But that's another book.)

In contrast, the only unified message that we regularly send to boys has nothing to do with doing well in school or achieving economic independence. The main message we deliver to our young men is that they should do well in sports—particularly team sports such as football, basketball, baseball, and lacrosse. Schools that barely have enough money for textbooks build stadiums for their (largely male) teams. Some of the same fathers who never attend a teacher conference boast that they never miss a game. Local newspapers run headlines praising solid play and winning seasons. And boys respond.

Don't get me wrong. I think that sports are important. All children, male and female, should have an opportunity to challenge themselves physically, compete hard, and learn how to function as part of a team. Every child should see his or her name printed in the newspaper, noting his or her participation in a particularly exciting game. Team sports provide participants with a sense of belonging and a valuable opportunity to be mentored by a caring adult. Many coaches are remembered fondly by boys and girls whom they influenced and encouraged. But I believe that school administrators and coaches who demand a robust sports program at the expense of academics may be suffering from a loss of perspective.

Some coaches claim that putting sports front and center is sometimes necessary to keep high-risk adolescent boys enrolled in school. But I believe that this argument is flawed and that their expectations, ambitions, and dreams for the boys on their teams sell those young men short. I recognize that I'm in the minority. But you only need to look at our sports-crazed high schools to realize there is a disconnect somewhere. As a nation, we're spending millions of dollars trying to figure out how to get more kids enrolled in college. At the same time, the Education Commission of the States reports that only seventeen states maintain any kind of athletic eligibility rules tied to academic achievement. Only three states—Arizona, Ohio, and Iowa—have a "one F and you're benched" rule. Surely as a society we want to halt the creation of underachieving male athletes who graduate from high school with bad knees and no future. A premier athletic program uncoupled from stringent requirements for academic achievement is a trap. We shouldn't allow our boys to fall into it.

Zach Heyl, who grew up in an affluent suburb of Pittsburgh, says that all through high school, he never saw a way to win respect as a male and to achieve academically. Not that this bothered him much back then. He was a gifted athlete. He played football and lacrosse, and for a long time he thought the cheering would never stop. Heyl is an earnest, good-looking young man who is eager to describe how his schooling went wrong in hopes that younger athletes, their parents, and maybe their principals can learn something from his experiences.

In high school Heyl was content to skid along at the bottom of his class. Every year, he failed a class or two and ended up in summer school. His parents worried. He's a smart kid, and they couldn't figure out why he was so unengaged in learning. They took him to doctor after doctor who diagnosed him with ADHD and prescribed a medicine cabinet full of attention-enhancing drugs.

"That was nonsense," he says brusquely. "Half the boys on my sports team had the same medications. We used to laugh about it."

When it came to lacrosse, his attention problems miraculously evaporated. On the field, his engagement was absolute.

The message Heyl says he got from his school, his community, and his peers was that life was all about looking good on the playing field.

"Our town just shut down for the games. It was like that show *Friday Night Lights*," he says. "Everyone came out to watch."

It made sense to him that the valedictorian of the senior class was a girl. "School was their domain. That was their area. They were expected to have success in the classroom," he says. "Ours was sports."

Shortly after Heyl collected his high school diploma—finishing nearly last in his class—the cheering stopped. He found that his athletic experiences, though heady, had prepared him for just about nothing. His appalling high school transcript made him ineligible for the kinds of colleges his friends were attending. He enrolled in a community college, but playing on the lacrosse team there was not cool. He longed for the approving roar of the crowd and at the same time began to wonder where he had gone wrong. He began digging around in his memory for other ways in which he might have lived his short life.

"What stuck in my mind was kids from private schools I'd met when we played them in lacrosse. The idea in their schools was that they had to be athletes and scholars. In retrospect, that really made an impression on me. It wasn't required of me so I didn't do it with my own life. But, looking back on it, I began to think that would have been better."

Heyl is one of the lucky ones. After he spent a few years struggling in community college, trying to learn the material he'd missed in high school and to develop some study skills, he eventually found his way to Hofstra University in Hempstead, New York. These days, he's intent on making up for lost time. He still plays lacrosse but says, "Being an athlete, it's not enough." His GPA is now as important as his lacrosse statistics.

Graduation Coaches

WHEN it comes to fielding a winning team, a dedicated coach can help all kinds of boys raise their game. So why not transfer the lessons learned on the football field into the classroom? That's what the state of Georgia has begun to do. In 2006, Sonny Purdue, the Republican governor, carved about $20 million out of the state budget and hired 330 "graduation coaches" to make sure that kids who may be in danger of dropping out go the distance and get a high school diploma. In order to understand the genesis of the idea, you need to know that high school football is very, very big in Georgia. In many communities, Main Street just about closes down during a football game. Players get plenty of attention. Football coaches dog their players to keep them eating well, sleeping enough, working out, and practicing regularly. Coaches step in to minimize any academic, social, or personal difficulties that might detract from a boy's performance on the field. During his reelection campaign in 2006, Purdue took a look at the number of dropouts in Georgia—about 23,000 of 450,000 high-schoolers drop out each year—and decided that kids who are struggling academically would also benefit from that kind of focused attention.

La Grange High School sits on a small hill in rural Troup County, an hour drive south of, and a cultural light year away from, metropolitan Atlanta. Tidy middle-class homes dot the beautiful, red clay countryside, but there are dilapidated houses as well. Unemployment has been high since textile jobs began to move offshore.

"It used to be that you could graduate from high school and get a job in a mill and live a pretty nice life," says Janet Greer, who oversees vocational training in the area. "These days, those jobs just aren't there."

When kids drop out of La Grange, they step from the buffed hallways of the high school into a life of struggle. But that prospect doesn't stop the early exodus. Last year, 30 percent of kids failed to graduate from La Grange in four years. Kelli Farrell, a youngish woman with kind eyes, became the graduation coach at La Grange under the governor's new program to staunch that flow. Instead of top athletes, her team consists of seventy-five at-risk kids—many of them male. For a yearly salary of $40,000, she's social worker, troubleshooter, and nag. But for seventeen-year-old Octavius Grisson, a lean, well-muscled young man, she's been a godsend.

When Farrell met him in September, he was resigned to dropping out of high school. The state required that he take and pass graduation tests to demonstrate proficiency in math and English. Grisson had taken the tests five times and never managed to pass. It wasn't as though he had a lot of time to study. Two years earlier, his girlfriend—then fourteen years old—had given birth. Since then, the hours he wasn't in school were spent caring for his daughter. Money was tight.

"It was crazy," he recalls. "I had to get home, then buy Pampers, then take care of myself."

Feeling frustrated and hopeless, Grisson began hanging out with a tough crowd known in the area for petty crimes and small-time drug trafficking. "They pull you down," Grisson says softly. "They say, hey, let's skip out on school, and then they make fun of you if you don't want to."

One of the first things Kelli Farrell did was meet with Grisson's mother, who works the night shift at the local Wal-Mart. "I could see this was a good kid who needed a break," said Farrell. School, she quickly figured out, was probably the only thing that would keep Grisson out of jail or worse.

Farrell started coaching—prepping Grisson not for the big game but for life. She found him a part-time job cutting lawns. She located a remedial course not far away so he could improve his academic achievement enough to pass the graduation tests. She loaned him $200 to pay for the course (a community member later reimbursed her). Week in and week out, she kept on Grisson. At their regular meetings she hassled him about showing up for school on time, and she asked whether he was getting his homework done on time and was studying. She was constantly nipping at his heels to make sure he turned out to be the best he could be.

"It was kind of annoying," says Grisson with a big grin. Then he adds seriously: "Miss Farrell? She helped me out a lot."

After a few months of hard work, the insurmountable obstacles that separated Grisson from a diploma began to crumble. In the spring of his senior year, a few months before he dons cap and gown, Grisson is making plans to move to Orlando with his girlfriend and daughter after he graduates, and to attend technical college. He's looking for a better life.

"People who stay here get hooked on drugs and have babies and call it a life. Not for me."

Kelli Farrell talks about the difference between girls and boys who struggle to get through high school: "Girls, especially those whose moms are head of household, get the message that men come and go, that they're going to have to take care of themselves and their kids. They're ready for the opportunity to step up. By their last year or two in high school, many boys have already steeled themselves for failure. They've checked out intellectually, mentally, and emotionally."

Getting boys to believe that school achievement can lead to a better life requires an act of faith. "Many of these boys," says Farrell, "don't know what it looks like to be an educated, successful, hardworking man." But since she became a graduation coach, there's been someone at La Grange who can tell them exactly what they need to do to get there.

There are signs that the program is working. Last year, the graduation rate in Georgia rose 1.5 percent—from 70.8 in 2005–2006 to 72.3 in 2006–2007, and statewide the number of dropouts—which includes all high-schoolers—fell to about 21,000 students. Last fall, Georgia state budgeted another $25 million for middle school coaches. And a few other southern states, including Alabama and Florida, are making inquiries about starting graduation coaching programs of their own.

CHAPTER 18

NOTES FROM THE FRONT

Learning to Be a Man

For over two decades, psychologist Michael Reichert, who runs the Center for the Study of Boys' and Girls' Lives, in partnership with the University of Pennsylvania, has been thinking about how a boy learns to be a man. He's worked with boys on street corners, in jails, on the basketball court, and in his office. He knows by heart the mental health statistics, the criminal justice numbers, and the graphs that represent how boys are underachieving in school. But mostly, he's seen firsthand the myriad ways in which boys seem to go wrong. As a consulting psychologist at the private Haverford School outside Philadelphia and as the father of two sons, he's come up with a novel idea. Boys aren't stupid. Boys aren't insensitive. To his eye, boys who are failing to meet the expectations of our society are behaving in the ways we tell them to behave. If we want to change the behavior of boys, Reichert says, we need to change the negative, self-destructive, and contradictory messages we give them: "I can see that in our society, we have deeply held ideas about boys—ideas that are traditional, ideas that are intergenerationally inherited—that are just not working. I thought it was time we acknowledged what they were, the ways in which they hurt our boys, and what we needed to do to change them."

251

In 1992, Reichert convened a conference of the most interesting thinkers on men, gender, and social change. His aim: to come up with a practical but very clear message for boys about what is expected of them. At first, all the conference participants were in agreement: The old one-dimensional masculine stereotypes were hurting young men. Women have changed. Female gender roles have gotten broader. These days, it is acceptable for a woman to raise a houseful of children, become a police officer, get an M.B.A., and run her own company. Boys still grow up wanting to be either Jay Z or G.I. Joe.

Reichert's group got down to business, envisioning a new, broader ideal for boyhood. The facilitator, a veteran of both the peace movement and the civil rights movement, coached participants to come up with what he called "commonly shared values" regarding boys. For hours, ideas were thrown out, then systematically shot down.

"Boys should be psychologically and emotionally healthy," someone suggested. But someone else countered that this shouldn't be a movement for wimps. Maybe emotional detachment and toughness should be part of the boy ideal. Discussion continued. "Boys should be protected from harm and threat," someone suggested. But wasn't a certain amount of bullying part of a normal boyhood? Besides, boys were expected to serve their country in time of war. Wouldn't that contravene the ideal? More discussion. "Boys should be free to determine their futures," someone ventured. But wait a minute, said another. "Don't we need boys and men to serve us? Don't we need to weave males more closely into the fabric of our schools, families, and communities?" "Boys should be moral, kind, and well-behaved." "But aren't rowdiness and pranks an essential part of boyhood?"

Back and forth the discussion went. In the end, although every participant was deeply concerned about the ways in which boys were not measuring up, the group could come up with no consistent set of values, no blueprint, that could be used to build a better boy. When it came to boyhood, these passionate advocates could agree on exactly nothing. In fact, they realized that society's ideas about boyhood were rife with contradiction. What we say we want for boys and what we really want for boys, it seems, are very different.

Another man would have been frustrated, but Reichert began focusing on smaller, more contained communities in which he could bring about some positive change. One community that he knew well was the school community. He set up a program at Haverford, then in 2001 expanded it to include six other schools. The objective was to take a hard look at what schools teach boys about being boys.

These days, Reichert and his colleagues offer schools—mostly private schools—a "boys' audit." It's a weird name, but the assessment is not as touchy-feely as it sounds.

"The idea of the audit," says Reichert, "is that boys base their behavior not on what we say we want them to do but on what we do ourselves as men, the kind of behavior that is modeled for them by authority figures. The kind of behavior that is ratified, and held up for praise, in their community."

The purpose of the audit is to figure out what boys are going through and then put a halt to the destructive experiences and enhance the positive ones.

For $15,000 or so, Reichert and his colleagues spend about six months at a school, talking individually and in small groups to teachers, administrators, and boys themselves. The process is simple but cuts very deep. Recently, administrators at a school knew that they had a common but troublesome problem—boys bullying other boys. Most school administrators express concern about bullying. The administrators at this school had seen the research showing that kids can't learn when they're constantly afraid of their fellow students, and they had done what school administrators typically did: They lectured students. They held meetings with a few culprits. They called mass assemblies in which students heard the predictable antibullying homily. The results? Nothing much.

Reichert's audit allowed the school to try a different approach. Reichert and his colleagues spoke with some boys who indicated why they felt bullied and why they believed that the school itself condoned bullying. The boys said that they learned how to bully from observing their teachers. How so? A popular teacher, thinking he was being jovial and informal, had humiliated a boy in front of his peers. The teacher thought he was engaging in lighthearted banter, but the boys around him heard his words in a different way. The boys saw the teacher as modeling bullying-type behavior. They felt free to emulate him, and they readily did so, bullying the underclassmen. Boys at this school told Reichert that one of their classmates who regularly bullied other kids was highly valued by teachers and administrators because he's a star athlete. Rightly or wrongly, the boys assumed that the teachers and administrators knew the athletic boy was a bully and condoned his behavior.

By talking to the boys, Reichert says, "we looked at the way the school culture ratifies a particular value—in this case being a bully—that they say they are trying to reduce." In the end, Reichert points out, it's up to teachers and administrators in each individual school to come up with a coherent list of attributes that they want to instill in their young men—and then rethink the dynamics of the school so that administrators, teachers, coaches, and upperclassmen consistently model those values.

So far, only a few schools—mostly elite private schools—have gone through the "boys' audit." The ones that have found the exercise an eye-opening experience. The concept is simple: Ask the boys what they are being taught at school about how to think and how to behave as men; then listen when they answer.

CHAPTER 19

COLLEGE

Where the Boys Aren't

When I meet freshman Chris Beck, I wonder if he's the new face of the American male undergraduate. He's a skinny guy with short wispy hair, a splotchy complexion, and a big, easy grin. Like many of the students at Towson University, a suburban campus outside Baltimore, he dresses casually—a worn T-shirt and polyester sweatpants. He doesn't seem to notice how out of place he looks sitting next to his adviser, Associate Provost Deborah Leather, a formidable woman in her fifties, on the third floor of the main administration building. He doesn't seem to realize that it is Leather who got him where he is today. Looking back on his first three months as a college student—he's getting B's and a C—he sounds confident, even cocky: "I knew I'd be OK." The administrators and admissions staff at Towson weren't so sure.

Compared to most Towson freshmen, whose high school GPAs tend to hover around B+, Beck had a poor academic record—a woeful C+ average. Because his SAT scores were on the high side—1240 compared to 1050, the TU average—he was admitted to Towson through the university's Academic Special Admissions Program—or ASAP—a controversial new program that allows less-qualified men to enroll alongside well-qualified women. The aim of ASAP is simple: to enroll men. There are three girls for every two boys on the TU campus, and to ensure the long-term health of the institution, which is part of the Maryland state system, TU administrators need to attract more guys.

College administrators are finely attuned to the desires of the young men and women who are their potential students. And nearly every bit of research on gender balance on campus shows that the overwhelming majority of freshmen—men and women—want to attend a college where there's at least near parity between the sexes. Once enrollment reaches 60 percent female, applications from both sexes begin spiraling downward. If men aren't applying because they aren't qualified, then women, who tend to be more qualified, don't apply because they want to attend a college that has enough guys to go around.

This is putting many college administrators in a tough spot. Those at TU first tried measures less drastic than ASAP to attract guys. When male enrollment cratered in 2003 to 32 percent, they amped up the football team and raised the profile of the science and technology programs. But there still weren't enough men. So in 2004, in a move that is being studied by college and universities across the country, TU started the Academic Special Admissions Program, admitting a group of men whom Leather says she used to call "white male goof-offs"—boys who, at least on paper, aren't as qualified as the female classmates they will sit next to.

It wasn't a decision the school took lightly. College admissions officers understand the crucial role they play in what's been called "America's sorting machine." For the most part, they tend to be thoughtful and deliberate in the way they make their decisions, knowing that for better or worse they are the gatekeepers of opportunity. They know how highly charged their decisions can be. Most of them consider their job well done when they can find young people who've succeeded in the face of discrimination or adversity, persuade them to apply, and then provide them with the resources they need to enroll. But increasingly, college admissions officers are confronting an awkward reality: Because of widespread male underachievement, colleges are forced to press a thumb on the scale when weighing applications from the type of candidates who used to have the most access to higher education: white males.

It's a shocking strategy until you look at it from the colleges' point of view. Every spring, despite their best efforts, most liberal arts colleges find that many more girls than boys apply. It then falls to the admissions officers to examine and compare candidates. How do the girls stack up to the boys?

First off, college admissions folks look for students who have taken college-prep courses in high school. A candidate without a strong course load in high school probably won't be able to handle college-level work. Currently, more girls than boys are on the college-prep track in high school. About the same number of boys and girls take calculus, but girls take more geometry, algebra II, trigonometry, precalculus, biology, honors biology, and chemistry. Second, college admissions officers look at how well applicants did in those classes. And on that score, girls sweep. On the whole, they get better grades than boys and graduate from high school with higher GPAs. Then college admissions officers look at standardized tests. On the SATs, boys do slightly better, but many more girls than boys take the test—a disparity that exists in kids from every family income level below $100,000. Finally, admissions officers look at extracurricular activities—where girls rule.

Public universities can't look at the gender of their applicants. In 2000, a federal court decreed that the application process at those schools is supposed to be gender-blind. Private colleges that are known as big sports schools and schools, such as Rochester Institute of Technology and M.I.T., that have strong technology and engineering programs, attract ample numbers of male candidates. Harvard, Yale, and other marquee schools aren't hard up for guys either. They attract so many qualified candidates—male and female—that the admissions staff could put together a qualified class three and four times over. But the applicant pool of a top school like Brown University, for example, is so overwhelmingly female (11,083 women and 7,233 men applied to be in the class that entered in 2007), and admissions officers are so determined to achieve gender parity (Brown enrolled 1,341 women and 1,190 men) that girls find themselves at a great disadvantage. Admissions officers at slightly less-sought-after schools face the unenviable task of rejecting well-qualified girls because they are girls.

Towson University, a state school, has found a way to make an end run around the law outlawing overt discrimination based on gender. TU long ago established a special admissions track for low-income inner-city students who graduate in the top 10 percent of their high school class. Once the admissions officers have created the freshman class, they admit some of these public school kids—sometimes bending TU's standards a bit to get them in. Poor kids don't have the resources for the SAT-prep classes and at-home tutors that upper-middle-class kids take for granted. So the trustees have given the TU admissions officers their blessing to give these kids a break. Using the same strategy, TU accepts boys whose grades ordinarily would keep them out. After admissions officers admit a freshmen class full of the applicants they want, they offer admission to less-qualified men through the Academic Special Admissions Program. Leather, the assistant provost, says that because ASAP accepts men and women, and because they are accepted on top of the freshman class, the university can argue, at least in court, that no qualified women are denied a place at the expense of less-qualified men.

In the late 1980s, Leather was in the administration of formerly all-woman Marymount University in Arlington, Virginia, when that school began to admit men. She explains how she came up with ASAP. "During admissions season, we look at each candidate on a grid based on grades and test scores. And I kept asking myself, what is it about these students—the ones that have traditionally sounded the warning bell for admissions officers? These are kids who can do the work but don't. What is going on with those boys? How do they sit in class and do next to nothing but be smart enough to absorb what they need to do well on tests? Is there something systemically wrong with elementary and high school that causes so many boys to disengage? Should they be denied a college education—and perhaps an opportunity to contribute to society—because of it?"

So TU, at the advice of Leather, is taking a chance on them. The idea is bold—it flies straight in the face of almost all national research, which suggests that high school grades are a much better predictor of college success than are standardized tests alone. And it may be foolish. Broadly speaking, boys tend to do worse in college than girls. Their grades aren't as good. They spend more time working out and playing video games and less time studying than girls. They drop out more frequently. So it's hard to see what makes these boys appealing. If a boy who doesn't have the perseverance and maturity to turn a C in his junior-year high school English class into a B, how likely is he, eighteen month later, to meet the challenges of higher education? Still, with the student population becoming predominantly female, the school decided to give underperforming males a second—and maybe even a third—look.

Some of Chris Beck's fellow students say they're surprised—and angry—that Beck got the opportunity to enroll at Towson. But the female/male ratio among freshmen is about 61/39, and many of the women say they'd like to see more men on campus. Sharon Leff, a TU junior from New Jersey, says 90 percent of the students in her communications class are women. She worries that a school that is so heavily female won't prepare her for the real world. "How many high-powered careers are going to be all female?" she asks. "I'd like to have some experience working around men." But the program through which Beck gained admission challenges her sense of fairness. "I feel the campus should be diverse, but if I got good grades and applied and got in, and someone—a guy—doesn't try, the question is, why should he be here?"

Beck is the first one to tell you that he's never been much of a student: "My teachers always told me, 'You're a smart kid. You should apply yourself.'" But Beck and school were never a great fit. As a child, he was too active. "I was hyper in class. Moving around a lot? That's me," he says. While he was getting yelled at for fidgeting, his sisters, who mostly got straight A's, seemed to be able to sit at a desk and pay attention in school. Beck liked to read—and did so avidly; but in school, his mind would wander. "I could pay attention," he says. "It just wasn't that interesting. They should make school to be more about what guys like." His parents, a hospital administrator and a teacher, tried everything to help. They put him on a no-sugar diet and made him take mineral supplements. They had him tested for ADHD not once but three times, and each time the neuropsychological work-up indicated that he was a normal, healthy male. His parents tried grounding him and cutting off his Internet access. They hired twice-weekly tutors to help him stay on top of his work.

"I was lazy," he says, grinning again. "It was more fun to do other stuff, social stuff with my group of friends, than to do schoolwork."

As one of sixty-five or so ASAP males (plus a couple of females admitted through the Academic Special Admissions Program in order to keep TU from being sued for gender discrimination), Beck has to maintain at least a 2.0 GPA, carry a full course load, attend a single learn-to-use-the-library seminar, go to study hall twice a week, and participate in two "personal growth" activities such as joining a fraternity, attending a sporting event, or going to a lecture.

Beck says he's trying. Getting up in the morning has never been easy for him, so he covered the shutoff button on his alarm clock with duct tape. "It's a start," he says, with a grin.

Leather says that as she's gotten to know the ASAP boys, she's developed a more sympathetic view of them: "Many of these kids had a bad year, or felt, for whatever reason, that they just didn't need to apply themselves in high school. We learned that these boys were really smart."

Maybe. But in the first year, nearly 20 percent of the ASAP group flunked out or transferred, and still that outcome didn't discourage the university from expanding the program.

Is this a remedy for the mismatch between boys and school? Is papering over young men's lack of preparation and admitting them to good schools a good idea? Ideally, each member of the freshman class will contribute something to the community of learners. What exactly does the ASAP group contribute to the life of the school?

I'm struggling to get comfortable with the existence of the Academic Special Admissions Program, and I'm not the only one. Leather clearly struggles with this herself. "They contribute by being here," she says defensively. Then she checks herself. "These were guys who just needed someone to help them get there. We believe they are going to be important to us and to society. Besides, we're getting a chance to watch them grow."

The Steep Cost of Underachievement

As I researched this chapter, what became clear to me is the end results of the mismatch between boys and school. Looking hard at who goes to college and what it will mean drives home for me that to a large extent both boys and girls will pay the price. As our most promising children stand at the threshold of adulthood, they enroll in colleges and universities. There, the real flesh-and-blood impact of boys' disengagement becomes clear. Most places of higher learning around the country, save

engineering schools, are becoming female-dominated institutions—
and not by a slight margin, either. U.S. census data tells us that there are
more college-age men than college-age women in the United States—
15 million versus 14.2 million. But today, 57.2 percent of undergraduates in college are female, and that disparity is expected to grow. The
U.S. Department of Education estimates that by 2016 the ratio will be 60
to 40. In sheer numbers, the difference between boys and girls in college
is staggering. More men and women attend college in the United States
than ever before, but the number of women attending college is rising
much faster than the number of men. In 2006, female undergraduates
outnumbered male undergraduates by 2.5 million, and that difference
has been growing by about 100,000 every year. The gender gap exists in
graduate school as well: Women now make up 58 percent of students
enrolled in graduate school. They make up 49 percent of students in
medical school, 79 percent of those studying veterinary medicine, and
49 percent of those in law school.

It's hard to overestimate the downstream economic effects of this
difference in educational achievement. College has long been the ticket
into the middle class, but never before has the differential between the
income of high school graduates and college graduates been so stark.
Back in 1979, the income of a person with a bachelor's degree was
roughly 50 percent higher than the income of that person's peers who
had only a high school diploma. By 2004, that income difference had
widened to 96 percent. Within the same period, the percentage of males
in college, as a percentage of the total population of males, has remained stagnant. In the past, young men obtained more education
than their father and were able to move higher up on the social ladder.
In contrast, as Pell Institute scholar Thomas Mortenson points out on
his Postsecondary Education Opportunity website, the present generation of young men is less likely than their fathers to get a college degree,
and women's enrollment will continue to rise.

What these statistics portend is nothing less than a massive shift in American culture. It's happening already. Education boosts earning power. One in three married, working women outearns her husband—up from one in ten in the 1970s. Expect more women to be bringing home the big bucks. Among workers in their twenties, 33 percent of women and only 26 percent of men have college degrees. Since 2005, young women in big cities, which tend to attract an educated population, have been outearning men. In New York, they make 117 percent more than men, in Dallas 120 percent more. Whether that news causes you to celebrate or worry depends on your comfort level with the changing roles of women. But it certainly augers a sea change in the way our children will work, how they marry and mate, and how they raise their children—a change that no one, male or female, seems willing to acknowledge or to prepare for.

Even now, the gap in educational achievement is changing and in some cases undermining the recruitment strategies and admissions processes at colleges and universities all over the country. Carlos Laird, associate director of admissions at Texas State University-San Marcos, says that when he visits high schools he's amazed by the differences he sees between boys and girls: "The boys seem content to move aside and let girls lead. It's as if boys decided at some point that girls can have school and they'll be content to have the football team or their rock-and-roll band."

In high schools in affluent communities where admission to a prestigious college is the brass ring—a reward for four years of diligent work—the fact that it's easier to get into college if you're a young man heightens the stress of young women. But before we begin to examine the broad effects of the achievement gap, let's see exactly which boys are missing from college campuses, how some boys get there, and why.

The Lost Boys

It takes some digging to get to the real picture of the American under-graduate. Independent students—older students who have returned to college after years in the workforce, "nontraditional students" in the parlance of enrollment specialists—are overwhelmingly (around 62 percent) female. For a moment, let's take those admirably ambitious men and women out of the mix and focus instead on traditional college students—young men and young women who graduate from high school, then two months later, bolstered by their parents' hopes, dreams, and considerable savings, take up residence on some leafy green campus. A full 57.2 percent of those undergraduates are female.

Where are the boys? It's worth drilling down into the numbers to see. Poor boys are disproportionately disengaging from the educational process that moves children from secondary school to higher educa-tion. The difference between the number of boys and the number of girls going to college gets bigger the farther you move down the socio-economic ladder. Girls from the poorest white families in America—those who make $32,000 or less—are attending college in greater numbers than ever before. But the percentage of white undergraduates who are male from that cohort of families dipped from 48 percent in 1995 to 44 percent in 2004. What's happening to white, working-class boys? When we allow our schools to broadcast the message that school is not for boys, it is internalized by our young men by the time they reach high school. It also is heard loud and clear by their anxious par-ents. As a result, poor families with limited resources and limited edu-cation tend to back the child who does best in school—invariably a girl.

This trend is a massive reversal. Forty years ago, working-class fam-ilies were more likely to stake their sons' academic careers at the ex-pense of their daughters'. These days, says Thomas DiPrete, chairman of the Sociology Department at Columbia University, parents with limited education and limited resources will not or cannot back the boys enough to offset the advantages girls have in school. To DiPrete, those decisions make sense. "Girls," he points out, "are quicker to mature, they have better social skills, they get in trouble less, they get better grades. They experience less discrimination. These families just don't have the resources—like tutors, for instance—to help boys overcome the academic disadvantage they face."

What is the impact of this shift? We've discussed the growing difference in earning potential for high school graduates versus college graduates, and I won't delve into that again. But the latest demographic figures are unequivocal: The surest way to keep pace with an increasingly globalizing economy is through college. Men without a college education find themselves floundering economically. When they work, they don't make as much. And without a college education they find it harder to stay employed in a rapidly changing work environment.

Uneducated men also find themselves floundering socially. Back in 1985, *Newsweek* ran a much-discussed cover story called "Too Late for Prince Charming." Coming hard on the heels of a skyrocketing divorce rate and a record number of women entering college, the gist of the story was that women pay a marriage penalty for attending college. There was, the writer suggested, a marriage crunch. The article quoted experts from Harvard and Yale who had distilled demographic numbers and figured out that a college-educated woman at age thirty had a 20 percent chance of finding a mate. Women ten years older, the experts told the magazine, had a 2.6 percent chance—a statistic that launched the now notorious line that a college-educated woman over forty "was more likely to be killed by a terrorist" than to find a mate. The story turned out to be dead wrong and was retracted in a cover story in 2006, but the notion of a marriage penalty for college-educated women took root.

Recent census data suggests that we could turn that old *Newsweek* story on its ear. What emerged in the years following the marriage crunch story is a strong link between educational attainment, marriage, and the stability of marriage. These days college-educated people of both genders are more likely to get married and are much more likely to stay married. A college education offers some protection against painful and costly divorce.

There is, however, a strong marriage penalty for men who don't have a four-year college degree. At all levels of education, Americans are marrying less. That's widely known. But what you might not know is that the decline in marriage rates has been greatest among men with less education. According to U.S. Census Bureau estimates, 18 percent of men with less than four years of college have never married, up from 6 percent in 1980. Among men ages 35 to 39 with less than a bachelor's degree, the portion of unmarried men has jumped from 8 to 22 percent. Among men 40 to 45 years old, the number who have never married has jumped from 6 to 18 percent. African American men without a four-year degree are most dramatically affected, but white men without a four-year degree pay a marriage penalty, too.

What's happening to these guys that marks them as undesirable mates? Women, demographers say, look for mates who have backgrounds similar to theirs, and increasingly they prefer to marry a man with a similar level of educational attainment. The more educated women become, the less willing they are to "marry down"—and to get hitched to a man whose lifetime earning potential is inferior to theirs. Indeed, census figures show this topic is not simply something women talk about over a glass of chardonnay in *Waiting to Exhale*. If you want to talk about a marriage penalty, take a look at black males who are single, unemployed, and high school dropouts. Their chances of getting married and staying married may be greater than their chances of getting killed by a terrorist, but not by much.

Men on the Way

WHAT stands in the way of working-class young men getting to college? To find out, I traveled to St. Petersburg College in Clearwater, Florida, which is grappling with its own version of the boys' crisis. In the last twenty-five years, this commuter college on the west coast of the state has gone from having about equal numbers of women and men in the 1980s to that crisis ratio of 60/40. Then the ratio dipped lower. These days, men make up 37 percent of undergraduates at St. Petersburg College, which is girl-heavy even for Florida, where only 43 percent of the students in the entire state university system are male. This year, more than 10,000 more women than men will receive a bachelor's degree in this state.

"This male gender gap," says St. Petersburg College president Carl Kuttler, "isn't getting better, it's getting worse."

On the quiet, well-maintained campus it's remarkably easy to find boys who will tell you exactly what makes it hard for them to enroll, and then stay, in college. The young men I meet speak of their female classmates with respect and more than a touch of awe. But they feel cowed by the increasing feminization of the campus.

"You can see that it's mostly girls," says senior Christian Vargas. "Every class, except maybe programming classes, is dominated by women."

"They know what they want. They're not sitting at home doing the housewife thing," says Nikia Smith, a junior. Many of the women in his classes, he observes, seem to have forged an identity around scholarship in high school—a role that somehow never seemed to fit young men. "When I went to high school, I didn't think about college. I thought about basketball. It helped me but it also distracted me," says Smith. "I played too much. I failed classes. A couple of times, I even had to go to night school to make it up." Instead of taking pride in eventually graduating from high school, he says, "you start to think that college is just not something you can do."

Every boy I speak to talks in various ways about being thwarted by a double standard. Society approves of young females living and working in poverty for a few years while they're going to school. But society expects college-age males to show rudimentary signs of being "good providers." Owning a car, being able to pay for gas, and having enough pocket money to take a girl to dinner and a movie is what separates boys from men. "It's a money thing," says Nicholas Sintes, a sophomore. A twenty-year-old college girl with no money in her pocket is someone who understands delayed gratification and is making sacrifices for a better future. A boy in a similar position is viewed less kindly: He's a loser, plain and simple, even if he's taking his first steps toward a Ph.D.

Considering the rampant gender imbalance at St. Petersburg College, I learn something that mystifies me. Plenty of loans, scholarships, and work-study programs are available to St. Petersburg students. Presently, about 80 percent of the recipients are girls. Why don't boys take advantage of these programs? The boys I ask look queasy. Many of them claim they don't know about the programs, and don't know whom to ask. But there's something behind their reluctance to find out about them, and in conversation, it becomes clear that the boys are backing up against another double standard. In their world, it's OK for girls to get handouts, but these boys are all desperately trying to be men. Real men are self-sufficient and independent. Real men, it seems, don't want to be seen scrounging for money.

St. Petersburg president Kuttler has heard all that. "When you talk to these young men, you realize how lost some of them really are," he says. In order for their horizons to expand, they have to go to college, but many boys can't break free of their own rigid gender stereotypes to take advantage of what is being offered.

So recently, Kuttler carved out a line in the college budget to create and implement a marketing strategy to lure men to St. Petersburg. "We sent out 30,000 e-mails to say that we are looking for men. We aren't talking affirmative action; that's too loaded. We are taking action—to articulate what we want." Men who enroll at St. Peterburg are able to sign up for "Men on the Way," the new little brother of a large and highly successful program called "Women on the Way," which helps girls get to college, stay in college, and make the most of their degrees.

Kuttler hired Rod Davis, a young man from the local business community, to run "Men on the Way." So far, Davis has recruited about 40 young men for the program and has targeted about 160 others. The first thing Davis realized is that boys need information. "A female student," he says, "is concerned with her grades. She knows where she's going. She's asking questions about scholarships, internships, and programs that will help her on her journey. Guys are too cool. They don't ask questions. They don't find out about tuition reimbursements."

So at the regular meetings of "Men on the Way," Davis provides information about work-study programs. He also brings in male speakers from the business community to remind students about why they want to be in college in the first place. Members of the group also see each other around campus, and friendships develop. No one wants to call it a support group—too girlie—but the boys agree that the program provides them with a sense of camaraderie.

"They know that when they hit a brick wall, they're not the only ones hitting it," says Davis. "And it's not so big or so wide that they can't get over it."

A Thumb on the Scale

COLLEGE enrollment ratios also show the way in which the underachievement of boys has become uncoupled from poverty and moved into the middle class. According to the nonpartisan American Council on Education, 50 percent of the families in this country are middle class—neither rich nor poor with an income that ranges between $32,500 and $97,500 per year. Among white families, the percentage of middle-class males going to college dropped from 48 percent in 1995 to 47 percent in 2004. Among middle-class African American boys, the ratios dropped from 48 percent in 1999–2002 to 44 percent in 2002–2004. It's less obvious among the wealthy. When we compare the numbers of male and female undergraduates from families who make $97,500 and above, we find that men still enjoy a tiny advantage: About 51 percent of wealthy students who attend college are male.

But let's drill down again. If we take a hard look at the way in which private colleges are admitting middle-class and wealthy boys, the boys' crisis reverberates all the louder. Middle-class and wealthy boys are not doing better than or even as well as their female counterparts. Rather, private liberal arts colleges and universities around the country are giving them preference over girls when it comes to college admissions.

Public universities are barred by law from considering gender in the application process. But the gender discrepancy in enrollment has grown so great in some states that boys are now being considered an "underserved population." In 2005 in Colorado, where the gender balance in state colleges runs 116,935 female to 94,716 male, the state's Commission on Higher Education told its two- and four-year institutions that they have until 2009 to come up with a plan to encourage the enrollment and retention of young men on campus. "We're trying to get our colleges to step up and see that there is a declining number of males—and that it's a problem," says Dr. Julie Carnahan, chief academic officer of the commission.

Many private liberal arts colleges and universities around the country have quietly begun channeling resources into attracting the population they want to bring to campus: boys. Sometimes the effort is subtle. Hoping to bring more males into the application process, Dickinson College in Carlisle, Pennsylvania, is aggressively marketing itself to men. The colors and images in the school's glossy brochures were changed to make them more male-friendly. A male candidate who shows interest receives a male-friendly mailing that features successful male graduates, and male graduates phone prospective male applicants. Mindful of national data showing that more men than women attend business school and enroll in technology, engineering, and computer science courses, colleges where men are scarce are beefing up those departments. Some community colleges are adding game design as a major and forensic science courses to capitalize on the popularity of the television show *CSI*.

Hampshire College, a highly selective liberal arts college in Amherst, Massachusetts, is casting a wider recruitment net. Like most schools, Hampshire buys a list of prospective applicants each spring from the College Board, which administers the PSAT to college-bound juniors. Hampshire asks the College Board for girls who have a B+ average or higher. For boys, says admissions chief Karen Parker, "we go one step lower—a GPA of B or above. We only have x number of dollars to spend, and we are trying to get more boys in the pipeline."

Some schools, like Towson University, add a football program. In the late 1990s the proportion of men at the University of Mary Hardin-Baylor, a small Christian college in Belton, Texas, was about 28.4 percent. "Alumni/ae and trustees—both male and female—wanted us to be more in sync with the national average," says college president Jerry Bawcom. So in the fall of 1998, Bawcom added a Division III football team. In the first year, male enrollment increased more than 4 percent. "We needed sixty men for the team, but the first year two hundred showed up." Requiring the expenditure of not one dime of financial aid money, Bawcom says, football became one of the school's best recruitment tools. "The football player bring friends, and those students in turn bring girlfriends. It's been very effective." By 2004, the proportion of men on campus had risen to 40 percent.

Other schools seem to be practicing a form of gender weighting. Don't call it affirmative action. Admissions officers say their decisions about whom to accept and whom to reject reflect more than gender. But it's increasingly easier for qualified boys to get admitted to college than for qualified girls.

For instance, it's easier for a man to get into Providence College, in Rhode Island, than for a woman. The school has a famous basketball team whose revenues support nearly all of the college's men's and women's sports program. In order to keep that team going and to meet the Title IV requirement that says that schools must spend money on men's and women's athletics in proportion to the number of men and women enrolled, Providence College's freshman class must be 43 percent male. Unfortunately for girls whose hearts are set on attending Providence College, the applicant pool runs 40/60 men to women. Last year, says admissions chief Christopher Lyon, the school accepted 48 percent of the men who applied and only 39 percent of the women—a 9 percent difference. It's easier for men than for women to get into Brown, Wesleyan, the schools of arts and sciences at Tufts University, and William and Mary College.

For a lot of reasons, however, we don't want to hear about this kind of gender weighting (or should we call it backdoor discrimination against women?). Jennifer Delahunty, admissions director at Kenyon College, in Gambier, Ohio, learned how deep and strong the taboo is. In the spring of 2006, she wrote an op-ed piece for the *New York Times* titled "To All the Girls I've Rejected" in which she tried to wrestle publicly and honestly with the issue of gender weighting. She described her uncomfortable position as the mother of a well-qualified daughter who was applying to colleges, while at the same time being part of a profession that struggles to increase the number of male enrollees. At Kenyon and at other colleges, "the reality is that because young men are rarer, they're more valued applicants." She wrote, "If there was a tie between two equally qualified candidates of different sexes, the male would be more likely to get the admit letter, and the girl would get wait-listed." She explains why she was motivated to tell the truth: "We have told today's young women that the world is their oyster; the problem is, so many of them believed us that the standards for admission to today's most selective colleges are stiffer for women than for men."

Delahunty was prepared for her article to spark some controversy, and she had taken the precaution of showing it to the president of Kenyon and to its board chairman prior to publication. Still, the outcry that arose, she says, "shook us to our timbers." For a while, she feared she might lose her job. But she's not the only admissions director resorting to gender weighting.

The University of Delaware's admissions director, Louis Hirsh, explains exactly how the process works. In an effort to create a gender-diverse class, the admissions office thinks long and hard before rejecting or wait-listing a male applicant. "We, and every other college these days, give a male applicant a second look," Hirsh says. And male candidates who are on what admissions officers call "the bubble"—that is, they are borderline cases—receive "a lot more scrutiny [than female candidates]. We look at test scores, rank, essays, letter of recommendation, even the writing sample on the SAT," says Hirsh. "As much as we're concerned about gender balance, we're still not at the point where we take a demonstrably less-qualified male over a more-qualified female."

That's cold comfort if your daughter was rejected on the first pass while an admissions officer dug through the dossier of a less outwardly accomplished male candidate to find a reason to accept him.

How Schools Really Shortchange Girls

WHILE working on this chapter, I began to see the reasons why all parents—whether they have boys or girls—need to think long and hard about how to address the problems of boys in school. And I began to believe even more strongly that academic feminists who airily dismiss earnest concerns about boys' underachievement as a kind of "moral panic" over girls getting ahead are perhaps willfully ignoring the very real distress it causes among young people of both genders and the parents who love them. The pipeline that carries boys from preschool to college is leaking, and that's bad for boys—all boys—but it's a catastrophe for poor Latino and African American boys. It's also bad for girls, especially bright, ambitious, hardworking ones from well-to-do families.

Jeffrey Durso-Finley, director of college counseling at the prestigious Lawrenceville School, near Princeton, New Jersey, says he tries to break the news about the anti-girl bias in college admissions to Lawrenceville girls and their families gently. In the middle of their junior year, he convenes a meeting at which he talks about the transcript of an anonymous white, high-achieving student from the suburbs, replete with high honors, AP courses, and strong but not stellar SAT scores. Then he describes for members of his audience what would happen to that student if he or she were to apply to, say, University of Richmond.

"If they're male, they'll get accepted," Durso-Finley tells them. "If they're female, they'll be rejected. And they'll also be rejected if they apply to Davidson, Middlebury, or Hamilton—any private liberal arts college where they are one of four thousand females with almost the same profile. There are just too few high-performing boys and too many high-performing girls."

I ask how the parents react.

"They're fine when we're talking about demographics. But when we're talking about their daughters—who have the grades and scores but will end up getting rejected from NYU, rejected from Haverford, and end up at Fairfield, a perfectly good school but certainly not NYU, then the parents start to get upset."

The biased admissions standard is taking a savage toll on the girls themselves. For several years, Mark Schoeffel, the new upper-school head of Shipley School, an independent school outside Philadelphia, and a longtime chair of the English Department at Lawrenceville, has seen disappointment crush some of his girls. In affluent schools that have a preponderance of ambitious, high-performing females, the focus on gaining admission to a highly selective college is intense.

From the very start, says Schoeffel, girls buy into the college application process more than boys do: "From freshman year, even before, a number of girls fall into this habit of meeting expectations. You give them something to do; some boys won't do it but most girls will, maybe begrudgingly, but they'll do it. After a while, they develop this way of being in school—they are constantly putting themselves out there, getting judged. They start to believe in the system. Then their older friends, the ones a grade or two ahead, apply to college. The girls, they see the same thing I see—boys, some of whom seem to have done next to nothing, get into top schools. But some of the more accomplished senior girls, who get good grades and have a wonderful array of activities and powerful interests, they apply to colleges that should be accepting them and then they don't get in. Once their friends get denied, the younger girls start to think, what does this mean for me? And they start to work fiendishly hard to do this thing that we've told them they're supposed to be doing. They get locked into a state of hypercompetitiveness between themselves and other girls. They become terribly vulnerable to self-castigation. They feel worse and worse about themselves. It warps them into a kind of overdrive. This is not one girl—any educators will tell you there is a huge group of strung-out high-achieving girls. The one thing that they are all doing is trying very, very hard. Then, in their senior year, what happens to some of their female friends happens to them. The girls who have worked so hard, who have met so many expectations laid on them from so many places, they don't get into the colleges they deserve to get into. And they take it hard. This happened at my old school, and even now, they come to me, and they have tears in their eyes, and they say, I don't understand. I thought colleges valued effort and doing your best."

Schoeffel pauses, then says: "These girls, they've sacrificed part of themselves. And ultimately, they end up feeling depleted and used."

The Boy Becomes the Man

AT THE end of many of my chapters I pass along tips on how we might improve the experience of boys at the stage of education we've been discussing. But I don't have much to offer you if your son is heading—or not heading—to college.

"In the end," says Kenyon's Delahunty, the absence of boys on campus is "not an admissions story, this is a larger societal story—but a larger societal story that has come to roost in college admission." Instead of counting the number of girls admitted to private liberal arts universities, Delahunty suggests we should ask, "How has K–12 education failed young boys, and why they aren't they seeking higher education?"

She knows that what parents of struggling boys fear is, in fact, coming to pass. Boys who are unenthusiastic about elementary school, who grit their teeth through middle school, and float along under the radar in high school grow up to become lackluster college applicants—students with mediocre grades, no leadership skills, and no strong interests. They are, compared to girls, ill prepared for the challenges of college, and most will be unable to perform college-level work. Having a shaky academic foundation, they not only attend college in fewer numbers but the ones who do enroll will drop out in greater numbers than their female counterparts.

After three years, Towson University decided that lowering the admission bar for boys was bad policy, and the Academic Special Admissions Program was closed down. Many of the ASAP boys turned out not to be college material. Around 30 percent of the 185 ASAP kids accepted over three years either stopped attending school or withdrew in order to attend a community college—compared to about 12 percent of the regularly admitted students. In a move that galled the Towson administration, a couple of the ASAP boys attended TU just long enough to build a decent transcript, then transferred to a more selective university, one where the gender balance was closer to 50/50.

Deborah Leather, who teaches a graduate-level organizational behavior class, says she often tries to engage her predominantly female students in discussions about what the growing education gap will mean to their generation. "We talk about how finally woman are in the place where they always should have been. But where are the men?" At first, there's a lot of laughter and jokes about Mr. Moms and Soccer Dads. Then, she says, her students get serious. "We have to ask ourselves the question—are we ready to see those traditional gender roles flip? And maybe that answer is yes. But then the question becomes, just how are we preparing for it?"

CHAPTER 20

THE FUTURE

Telling the Truth About Boys

In the end, it's impossible to look hard at the trouble with boys—and at the impact of their underachievement—without talking about the very real problems the issue is creating for girls. Academic achievement—and the economic stability it brings—is not a seesaw on which girls go up when boys go down and vice versa. When we talk about how boys are doing, what we are really talking about is the welfare of *all* children. When one group begins to falter—these days, our young men—both boys and girls pay a steep price. So here's a radical idea: For the sake of little Chance Furgerson, Ray Karen, and Kai Farquhar, for problem gamer Aaron Dona, and lacrosse player Zack Heyl, for the boys in Clearwater, Florida, who find it so difficult to stand on the first tread of the escalator that has long been lifting Americans out of poverty, for the sake of smart girls from Shipley and their high-performing sisters in Palo Alto, Shaker Heights, Rye, and Westport, who are being rejected by colleges in favor of boys, I propose that we start telling the truth about boys and school.

I believe our nationally elected leaders should show us the way. As of this writing, the federal government is projecting that $2.4 trillion will be spent waging war in Afghanistan and Iraq. The federal government should carve out a tiny portion of that amount and launch some thoughtful and well-funded research projects on male literacy in order to undercover the social, pedagogical, and maybe biomedical roots of the reading and writing gap. The government needs to hold interdisciplinary symposia to encourage people from different fields— education and social services and medicine, for instance—to begin thinking more broadly about how to address boys' problems. Educational researchers need to find schools that are teaching boys well and to come up with some real-life, well-tested classroom techniques that will work for boys and won't hurt girls—practices that all teachers can learn about and adapt to their own classrooms.

Before we start expending tax dollars on nationwide programs, though, we have to remember to bring some nuance to the discussion. A boy in the public elementary school in affluent Greenwich, Connecticut, may not be reading as well as his female counterpart, but he probably doesn't need the same level of intervention as an African American boy who lives in foster care and attends a crumbling school in inner-city Chicago. It's a matter of degree.

But make no mistake: In some school districts, the challenges that boys are facing are formidable, and the solutions must be well funded and far-reaching. With all the good intentions we can muster and all the resources at our command, we should intervene on behalf of poor white and poor black and poor Hispanic boys. Currently, in some school districts, especially rural and inner-city ones, boys are dropping out of high school at rates that are a national disgrace. Success at school is their only hope for lifting themselves out of a life of poverty, and it is falling through their fingers. We need to stop using the prison system as a catch basin for school failure and instead plow resources into creating new kinds of schools aimed at meeting the specific needs of at-risk young men.

Is change possible? You betcha. Back in the 1970s, girls lagged badly behind boys in academic achievement and educational attainment. Feminists and their supporters lobbied Congress to pass a host of bills authorizing money to be spent on improving their performance. Then they set about retraining teachers to minimize the obstacles standing in the way of women participating in higher education. Since the 1970s, the federal government has spent upwards of $100 million to help girls succeed in school. We need to adopt similar strategies to help boys.

At the very least, the U.S. Department of Education should stop acting as if girls are still an underserved population. Take, for instance, the department's exhaustive and costly report called *Trends in Educational Equity of Girls and Women*. The latest version, published in 2004 at the behest of Congress, compares in minute detail the achievements of girls and boys on multiple measures—from preprimary school through college enrollment and labor force participation. The result is an avalanche of data showing that girls are thriving and boys are lagging. Here's a passage from the executive summary of the report: "Females are now doing as well or better than males on many indicators of achievement and educational attainment, and the large gaps that once existed between males and females have been eliminated in most cases and have been significantly decreased in others." Why, then, is the government giving us a report on the state of girls in education while ignoring the problems of boys?

As I write this, two middle school girls I know are spending part of their summer at an all-girls science camp at the University of North Texas, in Denton. Around the nation, science camps for girls are on the rise—and rightly so. Despite the fact that more girls are taking college-prep science courses in high school, there are still relatively few female scientists and female physicists, and female computer scientists and engineers also are in short supply. Many of these science camps are run by female university professors who are well known in their fields. They serve as both teachers and mentors. Other camps are sponsored by Girl Scouts of the USA, which understands what is at stake when girls turn away from science and math. About 40 percent of the merit badges that 2.7 million Girl Scouts work so diligently to earn are connected to those fields of study. I propose that we establish a similar academic and social infrastructure to help boost boys out of their slump in reading and writing. We need literate and accomplished male university professors who are willing to invest in young men to take the lead—just as their female counterparts in the sciences are investing in young women. We need community groups to persuade them to do so.

Day in and day out, though, it is our schools and our teachers who will ultimately change the future for boys. For the last eighteen months, I've visited scores of schools and talked to almost two hundred teachers across the United States. I can assure you that there is no shortage of creative, energetic, innovative thinking. Teachers know that something is keeping boys from doing their best, and they want to do something about it. For the first time, the problem is something that teachers are willing to discuss.

Tim Shanahan, past-president of the International Reading Association, says he's sensing a thaw: "There are a lot of teachers out there, and a lot of them are women, who are looking at these statistics on boys and are starting to push back. They're saying, 'I feel uncomfortable about this.'" The "thaw" started out of concern among educators and leaders in the African American community about the male literacy deficit among black schoolboys. "Now," Shanahan says, "teachers across the country, from all kinds of communities, are saying, 'We have a problem with that, too'. It's become more respectable to study the problem with literacy and boys and come up with ideas about what to do about this."

Except in rare instances, we probably should not make wholesale changes, such as reorganizing our schools into single-sex institutions, as some schools in the United Kingdom have done. Rather, teachers need to fine-tune their lesson plans to make sure they are imparting material in ways that keep both boys and girls engaged. School administrators from elementary grades straight through high school need to keep the physical needs of all kids, but particularly boys, in mind. Specifically, they need to ensure that our children get ample recess— not just time away from schoolbooks but free time, preferably outdoors, to run around, socialize without restrictions, engage in imaginary play (yes, even tag), play ball, and make plenty of noise. We also need to make sure that more movement is integrated into the school day. An hour of daily physical education would be a good starting place. Classrooms should be set up to provide children with a comfortable place for reading and an opportunity to stretch their legs.

Teachers should be getting explicit, real-time information about the growing gender gap—in the nation, in the state, and in their schools. Until now, most discussion about gender difference in the classroom has focused on girls. That must change. Teachers must pay special attention to their young male students' progress in reading and writing. When it comes down to book choice and to the content of writing exercises, teachers need to stretch the boundaries of what they themselves might find interesting or acceptable. Learning to love reading is a most crucial precondition of student success. Teachers need to help boys as well as girls discover reading's myriad joys. As boys move into middle and high school, teachers need to heed their sometimes-irregular development—especially when it comes to organizational abilities. They need to pay attention to low-performing boys and take care not to write them off. Often, a boy's gruff exterior is masking confusion and fear. Teachers need to see how desperately boys need connection with each other and with adults. Constructive, thoughtful relationships with well-meaning mentors can help them on their path to manhood.

Principals should do their part. They need to identify the teachers who work best with boys—and help them mentor teachers with less success or less experience getting boys engaged and enthusiastic about learning. With good leadership and some training, teachers will begin to be able to tolerate—even celebrate—the natural behavior of boys. In time, the energy, humor, and peculiar sensibilities of boys may be seen as assets to a classroom rather than liabilities.

Many schools, especially ones in affluent areas, have begun this process. Others should follow suit. Teachers know they can do it. They changed the world for girls and provided a springboard for two generations of high-achieving females. They can help boys do better, too.

One more note: Teachers who express hostility toward the natural way in which little boys express themselves—even if it is sometimes noisy, noncompliant, quirky, rambunctious, aggressive, and, yes, a little irritating—should be removed from classrooms (and if possible from the profession). To teach children, you have to love what they are. And teaching little boys is part of the job.

Lessons from Maine

ALL the while, we need to be courteous and inclusive to the small factions of feminists who fear that calling attention to the new gender gap is a backlash against women. Their trepidation is understandable. Many worked tirelessly to win for women the economic and social independence that most of us now take for granted. And in the push and pull of our political climate, many of those freedoms often seem in danger of fading or being taken away. We must work with them to ensure that while we help boys, we protect the interests of girls as well.

Working to address the underachievement of boys is not part of an antifeminist agenda. And we need to stop acting as if it were. For too long, any discussion of the new gender gap has become quickly mired in a reactive and unsophisticated kind of gender politics. We need to change the terms of the debate. The feminist movement widened the horizons for girls, but when the tide of activism receded, it left a lot of young men unmoored. They remain adrift, uncertain of what the adult world expects of them and how they should move from boyhood to manhood. We need to give boys strong, positive, and coherent messages about how to become productive, useful members of society.

We need to resist the temptation to conflate the issues of gender equity in the workplace and gender equity in school. Women still face widespread discrimination in many professions. The goal of equal pay, equal access, and equal power for women at work remains frustratingly elusive. Much still needs to be done to open doors to women so that they can get equal access to top management, corporate board rooms, and Congress. But nine-year-old schoolboys are not the problem. We need to stop reacting to programs that support schoolboys as if they were.

It may be helpful to make comparisons between boys and girls. Comparisons were a routine part of the discussion when people were highlighting the struggles girls faced. But we need to remember that this is not a seesaw. There was no golden age of education for young men. The improved academic outlook for girls has not come at the expense of boys. And improving the lot of boys doesn't mean hurting girls.

The state of Maine got it right. In 2004, the governor commissioned a blue-ribbon panel to study the problems boys in school face in that state. The forty-member group was made up of educators, school administrators, state officials, women's studies researchers, and parents. At first the group was known as the Task Force on Gender Achievement Differences. Members renamed it Gender Equity in Education, and to the dismay of at least some members, the feminist minority insisted that the group consider sexual harassment and other problems that affect girls in school, as well as problems that affect boys. For a while, it looked as though the task force might be hijacked by feminist academics who feared that what was good for boys must necessarily be bad for the girls. But not so. After two years of wrangling, the task force issued a report. It included a look at the struggles girls still face in school but was clear, forthright, and unequivocal about the trouble with boys and schools and our responsibility to address it.

Here's what the report said:

> *Gender equity is often confused with gender equality. Achieving gender equality in schools requires that we provide the same resources and opportunities to all students regardless of their gender. This is a relatively simple task in comparison to creating gender equity in our education system. Gender equity goes beyond the expectations for gender equality. Gender equity ensures that boys and girls are given the necessary supports to achieve the same standards of excellence. Equity acknowledges that boy and girls may need different supports to achieve these outcomes.*

It's an ambitious notion—but one, I believe, whose time has come.

What Parents Can Do

WHAT boys need is a gender revolution of their own. But absent that, we as parents need to acknowledge to our sons, to our kids' teachers, and to each other that this is a tricky time to be a boy. And we need to stop letting our sons negotiate the changing demands of school alone. Stay alert to the warning signs. Watch out for boys who complain they are bored or afraid to go to school. Watch out for teachers who complain that boys are too active, who clamp down on boys' fantasy play, who allow boys to languish in reading and writing, who chastise boys for poor organization or bad handwriting. These are signs that your son may be in a school that doesn't respect him or that even discriminates against him.

Fortunately, those warning signs aren't difficult to spot. When we see them, we need to begin a dialogue with our sons' teachers and their principals, quietly insisting that the schools provide a healthy learning environment.

One of the easiest ways to ensure school culture isn't anti-boy is to bring more men into school, and that may not be as difficult as it sounds. Your PTA may be dominated by women, but there are dads who are eager to play a role. Since 1947, Kensington Hilltop Elementary School, in the West Contra-Costa school district in a middle-class suburb outside San Francisco, has had a Dad's Club—a group of mostly male parents who supply the brawn for any projects that teachers, administrators, or PTA members cook up.

"You don't have to have power tools to join," says Dad's Club president Rodney Dunican, whose son Shane attends the school. "You don't need any experience or need to be particularly good with your hands. Heck, you really don't even need to be a dad. You can be an uncle—or a mom, for that matter."

As an organization, the Dad's Club is short on structure: Dues are $25; planning meetings are laconic affairs where members figure out what projects are the top priority and who will take the lead on the work crew, then break out the beer. Still, the Dad's Club is a visible presence at Kensington. Several times a month, men wearing Dad's Club T-shirts can be found on campus fixing an easel, hanging posters, or setting up for a school event. When the school shifted classes into new rooms, the Dad's Club members were there to act as moving men. Big projects—last year the Dad's Club built an elaborate entrance to the room where the Halloween Movie Night was held—are celebrated with a late-night Dad's Club feast of pork barbecue.

The biggest reward, says Dunican, "is the kids get the sense that it's not just moms who care about school. That school is something both parents care about. That we're the dads, and we're there, in the school, working together, setting a positive example and having a good time."

Not up for hanging posters? There's plenty that men can do at home as well. Schools can teach our sons to read, and even to like reading, but we can teach them to love it. Dads need to encourage their sons to hit the books—whether it be a work by Tolstoy, by Stephen King, or by cartoonists at Marvel. Both parents must encourage sons to be fully engaged in school—and they must express the same level of enthusiasm for a well-done homework assignment as for a winning pitch. We must find new ways to motivate sons to move through secondary school and on to college, so that their education can anchor them more securely in the fabric of family and community life.

At first, you might feel conspicuously alone. But gradually, with a little luck, other parents of boys and girls will join in. We know that education is crucial for our boys and our girls. We need to find ways to help all our children succeed.

NOTES

INTRODUCTION

5 **Boys get expelled from preschool** W. S. Gilliam, *Prekindergarteners Left Behind: Expulsion Rates in State Prekindergarten Systems,* Yale University Child Study Center, 2005.

5 **four times as much as girls** "Identifying and Treating ADHD, 2003," U.S. Dept. of Education, http://www.ed.gov/teachers/needs/speced/adhd/adhd-resource-pt1.pdf

5 **twice as likely to get held back** "Trends in Educational Equity of Girls and Women, 2004," National Center for Education Statistics, U.S. Dept. of Education, http://nces.ed.gov/pubs2005/2005016.pdf

5 **Boys, though, continue to lag** "The Nation's Report Card: Reading 2007," National Center for Education Statistics, U.S. Dept. of Education, http://nces.ed.gov/nationsreportcard/pubs/main2007/2007496.asp#section2

6 **Boys are more likely to report** "Trends in Educational Equity of Girls and Women, 2004."

6 **They commit suicide** "Youth Suicide," U.S. Centers for Disease Control, http://www.cdc.gov/od/oc/media/pressrel/2007/r070906.htm

6 **They take harder classes** "Trends in Educational Equity of Girls and Women, 2004."

6 **More boys than girls drop out** "Drop-out Rates in the United States, 2004," National Center for Education Statistics, U.S. Dept. of Education, http://nces.ed.gov/pubs2007/2007024.pdf

6 **57.2 percent of all undergraduates in the U.S. were female** "Current Population Survey," Census Bureau, Table 10, www.census.gov/population/www/socdemo/school/cps2005.html

6 **that same year, 57.4 percent of all bachelor's degrees** "Digest of Educational Statistics," National Center for Education Statistics, http://165.224.221.98/programs/digest/d06/tables/dt06_257.asp

CHAPTER 2: THE SCOPE OF THE PROBLEM

23 **boys make up the overwhelming majority . . . gross motor disabilities**
D. Halpern, "A Cognitive-Process Taxonomy for Sex Difference in
Cognitive Abilities," *Current Directions in Psychological Science* 13 no. 4
(2004): 135–139.

24 **They are prescribed medicine** Courtesy of Medco Health Solutions, one
of the largest prescription drug benefit managers.

24 **Boys themselves report** "Trends in Educational Equity of Girls and
Women, 2004," National Center for Education Statistics, U.S. Dept. of
Education, http://nces.ed.gov/pubs2005/2005016.pdf

24 **Suicide rates among adolescent boys** R. McKeown, S. Cuffe, and
R. Schultz, "U.S. Suicide Rates by Age Group, 1970–2002: An Examination
of Recent Trends," *American Journal of Public Health* 96, no. 10 (2006):
1744–1751.

24 **Currently, between the ages of 5 and 14** "Suicide Trends Among Youths
and Young Adults Aged 10–24 Years, United States, 1990–2004," U.S.
Centers for Disease Control, Sept. 7, 2007, http://www.cdc.gov/mmwr/
preview/mmwrhtml/mm5635a2.htm

26 **It's no wonder that** J. Greene, and M. Winters, "Leaving Boys Behind:
Public High School Graduation Rates," Manhattan Institute, 2006,
http://www.manhattan-institute.org/html/cr_48.htm

29 **"One is closer to a B and the other is a C."** R. Rossi, "In City Prep Schools,
Girls Rule," *Chicago Sun-Times,* May 3, 2006, http://ccsr.uchicago.edu/
news_citations/050306_suntimes.html

30 **In high school, their grade point averages are lower** "America's High
School Graduates: Results from the 2005 NAEP High School Transcript
Study," National Center for Education Statistics, U.S. Dept. of Education,
2007, http://nces.ed.gov/nationsreportcard/pdf/studies/2007467_4.pdf

30 **In 1980, girls took slightly fewer science courses . . . boys still dominate
in physics** "Trends in Educational Equity of Girls and Women, 2004."

30 **By 2002, 56 percent of exam takers** Ibid.

31 **In 2006, an astonishing 26 of the 31 valedictorians** P. Smolowitz, "Best in
School? In 2006, Girls Rule: Valedictorian Disparity Mirrors National
Trend," *Charlotte Observer,* June 22, 2006.

32 **In the 1970s . . . about 2.5 million more girls than boys enrolled in college**
"Digest of Educational Statistics, 2006," National Center for Education

Statistics, U.S. Dept. of Education, http://nces.ed.gov/programs/digest/
d06/tables/dt06_175.asp?referrer=report

32 **At present, a full 33 percent of women** U.S. Census Bureau, "Educational
attainment in the United States: 2007," www.census.gov/population/
www/socdemo/educ-attn.html

33 **"We . . . should not simply accept with a shrug"** "Government Tackles
Boys' Underachievement," BBC News, Jan. 6, 1998, http://news.bbc.co.uk/
1/low/uk/44754.stm

33 Projections are based on data through 2005 and middle alternative
assumptions concerning the economy. For more information, see NCES
2007-038. See supplemental note 3 for more information on the Integrated
Postsecondary Education Data System (IPEDS). See supplemental note 9
for more information about the classification of postsecondary education
institutions.

CHAPTER 3: THE DOUBTERS

37 **The first court case** www.bernicesandler.com

37 **By 1970, about one hundred other groups and individual women** B. Wade,
"Women on the Campus Find a Weapon," *New York Times,* Jan. 10, 1972.

39 **In 1975, the number of high school seniors** Courtesy of the College
Board.

40 **By 1978, six years after Title IX** "Digest of Educational Statistics, 2006,"
National Center for Education Statistics, U.S. Dept. of Education,
http://nces.ed.gov/programs/digest/d06/tables/dt06_175.asp?
referrer=report

40 **"Most [girls] emerge from adolescence** *How Schools Shortchange
Girls—The AAUW Report: A Study of Major Findings on Girls and
Education:* Marlowe & Co., 1992.

43 **"Part of the boys-crisis alarm is about** K. Gandy, "There Is No Boy
Crisis," *USA Today,* Oct. 13, 2006.

43 **"The hysteria about boys is partly** S. Mead, "The Truth About Boys and
Girls," Education Sector, http://www.educationsector.org/usr_doc/
ESO_BoysAndGirls.pdf

44 **"The alarming statistics** C. Rivers, and R. C. Barnett, "The Myth of the
Boy Crisis," *Washington Post,* April 9, 2006, http://www.washingtonpost
.com/wp-dyn/content/article/2006/04/07/AR2006040702025.html

45 **According to the American Council on Education** J. King, "Gender Equity in Higher Education, 2006," American Council on Education, www.acenet.edu/bookstore/pdf/Gender_Equity_6_23.pdf

47 **According to U.S. Bureau of Labor Statistics projections** U.S. Bureau of Labor Statistics, http://www.bls.gov/ers/home.htm

CHAPTER 4: PRESCHOOL BLUES

57 **The average age of a first-time mom** U.S. Centers for Disease Control, http://www.cdc.gov/nchs/pressroom/02news/ameriwomen.htm

57 **In 1967, the average household** U.S. Bureau of the Census, http://www.census.gov/press-release/www/releases/archives/facts_for_features_special_editions/007276.html

58 **The Myth of Zero to Three** In this section, I relied on two books: John T. Bruer, *The Myth of the First Three Years: A New Understanding of Early Brain Development and Lifelong Learning,* Free Press, 1999; and Kathy Hirsh-Pasek and Roberta Michnick Golinkoff, *Einstein Never Used Flash Cards: How Our Children Really Learn—and Why They Need to Play More and Memorize Less,* Rodale, 2003.

62 **In 1945, Harvard University . . . admitted 2,175** With thanks to the Harvard University press office.

63 **Overall, retail toy sales had been dropping** Doug Desjardins, "Educational Toys Ride Healthy Sales Curve" *DSN Retailing Today,* Oct. 24, 2005.

65 **As toddlers, females learn to speak earlier** S. Lutchmaya, S. Baron-Cohen, and P. Raggat, "Foetal Testosterone and Vocabulary Size in 18 and 24 Month Infants," *Infant Behavior and Development* 24 (2002): 418–424.

65 **In a study conducted in 1991** J. Huttenlocher, W. Haight, A. Bryk, M. Seltzer, and T. Lyon, "Early Vocabulary Growth: Relation to Language Input and Gender," *Developmental Psychology* 27, no. 2 (1991): 236–248.

66 **Subsequent studies, though, including groundbreaking work** B. Hart and T. R. Risley, *Meaningful Differences in the Everyday Experience of Young American Children,* P. H. Brookes, 1995.

66 **Researchers at the U.S. Department of Education** "Trends in Educational Equity of Girls and Women, 2004," National Center for Education Statistics, U.S. Dept. of Education, http://nces.ed.gov/pubs2005/2005016.pdf

67 **Canadian developmental psychologist Warren O. Eaton** Eaton's work is well worth checking out. See "Sex Difference in Human Motor Activity

Level," *Psychological Bulletin* 100, no. 1 (1986): 19–28; "Sex Difference in the Activity Level of Infants," *Infant and Child Development* 8, no. 1 (May 1999): 1–17 and W. Eaton, N. McKeen, and D. Campbell, "Waxing and Waning Movement: Implications for Psychological Development," *Developmental Review* 21 (2001): 205–223.

73 **Gilliam collects national data** W. S. Gilliam, *Prekindergarteners left Behind: Expulsion Rates in State Prekindergarten Systems,* Yale University Child Study Center, 2005.

74 **Researchers have found** C. H. Hart, D. C. Burts, M. Durland, R. Charlesworth, M. Dewolf, and P. O. Fleegon, "Stress Behavior and Activity Type Participation of Preschoolers in More or Less Developmentally Appropriate Classrooms: SES and Sex Differences," *Journal of Research on Child Education* 12 (1998): 176–196.

74 **At ages five and six** Hirsh-Pasek and Golinkoff, *Einstein Never Used Flash Cards.*

75 **Dr. Rebecca Marcon, a developmental psychologist** R. Marcon, "Moving Up the Grades: Relationship Between Preschool Model and Later Success at School," *Early Childhood Research and Practice* 4, no. 1 (Spring 2002): 358–375.

CHAPTER 6: KINDERGARTEN

87 **In the early years of elementary school** "Trends in Educational Equity of Girls and Women, 2004," National Center for Education Statistics, U.S. Dept. of Education, http://nces.ed.gov/pubs2005/2005016.pdf

87 **They make up two-thirds** "Timing and Duration of Student Participation in Special Education in the Primary Grades," National Center for Education Statistics, U.S. Dept. of Education, http://nces.ed.gov/pubs2007/2007043.pdf

87 **In Texas, which has the largest number** J. Russell, "Far More Kindergarten Boys Repeat," *San Antonio Express-News,* Dec. 11, 2006.

88 **Diane Ravitch** *Left Back: A Century of Failed School Reforms,* Simon & Schuster, 2000.

88 **George Leonard** *Education and Ecstasy,* Dell, 1968.

89 *A Nation at Risk* U.S. Dept. of Education, http://www.ed.gov/pubs/NatAtRisk/index.html

90 **Abecedarian Project** For more information, go to http://www.fpg.unc.edu/~abc/

91 **In 2000, the National Reading Panel** For more information on the
National Reading Panel, go to http://www.nationalreadingpanel.org/
Press/press_rel_4_13_00.htm

CHAPTER 7: REQUIEM FOR RECESS

101 **These days, according to the U.S. Department of Education** "Calories
In, Calories Out: Food and Exercise in Public Elementary Schools,"
National Center for Education Statistics, U.S. Dept. of Education, 2005,
http://nces.ed.gov/Pubs2006/nutrition/tables/tab12.asp

103 **Taking test scores seriously** D. Johnson, "Many Schools Putting an End
to Child's Play," *New York Times*, April 7, 1998.

104 **Contact sports** E. Bazar, "Tag! More Schools Ban Games at Recess,"
USA Today, June 27, 2006.

104 **According to District Superintendent Richard Alonzo** J. Cromley, "Tag,
You're Out! Schools Try to Discourage the Game, but It Endures—For a
Good Reason," *Los Angeles Times*, Nov. 6, 2006.

104 **In New Jersey, an eight-year-old boy** J. Turley, "My Boys Like Shootouts.
What's Wrong With That?" *Washington Post*, Feb. 25, 2007.

105 **Anthony Pellegrini** A. Pellegrini and C. Bohn, "The Role of Recess in
Children's Cognitive Performance and School Adjustment," *Educational
Researcher* 34, no. 1 (2005).

CHAPTER 8: PAY ATTENTION

110 **According to the Centers for Disease Control** "Mental Health in the
United States: Prevalence of Diagnosis and Medication Treatment for
Attention-Deficit/Hyperactivity Disorder—United States, 2003,"
U.S. Centers for Disease Control, http://www.cdc.gov/mmwr/preview/
mmwrhtml/mm5434a2.htm

111 **In two southeastern Virginia school districts** G. B. LeFever, K. V. Dawson,
and A. L. Morrow, "The Extent of Drug Therapy for Attention-Deficit/
Hyperactivity Disorder Among Children in Public Schools," *American
Journal of Public Health* 89, no. 9 (1999): 1359–1364.

115 **In 2005, psychologist J. Michael Havey** J. M. Havey, J. Olson,
C. McCormick, and G. Cates, "Teachers' Perception of the Incidence and
Management of Attention Deficit Hyperactivity Disorder," *Applied
Neuropsychology* 12, no. 2 (2005): 120–127.

CHAPTER 10: GOOD-BYE, MR. CHIPS

126 **According to the National Education Association** National Education Association, http://www.nea.org/newsreleases/2004/nr040428.html

131 **In 2006, economist Thomas Dee** Thomas Dee, "The Why Chromosome: How a Teacher's Gender Affects Boys and Girls," *Education Next* 6, no. 4 (Fall 2006): 68–75.

132 **Researcher Laura Sokal** L. Sokal, H. Katz, L. Chaszewski, and C. Wojcik, "Good-bye, Mr. Chips: Male Teacher Shortages and Boys' Reading Achievement," *Sex Roles: A Journal of Research* 56, no. 9–10 (2007): 651–659.

CHAPTER 11: BOYS AND LITERACY

135 **John Locke** *Some Thoughts on Education* (1693).

137 **Right now in this country** *Reading: The Nation's Report Card,* U.S. Dept. of Education, 2002.

137 **It affects boys from every walk of life** Judith Kleinfeld, "Five Powerful Strategies for Connecting Boys to School" (paper for the White House Conference on Helping America's Youth, Indianapolis, June 6, 2006).

142 **In the fall term of kindergarten** "Trends in Education Equity of Girls and Women, 2004," National Center for Education Statistics, U.S. Dept. of Education, http://nces.ed.gov/pubs2005/2005016.pdf

142 **the "Matthew effect"** See Mathew 25:29: "For to everyone who has will more be given and he will have abundance. But from one who has not, even what he has will be taken away." See Keith Stanovich, "Matthew Effect in Reading: Some Consequences of Individual Differences in the Acquisition of Literacy," *Reading Research Quarterly* 21, no. 4 (1986): 360–407.

146 **Synthetic Phonics worked like this** J. Watson and R. Johnston, "A Seven Year Study of the Effects of Synthetic Phonics Teaching on Reading and Spelling Attainment," *Education Research,* 2005, http://www.scotland.gov.uk/Publications/2005/02/20682/52383

148 **But the answer was in the reading scores** P. Curtis, "Report Reveals Sound Method of Learning," *The Guardian,* Feb. 11, 2005, http://education.guardian.co.uk/schools/story/0,,1410888,00.html

149 **Here's the girls' story** Vivian Gussin Paley, *Boys and Girls: Superheroes in the Doll Corner,* Harvard University Press, 1984.

150 **Jon Scieszka** Check out his website: www.guysread.com

150 **In 2001, a Canadian researcher polled boys** L. Sokal, "Answer the
     Question, 'Which Boys?' A New Lens for Viewing Boys' Literacy Scores"
     (poster presented at the biennial meeting of the Society for Research in
     Child Development, Minneapolis, Apr. 19–22, 2001).

151 **English education researcher Elaine Millard** E. Millard, *Differently
     Literate: Boys, Girls and the Schooling of Literacy,* Routledge-Falmer, 1997.

156 **Fletcher crafted the writing program** R. Fletcher, *Boy Writers: Reclaiming
     Their Voices,* Stenhouse, 2006.

CHAPTER 12: THINKING WITH A BOY BRAIN

164 **boys and girls use different parts of their brains to read** A. M. Clements,
     M. O'Donnell, J. Abel, S. Rimrodt, J. J. Pekar, and L. E. Cutting, "Sex
     Differences in Cerebral Laterality of Language and Visuospatial
     Processing," *Brain and Language* 98, no. 2 (Aug. 2006): 150–158.

167 **Family physician and psychologist Leonard Sax** L. Sax, *Why Gender
     Matters: What Parents and Teachers Need to Know About the Emerging
     Science of Sex Differences,* Doubleday, 2005.

169 **All psychologists who have studied** S. J. Gould, *The Mismeasure of Man,*
     Norton, 1981

169 **The parietal lobes at the back** B. Bunch with A. Hellemans (eds.),
     History of Science and Technology, Houghton Mifflin, 2004.

173 **Because girls who get a super dose** S. Berenbaum, "Effects of Early
     Androgens on Sex-Type Activities and Interests in Adolescents with
     Congenital Adrenal Hyperplasia," *Hormones and Behavior* 35 (1999):
     102–110.

173 **the fetal brain, it seems** M. Hines, S. Golombok, J. Rust, K. Johnston,
     and J. Golding, "Testosterone During Pregnancy and Gender Role
     Behavior in Preschool Children: A Longitudinal Population Study,"
     Child Development 73, no. 6 (2002): 1678–1687.

180 **In 2005, two psychologists** I. Dar-Nimrod and S. J. Heine, "Exposure to
     Scientific Theories Affects Women's Math Performance," *Science* 314
     (2006): 435.

CHAPTER 13: (VIDEO) GAMES BOYS PLAY

187 **In a 2006 study, NPD group** "Report from the NPD Group Shows 45
     Percent of Heavy Video Gamers Are in the Six- to 17-Year-Old Age
     Group," Sept. 19, 2006, www.npd.com/press/release/press_060919a.html

187 **Senator Hillary Clinton spoke for many parents** http://www.senate.gov/
~clinton/news/statements/details.cfm?id=240603

188 **In his influential book *On Killing*** D. Grossman, *On Killing: The
Psychological Cost of Learning to Kill in War and Society,* Little,
Brown, 1995.

189 **Video games do indeed have effects** C. Anderson, D. Gentile, and
K. Buckley, *Violent Video Games Effects on Children and Adolescents:
Theory, Research and Public Policy,* Oxford University Press, 2006.

190 **In 1998, a group of researchers in Britain** M. H. Koepp, R. N. Gunn,
A. D. Lawrence, V. J. Cunningham, A. Dagher, T. Jones, et al., "Evidence
for Striatal Dopamine Release During Video Games," *Nature* 393,
no. 6682 (May 21, 1998): 266–268.

CHAPTER 14: SINGLE-SEX SCHOOLING

204 **When the Supreme Court of the United States** "VMI Says Yes to Women
in '97 Admissions," *Virginian-Pilot,* Sept. 22, 1996.

211 **While those complaints were percolating** For a thorough discussion
of the history of single-sex schooling, see Karen Stabiner, *All Girls:
Single-Sex Education and Why It Matters,* Riverhead, 2002.

212 **In 2001, Texas Republican senator**
http://archive.newsmax.com/archives/articles/2002/5/2/155112.shtml

213 **"It's been pretty rough"** M. Woodall, "All-Boys High School Off to a
Rocky Start," *Philadelphia Inquirer,* Feb. 26, 2006.

216 **Kids who attend single-sex schools** P. Robinson and A. Smithers,
"Should the Sexes Be Separated for Secondary Education?—
Comparisons of Single-Sex and Co-educational Schools," *Research
Papers in Education* 14 (1999): 23–49.

217 **In the early 1980s** C. Riorden, "Public and Catholic Schooling: The
Effects of Gender Context Policy," *American Journal of Education* 93,
no. 4 (Aug. 1985): 518–540.

217 **That is not to say** A. Sullivan, "New Research Dispels Myths Surrounding
Single-Sex Schooling," Economic and Social Research Council,
http://www.cls.ioe.ac.uk/news.asp?section=000100010003&page
=3&item=335

222 **What do all-boys schools have to teach us?** M. R. Younger and
M. Warrington, "Would Harry and Hermione Have Done Better in
Single-Sex Classes? A Review of Single-Sex Teaching in Coeducational

Secondary Schools in the United Kingdom," *American Educational Research Journal* 43, no. 4 (Winter 2006): 579–620.

CHAPTER 16: SMART BOYS WHO GET BAD GRADES

236 **"Collaboration, rather than individual competition** M. P. Sadker and D. M. Sadker, *Teachers, Schools, and Society,* 7th ed., McGraw-Hill, 2005, http://www.american.edu/sadker/teachingtips.htm

237 **The study of the writings of dead white men** J. Dixon, *Growth Through English,* http://steinhardt.nyu.edu/teachlearn/research/ncrll/Dixon.pdf

CHAPTER 17: BOYS ALONE

242 **rich, deep relationships with peers and adults** J. Chu, "A Relational Perspective on Adolescent Boys' Identity Development" (paper presented at the annual meeting of the American Psychological Association, San Francisco, Aug. 14–18, 1998).

242 **"single best predictor of psychological health"** Resnick, et al. "Protecting Adolescents from Harm: Findings from the National Longitudinal Study on Adolescent Health," *JAMA* 278, no. 10 (Sept. 10, 1997).

CHAPTER 19: COLLEGE

257 **On the whole, they get better grades** L. Sax, *The Gender Gap in College: Maximizing the Development Potential of Women and Men,* Jossey-Bass, 2008.

262 **In the past, young men obtained more education than their fathers** T. Mortenson, "The State of American Manhood," Postsecondary Education Opportunity, Sept. 2006.

263 **One in three married working women** M. Conlin, "Look Who's Bringing Home the Bacon," *Business Week,* Jan. 28, 2003.

263 **Among workers in their twenties** A. Beveridge, "No Quick Riches for New York Twentysomethings," *Gotham Gazette,* July 2007, www.Gothamgazette.com

264 **Girls from the poorest white families** J. King, *Gender Equity in Higher Education, 2006,* American Council on Education, 2006.

276 **Having a shaky academic foundation** A. Astin, L. Oseguera, L. Sax, and W. Korn, *The American Freshman: Thirty-five Year Trends,* Cooperative Institutional Research Program, American Council on Education, University of California at Los Angeles, 2002.

ACKNOWLEDGMENTS

Thanks are due to the many school administrators, principals, policy makers, teachers, educational researchers, experts, parents, and boys and girls who candidly and patiently shared their perspectives and experiences with me.

I would not have written the book without the unfailing support and generosity of my bosses and colleagues at *Newsweek:* Donald Graham, Rick Smith, Ann McDaniel, Jon Meacham, Daniel Klaidman, Mark Miller, Debra Rosenberg, and Julia Baird. Thank you for giving me a professional home— and the opportunity to do this important work. The idea for the article on which this book was based would not have been hatched without the guidance and support of some of my former bosses: Mark Whitaker, Dorothy Kalins, and Lisa Miller. It was initially reported with help from a group of wonderful reporters whom I have been privileged to work with: Vanessa Juarez, Andy Murr, Karen Springen, Anne Underwood, and Pat Wingert.

I am grateful for the intellectual stimulation and wise counsel of Barbara Kantrowitz, Jane Brody, Sharon Begley, David Bernknopf, Sally Charnow, Annika Holtan, Katharine Tracy Barnes, Nora Newcombe, Elizabeth McGrory, Betty Forero, Patricia Tyre, Dan Tyre, Betsy Nicholson, Julie Scelfo, and Sheila and Alan Weisman. Special thanks to Catherine Woodard and Honor Lassalle for their close and sensitive reading. Thanks also to Michal Lumsden, Robina Riccitiello, and Ben Witford for their able research assistance.

Thanks, too, to my agent, Richard Pine, and to my very capable editor Rick Horgan. Along with Steve Ross, they understood the importance of this idea right away.

I want to thank my two amazing sons, Mac and Mose, for urging me to write this book and for keeping me going when the going got tough. Special thanks to my husband, Peter Blauner. This book would not have been written without his support, patience, and love.

INDEX

Page numbers in *italics* refer to figures.

cultural myths on, 13–14
disengagement and self-defeating attitudes of, 2, 19, 20, 28, 31–32, 48, 86,
108, 118, 121, 133, 143, 156, 220, 236,
246, 250, 259, 260, 261, 263, 264, 267–
68, 276
drop out and expulsions of, 5, 6, 44, 53,
72–73, 87, 140, 220, 239, 277, 280
early development as slower in, 23, 65–
66, 68, 94–95, 99, 142
extracurricular activities as not participated in by, 30–31, 199, 257
as falling behind early in education, 14,
19, 21, 29–30, 48, 69, 72, 83–84, 87,
94–95, 141–44
fantasy and violence in play of, 70–72,
77, 81, 82, 104–5, 154, 286
fidgeting and high energy of, 8, 15, 21,
52, 66–68, 69, 74, 77, 80, 81, 96–97, 98,
102, 104, 106, 112, 114, 116, 179, 209,
260, 286
fine motor skills as poor in, 23, 52, 66,
68, 96–97, 108, 116, 235, 239
"fourth-grade slump" of, 19, 21, 142–
43, 147
gender-based admission programs in
favor of, 6, 29, 45, 255–61, 270, 271,
272–76, 277, 279
girls' struggles focused on at expense of,
3–4, 7–8, 24, 42, 47–48, 118, 140, 210,
281
inferior early verbal skills of, 65–66, 142
learning disabilities and special education classes of, 20, 21, 23–24, 44, 86,
87, 120
literacy skills and, see reading and writing
male teachers and role models as beneficial for, 123, 125–26, 132, 153, 160,
243–44, 250, 283, 287–88
movement and activity in lessons as
beneficial for, 53, 68, 76–77, 82, 97,
98–99, 116, 123, 138, 209–10, 215–16,
221–22, 283
organizational skills as poor in, 209,
233–34, 238, 239, 283, 287

in preschool, see preschool
recess as beneficial for, 81, 97, 101–6,
111, 283
short attention spans of, 1, 15, 106,
107–8, 109, 195, 260
video games and, see video games
see also education; gender gap; male
underachievement
Boys and Girls (Gussin Paley), 149
"boys' audit," 253–54
Boy Writers (Fletcher), 156, 161
brain science, 15, 62–63, 163–82
ADHD and, 107–16, 260
"Birth to Three" myth perpetuated by,
58–61
brain-based learning and, 169–70,
174–82
brain development rate and gender in,
65–66, 68, 181–82, 234
brain function and gender in, 164, 166–
68, 170, 175–82
gender behavioral differences and, 170–
74, 178–79, 180
gender discrimination in, 25–26, 168–
69, 179
gender-specific instruction based on,
167–68, 174–82, 212; see also single-
sex schooling
nature vs. environment argument in,
170–74, 178–79, 181
"stereotype threat" in, 179–82
on video-game addiction, 190
Broca, Paul, 169, 179
Brown University, 6, 258, 272
Brown v. Board of Education, 206, 207, 211
bullying, 24, 210, 252, 253–54
Bush, George H. W., 90–91
Bush, George W., 91, 140, 214

California, 87, 210, 233
Canada, 33, 132–33
Census Bureau, U.S., 6, 136–37, 243, 262,
266
Centers for Disease Control, 24, 110–11
Chicago-Sun Times, 29

About the Author

PEG TYRE is a veteran investigative reporter. After covering hard news for over a decade, she spent seven years writing about education and social trends for *Newsweek*. She is currently a fellow at Education Sector, a Washington, D.C., think tank. She is also the mother of two sons. You can reach her through her website: www.PegTyre.com.